SEEKING THE NORTH STAR

SEEKING THE NORTH STAR

Selected Speeches by John R. Silber

WITH A FOREWORD BY TOM WOLFE

DAVID R. GODINE, PUBLISHER · BOSTON

First published in 2014 by
David R. Godine · *Publisher*
Post Office Box 450
Jaffrey, New Hampshire 03452
www.godine.com

Foreword copyright © 2014 Tom Wolfe
Introduction copyright © 2014 Edwin J. Delattre
Copyright © 2014 John R. Silber
Frontispiece photograph of John Silber,
courtesy of *The Boston Globe*/Getty Images

LIBRARY OF CONGRESS CATALOGING-IN-PUBLICATION DATA
Silber, John, 1926–2012.
[Speeches. Selections]
Seeking the North Star : selected speeches / by John R. Silber. —
First edition.
    pages cm
Includes index.
ISBN 978-1-56792-507-4 (alk. paper)
1. Education, Higher—Philosophy. 2. United States—Civilization—1970-
I. Title.
LB2322.2.S545 2013
378.001—dc23   2013021213

FIRST PRINTING
Printed in the United States of America

To my students and colleagues

Contents

Foreword · Tom Wolfe   *xi*

Introduction · Edwin J. Delattre   *xxxi*

Preface   1

The Pollution of Time   5

A Tribute to Martin Luther King Jr.   22

The Humanities, the Crucible of Higher Education   28

The Tremble Factor   32

The Thicket of Law and the Marsh of Conscience   40

Generations on Generations   52

The Myth of Overqualification   66

Democracy: Its Counterfeits and Its Promise   72

By the Rivers of Babylon: The Mission of the University   84

The Next Parish Over   93

The University and the Defense of Freedom   102

Stretching the Envelope   114

Seeking the North Star   119

Parents' Convocation   126

Multiculturalism True and False   135

Obedience to the Unenforceable   140

The Need for Honesty in Confronting History   150

Character Education East and West 158

Such Stuff as Dreams Are Made On 169

"Drinking the Sun of Corinth and Reading the Marbles" 176

Procedure or Dogma: The Core of Liberalism 188

Roadblocks to Education Reform 204

Education and Spiritual Formation 229

Ethics and Corporate Responsibility 240

Life Is a Series of Surprises 263

Science vs. Scientism 269

The Choices Are Ours 280

Acknowledgments 291

Index 295

Foreword

I PLEDGE YOU my word, it came popping out of my mouth *just like that*, as if The Force had commandeered my voice box to make an announcement.

This was the evening of October 16, 2008, nineteen days before the presidential election, Barack Obama vs. John McCain, a matter of minus-ten interest to me at that moment. I was here in Chicago for a Chicago Public Library book program ... holding forth, as requested, upon a book about the original *Mercury* astronauts and their adventures half a century ago, *The Right Stuff*.

No sooner had I left the rostrum than an ace blogcaster for the online *Huffington Post*, Greg Boose, appeared: "Do you think that either of these candidates in 2008 have 'the right stuff'?"

Without a moment of reflection, without even a *Well* ... or an *Ummmm* ... my voice box said, "I'm voting for John Silber, a write-in vote. He was president of Boston University – not College – and he almost won the governorship of Massachusetts in 1990. He's a Democrat, but no matter what, he's like Epictetus the Stoic. He cannot assent to what he knows is wrong. He cannot disagree with what he knows is right."

"*Tom!*"

I turn about and it's a man whose face I recognize ... but I can't think of his name. So I adroitly come up with "*Hey*, Big Guy!" and we exchange pleasantries while mainly I'm wracking my brain to figure out who he is.... Then I turn back to the blogcaster, Greg Boose –

– and he's not here. Where's he gone? *Bango* – it hits me. He must have thought I had room to let upstairs ... telling him that in this election for president of the United States I'm going to write in by hand on a paper ballot the name of some loser who had last lost eighteen years ago ... and how much this loser was like Epictetus the Stoic, some maxim-mouthing Greek slave-turned-philosopher in Rome at the time of Nero, the first century A.D. –

– out to lunch, playing with half a deck, falling out of my tree, slipping off the platter or not, I was factually correct. Throughout forty-five years of a very public life in politics and academia, Silber might as well have been a sworn and tattooed Stoic. He refused to compromise, temporize, flatter, double-talk, or bleach the facts in order to make things go smoothly. He didn't merely anger vast majorities of his own constituents from time to time – students, faculty, administrators, alumni, librarians, service workers, not to mention the Commonwealth of Massachusetts's electorate ... no, he charged into them headfirst, like a bull ... and lost only two battles, one early in his career and one toward the end.

His father was a German architect who had immigrated to the United States and married an American girl with whom he raised two sons, John and his older brother, Paul, and created a family considered the very model of propriety, gentility, cultivation, and devotion to God, who, here in San Antonio, Texas, was a Presbyterian. Everybody's favorite explanation of why the second son, John, had such a combative and uncompromising nature had to do with his early grade school years. From the moment other children laid eyes on him, they teased and goaded him unmercifully. He was small and had a congenitally deformed right arm barely half as long as his good arm, the left, and ending in a clump of barely formed proto-fingers. His tiny tormentors called him "One-Arm Pete." His only recourse, he finally concluded, was to punch the little trolls out, small and handicapped though he was. He punched with his left fist and used his truncated right arm like a cattle prod. The bone was just under the skin of his proto-fingers, and when he jammed it into his little combatants' stomachs or kidneys – *Aha!* Thrust *PRODDDD!* – they would go *oof* or *arrrggggh!* or *ooomuggghhh* ... and if you rammed the bone hard enough just beneath any little fighter's rib cage in back and really *reamed out* his kidney and the adrenal gland on top of it, the teeny tough guy would start crying ... and as soon as somebody started crying bawling boo-hooing bubbling between gasps, the action would come to a halt, and little John Silber could take a break. If he didn't have a quick temper and a pugnacious side before all that, he sure did afterward.

The One-Arm Pete of yore grew up into a handsome young man with a square jaw and a challenging stare, no matter who he was staring at, a slender, fit body, even though he had only one arm to work out with, and a head of light brown hair that looked as if every cilium that ever grew on it had been nailed in for the duration. But his saving grace in all things was his IQonic intelligence. By the time he was ready to go to college, the Depression had all but finished off his father's architectural practice, and his mother had to take a job teaching. Silber had to settle for a local college, Trinity University. But he graduated with *laude* so *summa*, he had his pick of graduate schools and wound up enrolling in three, first, Yale Divinity, then University of Texas Law ... all the while teaching to pay his way ... before settling upon a third, the Yale Graduate School, receiving his PhD in philosophy in 1956. He was thirty-two years old and had a wife and a growing brood of children (eventually eight).

The University of Texas, known in Austin as UT, hired him as an assistant professor of philosophy in 1957. He was the sort of teacher who was painfully demanding ... used the Socratic method of confronting the student with barrages of questions to the edge of tears ... to the point where nobody dared come to class unprepared ... in fact, demanded such mastery of the material, it was hard to get top grades ... but also made the material – philosophy – seem so vital and terribly important that despite all the agonies, his classes were always heavily oversubscribed ... and Professor Silber took on the aura of legend. Three times classes nominated him for Outstanding Professor honors. He took off like a rocket – as time flies in academia. Five years later (1962) he was chairman of the philosophy department. Five years after that (1967), he became Dean of the College of Arts and Sciences.

Now John Silber was a player. The UT system was vast and complex, with a student body of 33,000. Sixty percent of them were enrolled in the liberal arts. So the Dean of the College of Arts and Sciences had an unusually eminent, potentially powerful position ... in the very highest ranks of the University's leadership. Silber wasn't modest or gradual in displaying his strength, either. He replaced twenty-two of the chairmen of the twenty-eight departments under his purview in no time.

Meanwhile, he was building up a reputation as a flaming liberal ... not that it was terribly difficult to light that fire in Texas. He cofounded the Texas Society to Abolish Capital Punishment. He called for greater racial integration at the University ... and stood out especially in the Barbara

Smith case in 1957. Barbara Smith, an undergraduate, had been chosen as Dido in *Dido and Aeneas*, a student production of Henry Purcell's famous seventeenth-century opera of romantic tragedy, ill-starred love, and, above all, passion, passion, *paff paff paff* passion and more passion. Barbara Smith was an immensely talented, ravishingly beautiful mezzo-soprano. She was also black … a member of the first contingent of black students to enter the University after it had been desegregated by law. In *Dido and Aeneas*, her lover, Aeneas, would be played by a white boy with blond hair and blue eyes. When the Texas Legislature got wind of this scheme to promote not just desegregation but also musical mis-cegenation, they ordered the University to remove the black girl from the production. The UT administration buckled immediately. The one outspoken voice of protest from within the UT ranks was John Silber's. Against the wishes of the University's president, he wrote a very public letter of protest … a brave try for a teacher his first year on the faculty, and a lowly assistant professor, at that … Nevertheless, Barbara Smith was duly canned as Dido. She went on to become one of America's great opera stars of the second half of the twentieth century, famous and fêted all over the world – and the subject of a 2009 documentary movie, "When I Rise," centered upon the UT incident. In the opera, "When I Rise" is the title of Dido's climactic aria of lament.

Oh, Dido's lament from 1957 got hauled back, revivified, rebooted, re-amped, re-risen in 1970, when the chairman of the board of regents, Frank C. Erwin, began to mount a campaign against Silber. The University of Texas was one of those cases in which the chairman of the board was *the power*, and the president stood by at attention. Erwin was a colossal donor. In Silber's two and a half years as Dean of Arts and Sciences, he and Erwin parted ways on many issues.… Erwin wanted to double the size of the UT student body from 33,000 to more than 60,000, in no small part to increase the size of the Erwin kingdom. Silber said that such a big student body would no longer be a university. It would be a population. Erwin wanted to divide Silber's domain into three, the Arts, Natural Sciences, and Behavioral Sciences. Silber argued that never had there been a moment in history that cried out more strongly for the opposite, for the cross-cultivation of all disciplines, for an inter-disciplinary approa – then he realized he was just talking into the wind. Erwin didn't intend to make him dean of anything, not even one of the three new pocket domains. He just wanted him to ... clear out ... and take his ambitions somewhere else. Something told Erwin that Silber was aiming to become not a dean but president of the University ... and he was right as rain about that. Erwin could see it now ... the end of the Frank C. Erwin era ... and this was no typical state university. UT was a Texas Giant.

Oddly, for such a clash, there appeared to be little personal bitterness between the two of them. If anything, they rather enjoyed their rivalry *pour le sport.*

"Now, you know," Erwin said to Silber, "if you resign, I'll help you in any way I can, because you know I like you and because you know I admire you. You'll still be on the faculty – and you can keep your salary as dean. So all you've got to do is resign."

Silber just laughed.

"Well, then," said Erwin, "the war's over. I'm going to have to make you famous by firing you." He added, "Next time don't take a job as Number 2."

And so, Erwin did ... fire him and make him famous. *Time* and the *New York Times* published long articles about his set-to with Erwin, casting Silber as the young maverick who fought for flaming-liberal ideals against an Old Ornery Guard still determined not to enter the new Civil Rights era in any but a begrudging way.

The dean had lost a job but gained a reputation. *John Silber* was now a *name*. It was against that background that Boston University – don't you mean Boston *College*? – no, Boston *University* – invited Silber to come for a visit. Their president had resigned, and the search committee was at its wit's end trying to find a suitable replacement. The job was not an easy sell. The Methodist Church had founded Boston University in 1869, and for the past twenty-five years, i.e., since the Second World War, it had been going downhill in a grim slide. By now, 1970, it was known as a "streetcar college," meaning that practically all students were the sort of locals who took the streetcar back and forth and had no college life. It was no joke. On the trolley system's "Green Line 'T' " there were still two Boston University stops.

After the tour, the search committee got its first dose of the Stoic who would not assent to what was false and refused to flatter or bleach words.

"This is the ugliest damn place I've ever seen," Silber told them. Not only that, the faculty was "full of deadwood," and the whole institution was about to go under. The committee took that glass of ice water in the face, braced, shuddered – and then decided this celebrated maverick was just what they needed. If so, Silber said, he insisted on complete control of hiring and firing faculty and the use of the endowment.

Looking back on it much later, Silber realized that one reason the committee had been so keen on him was that they had asked him something about Marxism, and he knew the subject backward and forward. There were several Marxists on the committee, it turned out, and they took great knowledge of the subject to reflect great enthusiasm.

If so, that was the last time they had the wonderful *huphuphuphupping* martial euphoria of marching shoulder-to-shoulder with their flaming fellow traveler toward a new world in birth.

Silber was sworn in as president of the University on January 1, 1971. The trustees immediately made available a small fortune so that he could recruit academic stars from all over the country to replace the aforesaid "deadwood" in the faculty. It was pretty obvious. He began right away, and right away the Deadwood began complaining that as soon as his "stars" arrived at Logan Airport, Silber inserted them in the lineup, ignoring such formalities as getting the approval of the existing chairmen of the departments. Before the summer break came, the Deadwood were already calling him, *sotto voce*, an autocrat.

The students didn't mutter behind their hands. Their hostility was an immediate outcry. In 1972 Silber invited the Marine Corps to return to the University and resume their ROTC recruitment program. As soon as they showed up, a mob of students set about hooting, howling, booing, intent on booting them out. Silber confronted the mob himself and told them this was not their decision to make. They refused to disband. So he did what few college presidents in that era of antiwar protests dared do except as a last resort. He called in the police immediately, and the police ran the wahoos off like hooligans. Silber, who steadfastly characterized himself as a liberal Democrat, said he had taken the only liberal approach available in the situation. Namely, he had called upon a duly authorized show of force to keep mob tyranny from shutting down freedom of speech ... namely, the freedom of the Marine Corps recruiters, duly invited to the campus, to be heard.

Oh, brother ... whatever happened to that *flaming liberal from Texas* we were supposed to be getting? – the one who spoke up for that black singer that time and for integration in general ... and against capital punishment ... in *Texas*, f'r godsake ... where they grow their Neanderthals Big. This choice item, our President Silber, turns out to be a stone-cold fascist ... or at least an extreme lunatic right-wing conservative who will double-talk you with perverted liberal rhetoric.

In fact, Silber was not a liberal, and he was not a conservative. He was a Kantian. The late-eighteenth-century philosopher Immanuel Kant had been the subject of his doctoral dissertation at Yale, and he went on to write three scholarly monographs about *der Meister*. Kant's ideal was "the autonomous man," the man who determines his own destiny. But he can achieve that freedom only inside a moral envelope that defines the outer limits of behavior. For example, the autonomous man must not try to undermine or destroy forces that exist to maintain the freedom and autonomy of one and all, in this case the Marine Reserve Officers Training Corps at Boston University. The Corps was part of an armed force, America's, created specifically to protect all of a society's autonomous people from the threat of attack by enemies. By the same token, Barbara Smith's autonomy in pursuing an operatic career must not be blocked by rogue elements, in this case segregationists who punched holes in the envelope in order to get at her.

So when Silber tried to protect the autonomy of the individual – Barbara Smith – he was hailed as a flaming liberal. When he tried to protect the integrity of the moral envelope – as in the case of the ROTC – he was excoriated as a right-wing dictator. Talk about flaming ... for the next five years Silber was all but immolated over and over as a flaming fascist. He never blinked. He had contempt for his critics. What were they compared to the tag team of John Silber and Immanuel Kant? In one of the twenty-seven lectures and articles before us in these pages – "The University and the Defense of Freedom" – Silber diligently spells out why a man's autonomous self depends so heavily upon what Kant thought of as "self-restraint."

This had nothing to do with a spirit of compromise on the issues. Silber had no such spirit! Every conceivable college creature called for his ouster, and in great numbers. At one time or another, students, faculty, librarians, clerical employees, and service workers demanded that the board of trustees fire him. Among the Deadwood the bitterness was intense. In 1974 they created a union and affiliated with the American Association of University Professors. Silber refused to negotiate with them. Two-thirds of the Deadwood demanded that the board get rid of him. The trustees backed Silber. The union went on strike, briefly. Then the clerical workers went on strike, and some of the Deadwood professors refused to cross their picket line. Silber singled out five of them to be disciplined. At this point faculty members from throughout the Boston area joined the Deadwood in a petition with a staggering number of signatures.

On the issues, Silber never gave an inch. He refused to avoid collisions. He made the shade of Epictetus gulp with admiration. From beginning to end, as the pressure mounted, he refused to assent to a single thing that struck him as false in light of his master plan for turning a moribund streetcar college into a major teaching and research institution in head-to-head competition with the two giants across the river, Harvard and MIT.

During that period, the 1970s, Silber was in the press continually … and came across as one hard case, unyielding when he wasn't in a straight-out *want-to-step-outside?* mode. At home and with friends, however, he was something else entirely, precisely the boy his parents had prescribed forty-five years earlier in San Antonio … a gentleman, courtly, congenial, the very picture of bonhomie … thoughtful of Kathryn and their children and generous to a fault…. In the morning the hard case, preparing for his return to the war front, liked to turn on the radio as he shaved, and one of his little girls, Rachel, loved to watch him. One morning the popular song "Hot Diggity (Dog Ziggity Boom)" came on, and he swept her up into his arms – his one and a half arms – he knew how to use his right arm to do such things – lifted her up until her head was level with his, put her little right hand into his left hand, and waltzed her around and around with ballroom whirls, singing, "Hot diggity, dog ziggity." When his children were with him, he was theirs. Then … back to the wars.

Diggity ziggity phyzzicality was merely one form that Silber's capacious sense of humor took. A second was his amazing gift for theatricality.

One year he invited a writer, Tom Wolfe, as the University's commencement speaker. Wolfe was known for his eccentric "habit of white suits," as he himself called it, believing that to be a highly refined pun, since *habit* meant both "a regular practice" and "a uniform." He wore white suits every day, winter and summer, except in the rare case when protocol ruled it out. Commencements, such as B.U.'s, were just such a case. The commencement speaker, like the faculty, was required to wear an academic robe, and Wolfe's, from his alma mater, Washington and Lee, was black. One afternoon near the end of March, Silber was in his office thinking about the upcoming commencement, just two months away, when he experienced an ahah! moment. All at once – *ahah!* – he could *see* it: in the ceremony would come a moment when the guest speaker would receive an honorary degree from the University. Just before going to the podium, the speaker would stop at a line painted on the stage for precisely that reason, stand as stock still, tall, and erect as he can, all the while gazing straight ahead out upon the audience, like a second lieutenant at attention ... whereupon stewards lift a long, silken, so-called hood symbolizing the degree – actually looks more like a monk's cowl – up majestically over his head and place it around his neck and aim him toward the podium for his oration.

Two months later comes the day Wolfe stands at that line on a stage in the B.U. stadium before thousands. On some pretext or other the stewards tell him *sotto voce* that they're going to slip his robe off and slip it back on in a matter of seconds, and this they do ... up to a point.

Silber has had a tailor custom-make an entirely white academic robe with red trim – the B.U. colors being red and white – and it's this they slip back on him from behind ... as Wolfe dutifully gazes straight ahead, as instructed. Immediately they bring the hood down over his head with a great blinding flourish in front of his face, slip it around his neck and not merely aim him toward the podium but add an as-if-unintended shove. Great applause from the crowd. At the podium Wolfe looks down slightly to gaze upon them ... down ... and *sees* it.... His black robe has unaccountably, inexplicably, mysteriously, miraculously turned pure white with red trim.... The man goes into catatonic shock ... can't speak

... can't move ... stands still as a clay-baked Statue of Liberty for what under the circumstances seems like five minutes ... with his mouth open and the tip of his tongue touching his upper teeth as if he had been about to say, "Thank you –"

He comes out of his catatonia in a state of enchantment ... bliss ... and proceeds to deliver a commencement address that can only be described as sublime. When he boards the airplane at Logan Airport for his flight back to New York, he is still wearing his sublime white academic gown, which comes to within inches of the floor. As he walks down the aisle to his seat, people stare at him with wonder in their faces ... or could that be wariness? A little girl says, "Mommy, is that the Pope?"

In the baggage claim area at LaGuardia Airport, he still has the magical white raiment about him. The looks he gets in LaGuardia are not so much full of wonder as dubiousness, disdain, suspicion, and free-floating resentment.

A beefy man – looks like he's in his late thirties – wearing a V-neck sweater over a T-shirt – he's had enough. He confronts Wolfe and says, "OK, and what are you supposed to be?"

"The Pope," says Wolfe.

The big man backs off ... in case the damn *what* bites.

Diggity phizzicality and ziggity theatricality, these two; but Silber's most lethal humor missile was the third, his heat-seeker: The Word. Just before another commencement – 1976, five and a half years into his presidency – his battle with B.U.-and-beyond's fractious factions reached the live-or-die point. For five and a half stormy years, Silber had been protected by a single but impregnable force, the board of trustees. For five and a half years, the board's 100 percent support had kept him untouchable. But barely a month before the 1976 commencement that solid bloc began to fall apart. Three board members made it well known that they were going over to the other side to join the insurgents and call for his ouster. Silber's imminent defeat and departure were now the talk of the B.U. gripevine. Two weeks before commencement he had a touchy and possibly ugly confrontation coming up ... an innovation of his own devising, the Senior Breakfast, a breakfast the president was to put on for the graduating class, his last chance to speak to them privately before commencement, which was of course a ceremony-ridden and motley-crowded event. Of all the anti-Silber factions, the students themselves were the most volatile, unpredictable, short-fused, riot-ready cherry bombs on the campus. Silber wasn't afraid of having a head-butting contest with them. He would have happily head-butted it out with them or anybody else. Just name the game, and he'd play it – and he'd win it. But having an ugly scene with the seniors two weeks before the commencement, on top of everything else, would be an unwinnable imbroglio. It would make it seem as if the whole University had erupted into Silber war and there would be only one quick cure for that.

So he thought he'd take a different tack. The seniors gathered in the dining hall, and Silber made sure they had a nice warm breakfast before he rose to speak:

"It is my pleasure to welcome you to this Senior Breakfast of 1976, and to have this occasion to speak to you.

"Ordinarily we anticipate that only the graduating class will be leaving the University. This morning, however, there is some anticipation that we may all be leaving. Your parents will be very disappointed if you do not depart, and my mother will be very disappointed if I do. It may have surprised some of you that I have a mother. Those of you who majored in biology know that all mammals have mothers."

He said he wanted them, the seniors, to get to know him better, even though recently the press had made his life "something of an open book, and in that way I think you have come to know me perhaps in a reasonably satisfactory fashion. I am abrasive, acerbic, ambitious, angry, arrogant, and autocratic. And that is just the a's."

He had no idea why he was perceived that way, he said, until he was listening to the car radio one day and heard the country music star Mac Davis singing "a song that fit my situation perfectly and would give you some understanding of the problem that I face, and I hope, though I have no license to practice singing, that you will let me try."

With that, he broke into song with all the gusto and quite a few of the same notes as Mac Davis himself:

> "Oh, Lord, it's hard to be humble,
> When you're perfect in every way.
> I can't wait to look in the mirror,

'Cause I get better looking each day.
To know me is to love me.
I must be a hell of a man.
Oh, Lord, it's hard to be humble.
But I'm doin' the best that I can."

With that, Silber cracked laughter out of three quarters of the seniors and actual applause, serious hand-clapping, out of at least half. There's no saying how many hearts he won, if any, but he sure softened up a lot of them.

When he then turned to "what is really on my mind this morning" – namely, those among them who were so obtuse they didn't realize that "real life" doesn't begin the day you leave college but the day you begin – they were like cattle. They didn't raise a peep. They just sat there staring at him and digesting their Senior Breakfasts and chewing their senior cuds.

By the time the board came to a vote, the rebellious Gang of Three were left out in the cold. For by then Silber had on his side the most powerful single ally a man could ask for at Boston University: the board's new chairman, Arthur G. B. Metcalf, a charismatic B.U. alumnus who had started off his career as an aeronautical engineer, inventor, and pilot. He had joined the B.U. faculty in 1935 for two years. That was all it took him to found two organizations, the Boston University College of Engineering ... and the enormously profitable Electronics Corporation of America. He was a mega-millionaire when he became B.U.'s chairman of the board and champion of John Silber in that crucial year, 1976. The board's vote backed Silber 100 percent – minus the Gang. Within the next five years the magnitude of his success began to be so overwhelming, not even his worst enemies could avoid seeing it.

His new faculty "stars" turned out to be precisely that, professors who stood out brilliantly in the firmament of academia. Two, Elie Wiesel and Derek Walcott, won Nobel Prizes not long after he recruited them. Two others, Saul Bellow and the mathematician Sheldon Glashow, won Nobel Prizes and then joined Silber's faculty elite.

As chancellor of the endowment, Silber increased the University assets fivefold, tenfold, twentyfold, so gloriously manifold, people were astounded. In the four decades of the Silber era, the endowment rose from $18.8 million to $430 million. He had overseen the construction of 13 million square feet of university space, including the Arthur G. B. Metcalf Center for Science and Engineering, the Rafik B. Hariri Building for the School of Management, the B.U. Photonics Center, and the Tsai Performance Center. He had turned the streetcar college into on outstanding research university, one of the very best in the country. Recruiting was no longer a desperate matter. Faculty and students from all over the world now rushed to what awaited them where the Boston trolley line went around the bend near the Charles River ... across the water from the competition, Harvard and MIT.

By 1988 this essentially new university was so solidly established that Silber – I wonder what Frank Erwin thought about this? – there is no record, but I doubt that he was too shatteringly surprised – Silber began organizing a campaign to run for the Democratic Party nomination for governor of Massachusetts in the 1990 election. In 1989 he took a leave of absence from Boston University and published a manifesto for his campaign: *Straight Shooting: What's Wrong with America and How to Fix It*. He had published his scholarly works on Kant, but *Straight Shooting* was his first book aimed at a general audience ... or as general an audience as he could reach in the Commonwealth of Massachusetts.

All three of Silber's opponents in the Democratic Party primary were Party officeholders who owed everything they had to the fact that they had been Party stalwarts from the moment they bawled James Michael Curley's name at birth. Silber entered the race for the nomination deep down in fourth place. He had no clout whatsoever in the Party and no ties to it beyond vague claims that he had been a "liberal Democrat" all his life.

Not only that, he seemed like a laughably amateurish campaigner. He kept committing the most politically incorrect gaffes you could imagine.

He'd say Massachusetts is a "welfare magnet" for "people who are accustomed to living in a tropical climate." In case you didn't know, that was how the town of Lowell had turned into "the Cambodian capital of America."

He cheerfully disclosed that when he was in Germany on a Fulbright Scholarship, he discovered that his father's side of the family was Jewish.

One of his aunts had died in the Nazis' notorious Auschwitz concentration camp. His father had hidden all that from the children. Then Silber torpedoed whatever sympathy this revelation might have brought him by adding that he had decided, initially, to convert to Judaism … but he gave up the idea, he said, because "the racism of Jews is quite phenomenal."

Party veterans had to laugh. This academic airhead was tooooo much. If you had a political nerve-ending in your body, you knew this guy was so busy offending every segment of the population, he didn't stand a chance. That wasn't the population's reaction, however. Yes, the professor stepped on some toes, corns and all, but he was the only man running for the nomination who was willing to do some straight shooting, just the way his book said. This happened to be a moment at which Democratic voters were grumbling that the Party leadership was getting too clubby by half. Silber may not be a smooth operator, but he's totally sincere and not afraid of speaking out. He's a breath of fresh air. He's lively. He makes you *want* to listen, and so on.

It was a huge upset when Silber won the primary by ten points, 53 percent to 43 percent over his closest competitor, the Massachusetts Attorney General, Francis X. Bellotti. Now he faced the Republican William Weld in the general election.

Success didn't tone Silber down in the slightest. The gaffes kept on coming. He said Jesse Jackson's oratory reminded him of Adolph Hitler. "If I were President of the United States, Jesse Jackson would have a place in my cabinet, because every president needs someone to write bumper stickers."

He said the Massachusetts public school system had gone berserk, steering children into special-education programs by the bus-load. By now, 17.5 percent of all school children wound up there. "It would lead one to believe that there has been a collapse of the gene pool in Massachusetts, because 17.5 percent of our kids are weird, are not capable of being educated under normal circumstances."

Gaffe after gaffe – but in politics a gaffe is a mistake a politician makes by saying what he actually thinks. By that standard, Silber's gaffes were not *gaffes*. Nothing he said came out by mistake. He was a miraculous creature, a politician who told you only what he really thought. So the press changed the word from gaffe to *shocker*. When Silber said that drugs had become a worse scourge than alcohol, the *Boston Sunday Herald* ran a headline on the front page that read "NEW SILBER SHOCKER: Gov Candidate in More Hot Water for Pooh-poohing Alcoholism." The press was going Silber-shocker-loony. In fact, Silber was the first gubernatorial candidate who had ever proposed that in driving-while-intoxicated cases, the police should not only take away the driver's license but also confiscate the vehicle. But what did that matter? ... SHOCKERS! ... The press just couldn't get enough SILBER SHOCKERS – and neither could the voters. The professor was different. He said it like it was.

Heading into the final weeks of the campaign, Silber led Weld by a comfortable margin, by close to 9 percent according to one poll. Two weeks before the election came a pair of television interviews that are legends in the annals of TV to this day. A Boston newscaster, Natalie Jacobson, thought up the idea of long "at-home" interviews with both candidates, and not the kind where you're just trolling for sound-bites or editing the video until you had cut it down into easily comprehended cubes. She wanted to capture the *real* William Weld and the *real* John Silber, the personality inevitably shielded or simply blocked off by all the usual dark suits and formal events and policy interviews and all the rest of the standard television settings. And Natalie Jacobson was *the* broadcaster to take on the job. She was not only extremely popular with her audience, she was extremely well-*liked*. She made her viewers feel that she speaks *my* language directly to *me* here in *my home*. If she hadn't been as young and pretty as she was, with big sunshine dimples in her cheeks when she smiled, she would have been known as belovéd.

When she arrived at Weld's house, he was in the kitchen at the stove, busy cooking some eggs over-light for his five children. His shirttail was out. He was right in mid-fry when she came in and couldn't very well just drop what he was doing and have a seat with the TV people. So he was busy doing a chore for the family when he greeted Natalie with a big smile ... a smile with frying-pan smoke drifting across it ... and she started asking him questions.

"What would you say is your greatest fault?" said Natalie. This was a personal interview. She wanted to find the man behind the tall WASPy certified-*Mayflower* Boston Brahmin impression Weld made on you when you saw him on an in-studio television interview.

"Ohhh ..." said Weld, eyes darting toward the frying pan so he could turn his children's eggs over lightly and just rightly, "I'm kind of a slacker."

Weld's running mate, his prospective lieutenant governor, Paul Cellucci, was watching the show at home. He couldn't believe it. "What the hell is he thinking?! Calling yourself *lazy*? That's not very bright!"

Then Natalie went to Silber's house to ask him the same question. This was a Sunday. Silber was at least savvy enough to wear a white shirt open at the neck and a sleeveless sweater, i.e., no necktie and no impenetrable dark suit. Since this program was supposed to be about the candidate and his family, Silber had three generations' worth seated about the dining room table, himself and his wife, Kathryn, three of his six daughters and their husbands and their children. Natalie was the only outsider. She was a small woman and looked even smaller sitting here amid a hive of family in-jokes and bantering and gesturing. Her familiar sweet-as-honey voice seemed diminished. But Natalie knew what she was doing, namely, running the show. She directed the conversation ... by questioning this one and that one and even the smaller ones. She asked one boy if he ever had to "defend" his grandfather at school. She asked a girl of about eleven, "What do the kids at school say to you about your grandfather?" When the girl replied, "Nothing," Natalie kept up and asked, "Nothing? Really? They don't tease you or anything?" She asked one of Silber's daughters how it made her feel when people said that her father was sexist, "that he really does not think of women as an equal to a man." As it happened, the children came up with perfectly innocuous answers, and no harm was done. But as far as Silber was concerned, that was not the point. That had nothing to do with it ... the heat ... the heat that was building up inside his head ... and nobody else could know what he was feeling. The woman had dared to use his little children as pawns in her smelly little TV game.

If you were acutely attentive, as soon as you heard the word "defend," you could detect a little *thoomp* as the gas ignited beneath the boiler. After the bit about kids teasing Silber's granddaughter, you could detect the *galoomph*, as a current of hot water rolled over into the stone cold depths.... After the word "sexist" you could hear the *shhhhhh* as the water began to turn to steam. Has she no ethical restraint at all, this woman? She's asking his little grandchildren *political* questions! Little children! She's *using* them, toying with them, trying to egg them on … to the point where they let slip some comment that shows what crude, sexist, racist, homophobic ideas they've been raised with – *Cut!* – *The End* – He'll swat you like a gnat, Gnatalie! Your time has come – but he can't let himself boil over in the middle of the woman's TV Family Portrait, can he…. He can't just set her straight in so many words and put an end to this outrageous *gaming* of his children and little grandchildren … right in front of his eyes! That means he's got to shut her up and take over the conversation himself and turn it around … but he's boiling! The rushshshshshshsh of the steam – it's filling his head! – and he's got to sound very *sensible* and remain very *calm* –

– so calmly, ever so calmly he walked right over Natalie's little honeysuckle voice and said, "I think that the Women's Movement has done very good things, because without it, I'm sure that my daughters would have had a much more difficult time living the kinds of lives they've had. But on the other hand, Rachel would not have had as difficult a time deciding to be a housewife and a mother if it hadn't been for the Feminist Movement, because they've denigrated those women who have decided to take their maternal responsibilities seriously. And there is no question" – this *feeling* he has! – the anger – the urge to throttle – "no question that we have a generation of neglected children, we have a generation of abused children, by women who have thought that a third-rate daycare center was just as good as a first-rate home" – something's happening … the steam is building up faster than his valves, his valves of good sense, can let it out.

Natalie jumps in: "But is that fair, though, Dr. Silber? Some of those women had to resort to the third-rate daycare centers, had to because they had to work – they had no choice but –"

The steam pressure mashes those last few words, *they had no choice but,* flat, and then begins erupting, overwhelming his entire venting system. "Of course not! I'm talking about the women who didn't have that as a choice. See, if I'm into another one of these Silber Shocker things, then *to hell with this damn program!* – because I don't need that. I thought we were having a fairly complex, objective discussion. Now, I'm talking about the case where you have a husband who is making a very good living, let's say, as a lawyer – a young lawyer making $75,000 a year when he gets out of law school, the first day he's out, which is about $40,000 more than he's worth –" Now, why did he have to add *that*? Makes him seem like a bitter old man. But the heat, the pressure – he's getting so damn hot ... like now there's steam building up faster than his valves can handle it. "– And he's already making more than a full professor at a first-class university. And here he is at thirty, and he gets married, and his wife – she's got to have a baby and she's got to have her career at the same time, and child neglect goes hand in hand with that kind of relationship over and over again. And we *see* those children."

Natalie says, "What do you see as your strength and, if you think you have one, a weakness?"

Silber concentrates on his valves – mustn't lose control – and steadies them long enough to say, "I think that my strength is competence and my strength is honesty –"

Then Natalie cuts him off, "And your weakness?"

Now it's Powder Valley for you and your whole damn family! It's blowing up, the boiler is! He had it under control until she sneaked the word "weakness" in under his voice the second time.... Now the damn pressure is stronger than he is – the pressure! the pressure! – the pressure twists his face into a pre-snarl mien – and then it happens – *He's blowing up!* –

"You find the weakness!" Him – he's lost it! He's snarling! Can't hold any of it back! *Kaboom*! It explodes from his lips! "*I don't have to go around telling you what's wrong with me!* The media have manufactured about 16,000 nonexisting qualities that are all offensive and attributed them all to me. Let them have their field day. *You can pick any one of them!*"

And that was it. Natalie had done it – completely outmaneuvered John Silber. The next thing he knew, her sweet honey-toned voice was wrapped around him like a comfy blanket, consoling her self-destructing adversary.

"Oh, you don't think that's a fair question?" said Natalie ... with the sweetest smile you ever saw ... with deep, full dimples ... the smile of a visiting nurse who has genuine sympathy for her patient. "If you ask me that, I can tell you what *I'd* say." Her smile begins to glow, and that glow says, *Now, now, little one, I'm not trying to hurt you. I'm not trying to trap you.*

"You don't think that's *not* a fair question?" says Silber. But he no longer sounds angry. He sounds peevish, as if he knows he's lost the battle and has no weaponry left, just a residue of sour feelings. "Well, maybe you don't *have* any faults." He swung his chin up and his face away from her gaze and looked like Patience on a monument, smiling at Grief.

"But I *do*," says Natalie, draping her sweet smile like a stole around his shoulders. "I *do* have some. That's why I –"

Even more peevishly: "I'm not interested in your faults."

Now her smile becomes an entire soft baby blanket, and she swaddles Silber in it.

"I wish you weren't so defensive," my baby, said Natalie, "because this is not a defensive posture here that I'm hoping to create. Rather, I want an understanding so that people watching this could get a better sense of who you are. Now, if you would ask anybody, 'What do you see as your strengths and weaknesses?' that's not meant as an antagonistic question. It was meant, rather, to have some insight into how you view yourself."

There were not only warmth and tenderness in her smile but also pity. She was ever so concerned by his hurt feelings and had done everything she could to encourage Baby to be a big boy:

Silber's little earphone was still in his ear, and he heard a man's voice: "OK, we've got what we wanted. Let's wrap it up."

He wasn't hearing things, either. He *heard the man say it*, "OK, we've got what we wanted. Let's wrap it up."

And there was nothing he could do about it. His humiliation was now *total*. The next thing he knew, little Natalie was looking right into his eyes with the sweetest, most profound smile. Pity dripped from her lips as she extended her clean hand in solace.... Her lips said, "Good-bye," but her eyes added, "You poor thing."

The words can't convey what it came out like on-screen. One of the first media lessons politicians learn is, "Never get angry on television." Even if it's completely justified, it comes across to the viewer as mad-dog rudeness toward the host, rudeness and a rabid temper.

To Silber, he was merely doing what he always did, calling it as he saw it, being a straight shooter. *Tell me what's your greatest fault....* Mygod how videotic can these people be?!

And the viewers called it as *they* saw it. How insufferably rude can the man be to our Natalie? *Our Natalie....*

From that moment on, Silber's poll numbers began sinking like a stone. His campaign's "continuing polling" people could see it happening in real time. His numbers *really* sank after the channel showed it again on October 31, on the eve of the weekend that led to Election Day. Weld got it right away. Right away he got hold of his PR consultant, Dick Morris, and his ad man, Stuart Stevens, and told them to make a killer commercial immediately using the TV footage of Mad-Dog Silber. They played it on every channel over and over and over for the entire weekend until nobody who watched television in the Commonwealth of Massachusetts could possibly miss it ... Silber snarling ... the real person behind the "refreshing" approach to politics ... and Weld won, 51 percent to 48.

To make it worse, this was the first time a Republican had won the race for governor in sixteen years.

If Silber had only been so kind as to assent to what was false, as Natalie Jacobson's cameras beamed their red eyes at him, and say something self-deprecating, such as *I'm a slacker*, and stand at the stove or in the cellar or up in the attic while doing something like cooking to feed your brood, thereby visually canceling out the "fault" you're revealing for the first time – if he had only pretended to be a typical politician for that one brief moment with lovely Natalie – the history of not just Massachusetts but the nation itself would have been very different ... or so I am convinced. John Silber could not have held himself back once he became governor of the Commonwealth. Massachusetts would have become the platform from which to ascend to a yet higher rostrum ... in order to convey to the nation the warnings he gives over and over in these pages ... and, considering his tenacity, to do something about them.

But then he wouldn't have been John Silber, would he. Like his spiritual godfather, Epictetus, he knew you can't just turn The Force on and off at your convenience.

TOM WOLFE

Introduction

THIS SPLENDID SELECTION of John Silber's speeches spans forty-two years—from 1971, when he assumed the presidency of Boston University, through 2012 when his last speech was written but, as his health declined, never delivered. Various as they are, these speeches together reveal the intensity of his focus on the young and the constancy of his concern that they should become able to lead fulfilling lives despite the difficulties of our times. They span John's presidency and chancellorship of the university, his emergence as a national figure in discussions of education, his service on President Reagan's National Bipartisan Committee on Central America, his leadership of Boston University's partnership with the Chelsea schools, his nearly successful run for governor, and his tenure as Chairman of the Massachusetts Board of Education. John was, by his own account, an intellectual pessimist and a congenital optimist. He saw clearly the problems we face yet never faltered in his belief that, as the title of his last speech says, the fundamental choices about the fate of our culture, our country, and our people are ours to make.

John believed that a teacher is obligated to live up to high standards of intellectual honesty, courage, and integrity in speaking to students and that the same obligations apply in speaking to the public. He was as meticulous in the preparation of his public addresses as he was in preparing his classroom lectures. His speeches were an "extension" of his work as a classroom teacher, "an inducement to reflection and dialogue." Had he lived, he would have welcomed the dialogue with his readers that he invites in his Preface.

Readers will see John's intellectual humility in his learning from the insights and character of others – from Plato and Aristotle to Martin Luther King Jr.; from Shakespeare and Immanuel Kant and Yeats to John Fletcher Moulton, Zeffirelli and Jacques Barzun; from Macaulay and Jefferson to Oliver Wendell Holmes Jr. and Duff Cooper; from Thomas More and Louis Brandeis to Paul Freund; from Marcus Aurelius to John,

Abigail, and John Quincy Adams; from the courage of Hector in Troy and Socrates in Athens to the courage of the Bible's Esther.

With some academics and public speakers, references to classical figures and sources are no more than showmanship, mere ornamentation that has little or nothing to do with how they actually live. Not so with John. He lived in accordance with his own insistence that "no teacher can affect the lives of students unless … he or she gives meaning to courage and integrity and intellectual curiosity by the embodiment of these values in his or her own life." He was understandably disdainful of people who seek the authority and status of high offices such as teaching and educational administration only to behave with indifference toward the obligations of courage, integrity, and competence they have voluntarily undertaken.

John stressed to students the singular importance of learning to read slowly, with great attention to every word, and often emphasized how much his own learning depended on doing so. Finding many students enamored of speed reading, John sometimes brought noted teachers of that faddish technique to our sophomore philosophy classes when students were reading and discussing Søren Kierkegaard. When John had them tackle passages from that Danish theologian and philosopher, some of these experts speed-read the passages several times; but until they slowed way down and paid attention to every word, they remained completely in the dark about Kierkegaard's meaning. In this and many similar ways, John showed students that he was willing to have them test the truth of what he said. Throughout his career, he was never afraid to publicly test the truth of his assertions.

John was likewise emphatic about the imperative to listen to others with the same intense concentration and patience necessary in reading books. He was a master of the art of conversation, what the philosopher William James and the intellectual historian Jacques Barzun called "sifting" ideas. This process involves speaking to each other as precisely as we can, listening intently, doing our best together to understand what we mean and to assess the merit of the ideas under discussion. Such sifting is the basis of all genuine dialogue, that cooperative search for the closest possible approximation of the truth. It is utterly and completely distinct from the fiery intellectual competition of debate. The purpose of dialogue is to learn together and escape error. The purpose of debate is to win a contest. John ensured his students understood the difference by bringing it to light in dialogue with them.

The achievement of mutual understanding through dialogue takes concerted effort to see things from another person's point of view. John was especially good at this; his teaching was a model of Immanuel Kant's categorical imperative: "Put yourself in thought in the place and point of view of the other." This formal expression of the principle of the Golden Rule is incompatible with any kind of condescension. So thoroughly had the categorical imperative become second nature to John that, in the forty-eight years I knew him, first as his teaching assistant and later as his colleague and friend, I never saw him speak condescendingly or listen carelessly to a child.

One time in Texas, John and I were in a car with several of his seven young children. One of his daughters asked, "Daddy, what's a mascot?" John deferred to me. I said, "Lots of sports teams have names like Longhorns and Bulldogs. A mascot is a real longhorn or bulldog that all the team's fans like to see and cheer for." The little girl then said, "Daddy, what's a mascot?" John replied, "It's a pet that a whole lot of people own together." She then looked impishly at me and said, "Well, why didn't Ed say that?" The car suddenly filled with happy laughter.

Such was John's insightfulness in replying to children in ways appreciable to them. Fidelity to the categorical imperative brought him an intellectual and moral power that stretched throughout his teaching and learning with students of all ages and experience.

John's focus on thorough preparation, precise speaking, slow reading, intent listening, and patient effort to grasp the thoughts of others pointed the way to his more comprehensive lesson that living for instant gratification is self-destructive: "An instant culture moves by nature toward its own destruction ... when the structure of time is destroyed, the basis for significance in our lives is likewise destroyed. All meaning is lost in the instantaneous...."

Human beings, he taught, are not creatures of the instantaneous. "We, because of memory, foresight, and thought, live in a past, in a present, in a future.... Our overarching project becomes that of building a structure or pattern of significance into our lives." Deliberately and forcefully, by his words and by the assignments he gave, John led students to understand that this overarching project never comes easy. Such an undertaking demands consideration and discussion of "the human verities: the mysteries of birth, love, suffering, joy, and death." No generation, he taught, "can find meaning unless it is informed by what it inherits and accountable for what it bequeaths." He encouraged students, as part of their projects in self-discovery, "to take knowledgeable risks in order to discover [their] capacities and limits." Over and again, in convocations and other public forums, in classrooms and seminars, he told students they "have the obligation, if they are to get the most out of their education, to select the most demanding professors, the ones who give not the easiest but the hardest assignments" and to work as hard as they can in their laboratories and classrooms, to take advantage of the extracurricular activities available to them in lectures, plays, and concerts, and to push to the outer limits of their capacity to learn, to absorb, to assimilate.

John never pandered to students; but he earnestly praised good work and progress in learning. He believed that genuine self-esteem and self-respect, like warranted self-confidence, have to be earned through arduous application and exercise of individual potential. Real self-esteem cannot be bestowed by flattery or any other technique of deceit.

John's vision of the project of self-discovery and of building a fulfilling life went far beyond reading, discussing, and writing about intellectually demanding books. It called for action, and structured his undergraduate and graduate courses at the University of Texas at Austin, his presidency of Boston University, his transformation of the Boston University School of Education, his leadership of the Boston University/Chelsea Public Schools Partnership, and his chairmanship of the Massachusetts State Board of Education.

In childhood, John, along with his parents and his brother, knew the hardships of the Great Depression. Jobs while a teenager taught him about people whose circumstances were very much worse than his own. Later, teaching in Yale's Master of Arts in Teaching program introduced him to shockingly bigoted and incompetent school teaching and administration.

Broader experience led him to share, but only up to a point, Francis Bacon's assertion, "Luxury doth best encourage vice while adversity doth best encourage virtue." He knew luxury deserved to be feared; but he also knew that too much adversity too early in life – desperately unhealthy conditions before and after birth, including prenatal drug addiction, malnourishment and disease, deprivation of sound parental guidance, absence of educational opportunity, constant exposure to vicious discrimination and threats of violence – destroys human potential, blights freedom, and thwarts aspiration by blinding imagination to possibilities.

In the summer of 1948, John worked in San Antonio conducting a survey as a census enumerator: "As part of this survey, I assisted the *patron* of a tortilla factory with his census forms. Leaving his small establishment, I entered a narrow doorway and was suddenly inside the same block of buildings I had been viewing from without. Behind all the storefronts, unseen from the streets, was a fetid barrio of hovels occupied by scores of families, a barrio without proper sanitation, and in which all the families drew water from a single spigot."

Slumlords were clearly in violation of sanitation and fire codes, not to mention codes of basic decency; and when John tried to find out how to improve things, he learned how successfully and dismayingly resistant to change entrenched interests can be.

Later, as part of his teaching at Yale, John spent time in a New Haven elementary school where he was "appalled at the way some teachers treated minority and poor children." Such experience alerted John to the persistent lack of educational opportunity – let alone equal educational opportunity – for poor and minority children far beyond New Haven. He subsequently became involved in the early stages of the Head Start Program. Throughout his life, his mission as a teacher and administrator took all children, fortunate and less fortunate, into account.

As a professor and chairman of the Philosophy Department at the University of Texas, John taught in Plan II, among the oldest and finest honors programs in American Higher Education. The Plan II curriculum in the academic and scientific disciplines brought together each year 150 of the University's most promising matriculating undergraduates, so that there were 600 students in the program at any one time, studying with professors known for the excellence of their teaching.

John's 150-student sophomore course was "Philosophy 610Q: Problems of Knowledge and Valuation." In it, students and John's four teaching assistants read, discussed, and wrote about the works of philosophers from ancient Greece through the Enlightenment. In his lectures, arguing against what many students had, unfortunately, been previously taught, John described the ways in which facts and values are interwoven, not separable, not meaningful in isolation from each other. Study of these ideas began with reading Platonic dialogues.

In the second semester, after students had done a great deal of reading, listening, talking, and writing, John made the largest assignment of the course, the "Slum Project." Students, many of them advantaged and sheltered, were assigned to choose, go to, and learn about slums: who lived there, why they lived there, how they lived, what health and educational conditions prevailed in the lives of children there, why slum dwellers did not leave, who profited from slums, and such other questions as they realized had to be asked. Where necessary, a teaching assistant talked with local police to determine whether a student could safely do the work.

The slum projects yielded some of the best undergraduate work I have ever seen or evaluated, deeply insightful and moving, with a mature sense of conjoined facts and values, penetrating in the application of serious philosophical concepts of justice and equality in frightening, dire, and dangerous circumstances of life. The work rubbed away some of the innocence and naiveté of many students and sometimes shed light on prejudice. A significant number of students became much more aware of the vitality, reach, and depth of the philosophers they had studied throughout the course. Few of the students I came to know as a teaching assistant were inclined after the slum projects to disparage classrooms by claiming they were separate from and less important than "the real world," not only because of what 610Q was, but because they had seen how dreadfully real – that is, destructive of human spirit and potential – some slum classrooms can be.

In 1986, John and I returned to Austin together for him to deliver the keynote address at the celebration of Plan II's fiftieth anniversary. We went again in 1996 for me to deliver the address at the program's sixtieth anniversary celebration. These reunions were delightful in bringing us together with many Plan II alumni we had taught years before, men and women who had clearly benefitted from the program.

By the time John became president of Boston University in 1971, he had learned a great deal about deficiencies in public schooling at all levels. He had already known about failings in higher education – shallow curricula without required core courses, area studies instead of real disciplines, faculty self-indulgently teaching their narrow specializations instead of subjects students need, lax standards for tenure, courses taught by teaching assistants rather than faculty members, grade inflation, too little homework and too few demanding assignments. He set out to remedy such failings as he found at Boston University. Twenty-two years into his presidency, he told parents of matriculating students, "The recruitment and retention of outstanding faculty has been our highest priority and our single greatest investment over the past 22 years.... We have never made an appointment on the basis of quotas ... yet we have the largest percentage of female faculty of any major research university in the country."

He repeated to parents and students, "Self-discovery is the primary function of undergraduate education"; and he expressed his heartfelt hope that their daughters and sons would share the experience and resolve of Oliver Wendell Holmes Jr., who said, "Through the great good fortune of our youth, our hearts were touched by fire. It was given to us to learn at the outset that life is a profound and passionate thing. And we were permitted to scorn nothing but indifference."

In John's abiding concern for the achievement of good character as part of the project of genuine self-discovery, he taught that no form of indifference more deserves scorn than indifference to doing the right thing. At times he framed this as John Fletcher Moulton had done in referring to "obedience to the unenforceable" – that domain of morals and manners that falls between the domain of positive law that governs our conduct and the domain of mere taste where we are free to do as we please. In obeying the unenforceable, living up to our duties in public and private life, we do what is right because it is right, "when there is no one to make us do it but ourselves." John warned that there is always the threat of encroachment on the domain of morals and manners, on the one hand by those who would enact laws destroying freedom and on the other by those who would insist nothing is really right or wrong and exhort us, "If it feels good, do it." So important is it, John taught, to protect the domain of the unenforceable from encroachment and to achieve the integrity to do the right because it is right, that "the future of our country, our future happiness and that of our children depends decisively on whether we as individuals and as a people practice obedience to the unenforceable."

The excellence that John cultivated in Boston University provided the template for restoring high quality in the Chelsea Public Schools. By 1989, when, at the invitation of Chelsea, and under state laws enabling the project, Boston University undertook the Boston University/Chelsea Public Schools Partnership, the Chelsea schools had fallen into disrepair physically and educationally. No new schools had been built since the World War I era, immigration had dramatically altered demographics and overwhelmed the schools' capacity to provide real educational opportunity, and urban corruption had gutted city resources. Shortly after B.U.'s entry into the Partnership, Chelsea went bankrupt and became the first New England city since the Great Depression to fall into receivership.

At that point, the Partnership grew from restoration of schooling into restoration of a city's capacity for self-governance. Neither John nor the B.U. personnel he had named to work in the Partnership, nor their counterparts from Chelsea, flinched. Reversal of the conditions that had caused bankruptcy required successful criminal prosecutions of public officials and the drafting of a new city charter with the provision that no one convicted of a felony while in public office could hold public office again. This provision was tested by a public official convicted of income tax evasion while in office who claimed his civil rights were being violated and also that income tax evasion was a "private felony" having nothing to do with his holding public office. Boston University fought his suit to the Massachusetts Supreme Court and prevailed. Thus was Chelsea safeguarded from repetition of some earlier criminal exploitation.

Both state and private funds raised by Boston University (which they put directly into Chelsea projects without deducting a single penny) went into building new schools, transforming the teaching faculty and administration at all levels, and providing new educational opportunities for both veteran staff and newly appointed personnel to work with accomplished faculty at Boston University and in cooperative teaching in Chelsea classrooms. State legislation spared Chelsea from "last hired, first fired" and similar contractual requirements that typically safeguarded incompetent personnel from accountability. Thus, unlike in many other school districts, in Chelsea accountability became the norm, as it had become already inside Boston University. With it came improved student performance, reduced drop-out and fade-out rates, and more students continuing their formal education beyond high school.

Student literacy rose as, at John's insistence, phonics took the central place in reading instruction and as genuine bilingual opportunity took root. Nothing in schooling took precedence over the establishment of a state-of-the-art early childhood learning center with unsurpassed instruction and guidance for children.

Improving the Chelsea police department through providing trustworthy and experienced leadership and some new replacement personnel reduced weaknesses and added to the cadre of decent police already there. Bringing school and religious leaders, police, medical personnel, nutrition specialists, business figures, parents, public officials, students, and their Boston University counterparts to work together to improve safety and health conditions in Chelsea enabled the city to repulse attempted incursion by dangerous gangs such as the Latin Kings, reduce rates of teenage pregnancy and sexually transmitted disease, improve dental health, limit drug trafficking and related crimes, and make schools into real and safe centers of learning.

All of this depended on earning trust in Chelsea, above all the trust of parents. Many parents saw the good that was being done and were pleased that, at the city of Chelsea's request, Boston University stayed the course, continuing the partnership for twenty years. In that time, the partners addressed all the necessary conditions of good education in the home, the schools, and the streets. When the formal partnership ended, cooperation between the university and the city did not. Friendships and mutual trust have secured longer-term affiliations.

Despite Boston University's record of successes, of difficult challenges faced and met, of learning from mistakes, of growing mutual cooperation and trust – and the actual restoration of a city's capacity for self-governance under very difficult conditions – no other university in the United States had the courage during the life of the partnership to attempt anything on a similar educational and civic scale.

The partnership included extensive participation by faculty from the School of Education and the College of Arts and Sciences. Throughout his presidency of the University, John had elevated the quality of faculty in both. SED, as the School of Education is called, had been a very high priority from the start. In addition to his experience in schools, John had studied the most reliable research on schooling. It showed that precipitous declines in student achievement in literacy, mathematics, and sciences in America, beginning perceptibly in 1963, matched declines in educational achievement and demonstrated ability among many people entering teaching. In many schools of education the admission and retention standards, in terms of SAT scores, high-school GPA, and class standing, were the lowest in their universities.

John made the situation at Boston University far different. By 1996 he could say, "The combined SAT score for students entering our School of Education is 1238, 240 points above the national average and even higher than that above the Massachusetts average. To achieve these results, we were forced to restrict freshman admissions. We reduced [entering] enrollment from 489 students in 1970 to 98 in 1996, costing us about $35 million. We now have about 100 exceptionally well-qualified individuals in each undergraduate class where we could have had at least 200 if we lowered our standards. But there are not many universities willing to forego about $35 million in tuition to maintain the integrity of their program."

The investment in SED did not stop there. In addition, B.U. awarded ten four-year full-tuition scholarships each year to students the University and SED particularly wanted to attract. These outstanding students, known as Presidential Scholars, enriched class discussion, helped to attract very strong faculty, and encouraged other students.

Furthermore, by the early 1990s, John had approved the appointment of humanists in SED – scholars and distinguished teachers in literature, philosophy, history, and the fine arts, whose courses in SED added much to the intellectual power of its curriculum for both undergraduate and graduate students. Some of these faculty also had appointments in the College of Arts and Sciences, thereby increasing cooperation between the two schools in ways that had salutary effects on teaching in Chelsea.

The challenges during John's chairmanship of the Massachusetts State Board of Education were certainly as difficult as those of transforming Boston University and restoring Chelsea. Eleven years before John and I joined the board, Massachusetts had enacted a law requiring state certification testing for teachers; but the law had never been implemented or enforced. In the face of fierce opposition from entrenched interest groups and their political allies, John led the state board to successful implementation of the requirement for certification. This set limits to educational incompetence and forced schools of education to try to raise their own standards of admission and standards for faculty and student performance.

At the time that John became chairman, public school curricula in many districts were in disarray; administrative edicts that came fast and furious led to little but confusion and financial waste; chasing educational fads made everything worse. In the face of such debilitating habits in schooling, the board saw to the drafting by excellent scholars and teachers of extremely reliable curriculum frameworks for academic subjects and sciences. These were of great assistance to teachers and administrators designing and teaching courses, including courses in subjects to be required by the state at various grade levels. The board then implemented MCAS, the Massachusetts Comprehensive Assessment System – achievement tests in various subjects at various grade levels that would measure certain dimensions of student learning and of school and teacher effectiveness and that would also establish minimum graduation standards. While some of this work broke new ground in American schooling, we did not everywhere reach the highest goals we had set; but we did improve educational opportunity for many Massachusetts students and teachers.

Much of the resistance to these steps was resistance to accountability itself. We took this resistance head on. John's work everywhere centered on the inseparability of accountability and the achievement of excellence: "The more competent the teacher, the more easily he or she can make claims on the time, attention, and efforts of students." Whatever the other circumstances in the lives of students, no matter how inimical to learning their environments outside school, it is competent teachers and administrators who have the best chance of doing them some good. And at Boston University, in Chelsea, and in Massachusetts, we tried to improve the outside environments as well, always focusing on accountability of the people responsible.

The image of accountability John often used was "The Tremble Factor." By it, he meant the *frisson* that comes with facing reality. Specifically, in ancient Rome, architects and builders of arches had to stand underneath their arches when all supports and scaffolds were removed. If the arch fell, it took the people underneath with it. That, he insisted, is really facing reality, including the possible reality of your own incompetence. Having to face reality is a hugely powerful inducement to achieve competence and do your work to the highest standards of which you can become capable.

Add accountability to integrity, combine having to face reality with obedience to the unenforceable, and each of us has the greatest chance of a fulfilling life, the satisfactions of work well done and life well lived, the realization of our aspirations in public and private life. These were John's beliefs.

The intellect and character, the resolve and dedication that John Silber brought to the conduct of his life made scholarship and teaching a calling for him. Every institution in which he worked shows the depth of his commitment. So do the lives of his family and friends, to whom his commitment was equally deep, his devotion, if anything, stronger.

John had no time for hobbies, because his work always transcended the duties of the offices he held. In this, he was different from many college and university presidents who abandon any scholarly or intellectual interests they may have had on the grounds that they are too busy for them. John never did this. When he retired from executive duties inside and outside Boston University, he could not be said to "return" to philosophical work and to scholarly reading and writing, because he had never left it. He gave priority to completing the manuscript for his highly regarded book, *Kant's Ethics: The Good, Freedom, and the Will*, published in 2012.

That book and this one confirm that John's mental powers never diminished. But with age, his physical health drastically deteriorated.

Years before, during the gubernatorial campaign, a reporter had asked John's opinion of organ transplants for the elderly, and he had replied that in his old age he would not seek a transplant. He would feel guilty, he said, taking an organ desperately needed by a younger person with much life yet to be lived.

So, as John's body failed and caretakers asked about an organ transplant, it was a question he had faced and answered long before. To the end, he remained faithful in private life to the answer he had given as a public figure.

Readers should not be surprised that John Silber died as he lived. Throughout his life, he took mortality seriously, just as he encouraged others to do in the quest for self-discovery. In his last days, he did not flinch. He faced death's reality as other exemplars of courage have done: Socrates in Athens, Hector in Troy, Eleazar in Egypt.* With his loved ones, John was cheerful, even humorous, to the end. In his final correspondence with intimate friends, written when death was imminent, he expressed gratitude for his opportunities to pursue his goals and appreciation for the enrichment of his life by his friendships. He reminded those closest to him how full his life had been and urged them not to be sad at his parting.

EDWIN J. DELATTRE: *Professor of Philosophy, Emeritus, Boston University. Dean, Emeritus, Boston University School of Education. President, Emeritus, St. John's College, Annapolis, MD, and Santa Fe, NM.*

* II Maccabees 6:18–31.

SEEKING THE NORTH STAR

Preface

THIS BOOK consists of speeches delivered over forty-some years, from 1971 to 2012, addressing a variety of problems, occasions and opportunities that seemed and still seem to me worthy of careful and enduring consideration. While the speeches were delivered in a variety of venues, each is, in some way, an extension of my work as a teacher – that is, an inducement to reflection and dialogue. Many of these speeches were followed by lively question-and-answer sessions, and I would welcome the equivalent of these from my readers. The issues are worthy of serious discussion.

Out of more than 200 speeches, I have chosen those whose ideas concern the future of our nation, with a particular emphasis on the future of our youth. When, prior to running for governor in 1989, I wrote the book *Straight Shooting,* I did so because I was alarmed at what I felt was happening to our country. This concern has remained with me from the late 1960s forward.

In 1960, I returned to the United States after a year in Germany as a Fulbright Scholar. I had taken my family with me; and while I had enjoyed participating in the life of ordinary Germans while also teaching and writing in the University of Bonn, I returned home to a country that inspired me by its dynamism, habits of hard work, and idealism.

Shortly after my return, I as a Democrat supported the candidacy of John F. Kennedy in a debate with the late Charles Alan Wright, who was a staunch supporter of Richard Nixon. I believe I won that debate, not because of my eloquence but because of the superior qualities of my candidate. I said as much to Charles. Unimpressed, he replied, "But I won the debate." In any case, we both thought our nation would be in good hands no matter which candidate won. Both candidates were capable of decisive leadership and, inspired by the legacy of the presidency, would try their best to meet its high expectations. Both were men of political skills who could garner support of a Congress which had been dynamically

1

led by outstanding individuals: Sam Rayburn, legendary Speaker of the House and Lyndon Johnson, Senate majority leader. Their political skills and commitment to the good of the nation greatly benefited the presidency of Dwight Eisenhower, who by consulting with the majority and minority leaders of the House and Senate had the advantage of knowing what he could accomplish as president. Consulting with no more than four individuals, he learned the limits of the art of the possible. As a result he had a colorless administration that disappointed those who liked fireworks, but important legislation and useful programs were passed, and our nation prospered and was at peace.

In the administration of Lyndon Johnson, extraordinary achievements in civil rights were offset by our involvement in the Vietnam War. The former began to heal a division in our country, while the latter began to divide us. In the late sixties and early seventies a chasm developed in the perception of our country between the older and younger generations.

As a member of the older generation, I accepted the presidency of Boston University in 1970 with the need to develop some rapport with the younger generation as it engaged in responsible and irresponsible activism. I became more and more aware that I and other Americans felt that something was terribly wrong – the way we might know in our own bodies that we are seriously ill. I wished in these speeches not only to diagnose some of the problems besetting our country but also to evoke what is splendid and strong about America, its traditions and political institutions. I offered suggestions to make our country whole and home to a flourishing people. While each speech was written with the general listener in mind, I paid particular attention to the perspective of the younger generation. Our country has always been able to live with divisions that arise between conservatives and progressives. But I do not believe we can survive as a house divided between the young and the old.

Because I am by habit a teacher, I do not engage in assertions so much as in facts and arguments by which I try to explain and justify the positions I have taken. In offering this justification, I frequently refer to other sources, individual thinkers, politicians, writers, and poets who have contributed insight on the issues I discuss. Those who wish to explore further the ideas of those whom I have quoted will know where to turn.

This book may be read a chapter or two at a time, or straight through. Readers will find, I think, a progression of thought and concerns in reaction to events from 1971 forward; and two themes carry through this entire series of speeches. One is the issue raised in "The Pollution of Time": I believe the ordering of our lives in a temporally meaningful way is essential to human happiness. I also think that our civilization depends absolutely on obedience to the unenforceable, on the necessity of obeying sound practices that cannot be enforced by law. Without that, we descend into dissension and chaos. In every speech these concerns are implicit if not explicit.

The last chapter of this book explains, as best I can, that although I remain an intellectual pessimist, I am at the same time a congenital optimist. My parents and grandparents accepted life as it came, with courage and determination to make the best of it. They lived in a nation that believed that we can not only overcome our problems, but can create a future better than our past. This, I suppose, is my inheritance which I commend to my descendents.

The Pollution of Time

"An instant culture moves by nature toward its own destruction."

The first essay in this collection, "The Pollution of Time," was my inaugural address to the University, delivered at Commencement in May 1971. This was a time of student unrest – indeed, student revolution – and the common theme of the day was the so-called generation gap. There was profound alienation between parents and students, between older and younger generations. This seemed to me a state of affairs inimical to, even destructive of, well-ordered life for individuals and for the nation.

The alienation between the generations began in the early sixties. Its beginnings included idealistic sentiments, many of them expressed in the 1962 Port Huron statement of the Students for a Democratic Society. This idealism persisted but became mixed with self-interest as some of those privileged to attend universities found themselves exempt from military service and entered the university not primarily to study but to avoid the draft. The draft law had the effect of dividing the country between those who served and those who took advantage of academic exemption. The Vietnam War, which deserved to be questioned, became the focal point of student protests that eventually developed into violent confrontations, including, in 1970, a homicide, as the Weathermen bombed a laboratory at the University of Wisconsin. It was in this atmosphere that I addressed the students, their parents, and the faculty at my inauguration at Boston University.

THINGS FALL APART

We are living in a period that is unique not merely in the life of this nation; it is unique in the history of humankind. We have reached the cultural watershed our artists anticipated. Fifty years ago Yeats wrote:

Turning and turning in the widening gyre
The falcon cannot hear the falconer;
Things fall apart; the centre cannot hold;
Mere anarchy is loosed upon the world,
The blood-dimmed tide is loosed, and everywhere
The ceremony of innocence is drowned;
The best lack all conviction, while the worst
Are full of passionate intensity.

Our times render these now familiar lines terrifyingly apposite. Yeats, you will remember, in his vision that "Things fall apart," perceived a revelation, possibly an occasion no less momentous than the Second Coming itself. He asked:

And what rough beast, its hour come round at last,
Slouches towards Bethlehem to be born?

Possessed of poetic prescience, Yeats feared that if it were the time for a Second Coming, it would be the coming not of a sweet babe in a manger, but of something monstrous.

The gyre has widened!

Twenty-five years ago my generation spent Saturday afternoon at the movies watching Henry Fonda play Frank James in *Jesse James*. Later they watched him play Frank James in *Frank James*; and still later, Frank James in *The Return of Frank James*. And it was always the Robin Hood legend – a poor citizen oppressed by the rich, saved by a man who would preserve right and justice even though he chose the way of an outlaw. This assault on the "Establishment" was not regarded as subversive, for it was part of the Robin Hood legend, a socially accepted form of protest learned at our mother's knee. The Robin Hood legend, 800 or 900 years old, was still believable and exciting only twenty-five years ago.

Not long ago, today's graduating class saw Henry Fonda's son, Peter, in *Easy Rider*, a movie about outlaws, but not about Robin Hood. There are no Merry Men; a few gay ones, perhaps, but none that are merry. No fair ladies. There is none of that simple, optimistic poetry of the Frank James–Robin Hood era. Rather, *Easy Rider* is a restatement of the Faust legend, a new version of Peer Gynt or of Jurgen – all dramatic attempts to express humanity's insatiable quest for meaning and the difficulty of finding it, whenever and wherever one lives. At the climax of *Easy Rider*, in the midst of an ecstasy brought on by drugs, we find Fonda, who plays Captain America, weeping in the arms of a large, stone, female figure. The figure might be seated before the Supreme Court building in Washington: clearly, she is Columbia, with her weeping son on her lap. But in the background we hear the children at the nearby church school, reciting their Hail Marys and singing the "Kyrie Eleison." And we recognize that this woman must also be Mary, Mother of God – a Pietà after Michelangelo. The associations converge. Fonda is saying, "Mother, I hate you; Mother, I love you," expressing the profound ambivalence of today's youth toward parents, society, and their religious and political heritage.

SCIENCE AND THE INSTANT CULTURE

Youth has good reasons for its ambivalence. We are in danger of losing our center as changes overwhelm, confuse, and ultimately debase our social and cultural order. I have time this afternoon to cite only a few of these changes, hoping that the mere citation will evoke elaboration by your own imagination.

We have witnessed the ambivalent triumph of science and technology that has carried us from an uncertain world, in which we looked at nature in confusion, impotence, and fear, to the point at which we see nature as essentially under our control. This triumph of science has brought with it a quasi-religious scientism. Its creed runs: we can get at the facts and thereby control anything. This overlooks the fact of our own presence in nature and our inability to control ourselves. Its inflated rationalism has put an inordinate value on efficiency and an inconsequential value on admirability. Overlooking the human, the scientific creed also overlooks the significance of human time. By focusing on the rational ordering of discrete facts, it has disregarded the process or passage between them. Science has in part caused and in part abetted a corruption of time by the promise of instantaneity.

The Janus face of science was only gradually revealed. For a while its development seemed altogether ennobling, uplifting to humankind: Galileo, Kepler, and Newton made marvelous predictions concerning the heavens. The Newtonian era opened up a whole technology, resulting in the invention of the steam engine and of thousands of devices that made life healthier and more productive. The development of wonder drugs promised great advances in health.

But with the outbreak of World War II, suddenly there was the other face: instant death through the development of atomic and hydrogen bombs. The limiting point was reached in this century as science became the dominant cultural force controlling nature, minimizing the contingent or accidental elements of human life, and aiming at instantaneous control over nature. Fertilizers and insecticides produce instant abundance, even if it means flavorless plenitude and indiscriminate poisoning; television and radio offer instant communication, even if it means instant boredom and vulgarity; rockets and airplanes facilitate instant travel, even if it means instant death. Instant death, of course, is rendered tolerable by the scientific, business, and advertising interests which educate a society on wheels and on wings to accept casually a frightful carnage as a part of instant living – over 50,000 deaths each year on the highways, an annual toll that in each of several recent years has exceeded our total battle casualties in World War I.

The development of pharmacology has led to our increased reliance on drugs, with the promise of instant "mental health." The Food and Drug Administration did not require persons on Miltown to hang a sign about their necks saying, "My personality is chemically derived." And Miltown was but a pastel daydream preceding the nightmare adventure with drugs. Casualties in Vietnam and at home include the growing mass of users of marijuana, LSD, and heroin.

The vastly increased use of hallucinogenic and pleasure-inducing drugs has led to the development of instant religion promising instant ecstasy. Where Plotinus would persist in spiritual discipline for a long lifetime to achieve three experiences of religious ecstasy, in which by transcending his own individuality he achieved union with God or Being, a young person today achieves instant ecstasy at a needlepoint: an instant escape, not into Being, but into nothingness.

Even our traditional eating habits have been transformed by the instant culture: we now have instant foods leading to instant indigestion, for which there is an instant cure – the noisy bubbling of which brings to mind the witches' brew in Macbeth. Americans reach an uneasy truce with their ugly digestion through the intercession of Alka Seltzer.

The corruption of time is evident not only in the overreaching of science. More seriously, we see it in the development of instant politics – politics by assassination and creedless revolution. We see it in our loss of a sense of history, in a loss of the recognition of the past as our own, in the loss of the awareness of any past, in the loss of the past in general.

INSTANT CULTURE AND THE POLLUTION OF TIME

An instant culture moves by nature toward its own destruction. Ours moves towards the last moment of its short existence by throwing away its heritage, its institutions, and the patterns marking a meaningful ordering of time in the passage of the individual from infancy through childhood to adulthood and old age. All over the nation we hear cries of alarm about the pollution of air and the pollution of water, but we hear little or nothing about a pollution far more serious – that of time itself. We can, after all, recycle air and water through filters. But we cannot recycle time. We can live meaningfully – though painfully, unpleasantly, and briefly – in dirty air, drinking dirty water. But when the structure of time is destroyed, the basis for significance in our own lives is likewise destroyed. All meaning is lost in the instantaneous.

The human concern for meaning, for a life that makes sense, is what lies behind the demands of youth for relevance and the demands of the elderly for law and order. In the search for meaning, all of us are essentially concerned with time, for time is the very matrix of human existence. And this initially unstructured matrix must be given content if our lives are to have meaning. Unlike us, the animals are timeless. As Nietzsche says, "they graze, they fight, they procreate and die in an eternal present." But we, because of memory, foresight, and thought, live in a past, in a present, and in a future. We endure. Our overarching project becomes that of building a structure or pattern of significance into our lives.

This unavoidable quest for meaning is best pursued by ordering our lives in a manner faithful to our temporal natures. Since we live in time, we have different responsibilities, obligations, and functions, depending on our changing age. A child should be a child and not an adult; an adult should be an adult, occasionally childlike perhaps, but never childish. Our lives are blighted or even destroyed when the temporal order is not respected. A child can be ruined or his or her adult life made unbearable by being propelled into an adult world for which he or she is not ready. Children's sexual immaturity must be acknowledged in the organization of society and in childhood education. In adolescence sexual problems are dominant and must receive attention in our institutions. Special problems likewise attend the aged, and the concerns of the old have as much relevance to the search for meaning in life as the concerns of the very young, for the very young will surely be old if they live long enough.

But the instant culture allows no time for the development of a variety of human relationships at substantially different levels of intensity: all associations, including the most profound and the most intimate, are placed on an instant footing. We indiscriminately use first names in addressing total strangers; we have become experts in instant friendship, instant sex, and even instant marriage – marriage that can be dissolved immediately after instant consummation.

We see the pollution of time in the loss of the myths of childhood. As rationalistic devotees of scientism, we cannot afford to rear our children on Grimm or Andersen, on the myths of Santa Claus and Bethlehem or of Easter and Passover. We do not believe that there is a time and a place for everything – a time to be born, a time to be a child, a time to be an adult, a time to be old, and a time to die. We cannot take time to observe the rites of passage. Only thirty years ago, long pants for boys was one such rite. Now long pants are issued to toddlers. So how does a boy know when he is a man?

In this instant culture, little attention is paid to the rites of baptism, confirmation, engagement, marriage, or even of death. What then is left of the meaningful structure of time? Time, that great river of life, is polluted and fouled to a degree threatening all possibility of meaning in human existence.

The philosopher of instant culture is Diogenes. He needed a lantern only for rhetorical purposes, to remark on the scarcity of honest men. He never dined; he only ate. He wouldn't make love; he would only rut. He was also an intellectual ascetic. Diogenes was said to have remarked to Plato, "Tables and chairs I see, but the form of table and the form of chair I do not see." To which Plato replied, "Of course, Diogenes, for tables and chairs you have eyes, but for the form of table and for the form of chair, a mind is required." Diogenes recognized only what he could see and touch. He recognized only isolated perceptions and experiences, and not meanings, which depend on development and continuity through time.

Having nothing to sell, Diogenes prided himself that he could not be bought. And the modern Diogenes, scorning all idealism, is exquisitely honest, if honesty means simply the absence of hypocrisy. However, if the absence of hypocrisy means only that one has espoused no ideals, there may be some value in recalling La Rochefoucauld's aphorism: Hypocrisy is the tribute vice pays to virtue. One must at least espouse an ideal to achieve the level of hypocrisy; hence, a hypocrite may excel a mere cynic. In our fully developed instant culture sincerity has become the only virtue – for sincerity alone among the virtues can be assessed at a given moment. Sincerity, however, is no substitute for integrity; and integrity, or moral character, can be assessed only through time.

Diogenes scorned marriage, and today commitment has become a dirty word in the mouths of those most sensitively reflecting the instant culture. For how can one whose primary virtue is sincerity be committed to a lifelong bond like marriage? How can one who prizes only sincerity promise to love and honor indefinitely when he or she may not feel like doing this years, months, or even minutes from the time of making that avowal? No one stays in love for long except through commitment. Hence, the anomaly of marriage in an instant culture.

Our society's pattern of two-generation families – and this for only a few years – is typical of the instant culture. Children are denied the important discoveries that are to be made about human existence by observing old age and death. The very old are denied the sense of renewal implicit in birth and childhood. Children are deprived of wisdom and grandparents of hope. Persons, bereft of the sense of enduring family ties, spend most of their lives in isolation from those who care most about them.

THE POLLUTION OF TIME IN EDUCATION

This atomistic tendency is evident as well in our universities, where strategies of inquiry dominated by inappropriate models of the scientific enterprise have produced specializations in the humanities, the social sciences, and even in the sciences themselves that are so narrow as to resist combination into a coherent body of knowledge.

Specialization which atomizes learning and thereby renders it non-meaningful has been encouraged by programs of quite deliberate incoherence. The cultural pursuit of non-meaningful phenomena, which Marshall McLuhan has called to our attention, is only another expression of the instant culture's disdain for temporal process. McLuhan, as the diagnostician of the instantaneous, has shown the fragility of meaning in a post-electronic age that stresses instant perception and thought. As if human beings thought any faster today than in pre-electronic times! As if they could transcend the brackish water of their nervous systems in which currents move, not at the speed of light, but at the same modest pace of pre-electronic years!

Failing to recognize McLuhanism as an intellectual diagnosis, many educators have embraced it, plunging headlong into meaninglessness with light shows and multimedia extravaganzas on almost any subject from psychedelic chemistry to *WOW* freshman English. The formula is simple: turn on three speakers, light up three screens; set a couple of strobe lights flashing; set up the overhead projector and a series of transparencies; then, and only then, begin lecturing in the midst of confusion and diversionary activity!

All we know about the psychology of perception and of concentration has been set aside in the name of simultaneous absorption. Recently, I had occasion to evaluate a lecture on the language of fish. It included a stunning movie with fish swimming by, making a babble of fishy noises. Some sang from their swimbladders, little bubbling, gurgling sounds like a coffee pot; others swam by with snaps and clicks, tiny aggressive sounds, little tap, tap, taps; still others made amorous noises too subtle for description. Eighth- and ninth-grade students watched the film. But on its sound track was also the noise of a rock band! (The imposition of Schubert's "Serenade" would have been equally distracting.) When I asked why rock had been added and why students were expected to distinguish fish sounds from all the implausible noises of the band, I was told that rock music would increase the children's interest!

The assumptions were clear. So was the condescension toward children. Without distracting gimmicks, no eighth- or ninth-grade child could be interested in the possibility that fish use sounds in order to communicate. No normal children would want to watch the fascinating movements of the fish or hear their entrancing sounds. It was assumed, in short, that the young have no intellectual curiosity, no interest in organized and meaningful data – that instantaneous, non-meaningful education is not merely acceptable but ideal. The assault on time through muddying its contents was made an essential feature of the educational program.

This experience is not isolated; it is symptomatic of a current trend in teaching that defeats its purpose by masking out temporal organization. The multimedia approach is increasingly adopted without any qualms about the mind's power to absorb confusing and conflicting data. Adherents of the movement are not embarrassed by saying and showing what cannot possibly make sense.

I am not suggesting that temporal structures need be spare. Leonard Bernstein pointed out some years ago that one of the marvels of opera is its power to present several conflicting points of view simultaneously yet coherently. In the quartet from *Rigoletto*, for example, two people sing inside a hut and two people sing outside; yet all the voices fit together. This concentrated melding of diverse viewpoints is the work of the music, which provides a coherent temporal and tonal organization. Full analysis of the quartet is possible only for those who have read the score and the libretto; yet through the power of opera a listener can, without analysis, experience the simultaneous presentation of four viewpoints with a sense of intense meaning.

In sharp contrast to such orchestration, the multimedia faddists throw raw, unordered data at our students. This unhappy consequence of the instant culture, this pursuit of simultaneous chaos, defeats our ability to discern coherent meaning.

WHAT UNIVERSITIES CAN DO ABOUT
THE POLLUTION OF TIME

It is the purpose of education to awaken each generation to the possibilities of a coherent and meaningful life. The program of our universities must therefore be to instruct students in the importance of time in its lived concreteness, and in the way in which scientism has corrupted time by treating it as a mere "independent variable," ignoring the processes of duration and transformation and focusing instead on mathematical descriptions of regular patterns whose only manifestations are physical. The process of life, the process of maturing and dying, is no less spiritual and intellectual than physical, and is individual rather than abstract. Just as the biological development of the individual may be said to recapitulate the development of the species, so the individual may be said to recapitulate aspects of human history in his or her intellectual and spiritual development. If the individual is to develop to a significant degree, he or she must discover, live with, and then discard some of the fundamental responses of the race to human existence. Otherwise, an individual may simply repeat those responses in their least significant and least satisfying forms.

Education, then, ought to involve a systematic recapitulation of specific stages in the spiritual development of human beings. We have a substantial choice in determining the direction and content of intellectual recapitulation. But unless important stages of thought and experience are lived through and rejected, growth may be superficial or crippled. And there is a rough correlation between the number and quality of stages recapitulated and the extent and profundity of the individual's development. Only after living through a carefully selected series of developmental stages do human beings acquire depth, range, strength, and flexibility as persons. Only then is there a chance for meaningful existence in a sustaining temporal order.

In ethics, for example, we may introduce students, first, to the claims and attractions of hedonism – the only major ethical system congruent with instant culture. After the attractions of hedonism have been dampened by ancient and modern refutations, the student may be ready for a deeper response to the problem of human existence. We cannot teach an ethics class by giving students the latest word on ethics. If we did, they might mouth the right conclusions, but they would likely regress to earlier positions merely because they had not grown through the previous stages. Students must live through intellectual and spiritual positions and grow out of them just as they once grew notochords and gill slits before discarding them for spines and lungs.

Recapitulative principles have an important and unrecognized part to play in the design of interdisciplinary courses. A course in law, history, English, and political science, for instance, might be developed according to these principles. A full year's course could be meaningfully devoted to the study of English and American history from Henry II through the American Civil War. In it students would study the emergence of that English common law which still provides the legal framework of our lives. As they retraced the growth of the common law, they would also study the historical context in which it matured. The historical narrative would, at the same time, reveal how the parliamentary system developed and the way in which political philosophies offered rational justifications and summaries of the unfolding stages. Combined with these studies there might be lectures and discussions in political philosophy, reviewing the contributions, for example, of Hobbes, Milton, Locke, and Mill; the English Bill of Rights, along with those of Massachusetts and Virginia; the Federalist Papers, the Declaration of Independence, the Constitution, and other documents crucial to the shaping of our political system. Students would not be primarily concerned with history as such, but with the development of those ideas that legitimate government, and with the growth of Parliament and Congress and of the common law, which together give substance to government. In short, the course would provide a comprehensive study of the domestication of political power, the process whereby political power can be transferred from one generation to the next without bloodshed – a study of the transformation of power into right. Educated persons will have learned this fundamental distinction. They recognize that great and good things are fragile and often perish, while corrupt persons and illegitimate movements sometimes triumph; consequently, they do not argue from the way things are to a justification of the way they ought to be. For our time and our society such knowledge is essential.

In sum, education must change in profound ways to meet the cultural changes that threaten our humanity. We must regain the same respect for time that the American Indian had for nature, for time is a part of nature. The Indian said that the earth was his mother, the sun his father, that nature was his law, and that all but human beings obeyed. In our instant culture, in which we have polluted not merely air and water but also the very temporal fabric of our lives, we know that recovery of respect for time requires the recovery of our past, the seeing of our present in terms of that past, and a strenuous effort to anticipate the future in the light of both.

THE OLDER GENERATION'S RESPONSIBILITY

It also requires the courage that we in this generation have lacked – the courage alluded to by Yeats. Survival is not possible if the best of us "lack all conviction, while the worst are full of passionate intensity." We sorely need conviction, a conviction that will prompt us – self-consciously and no doubt with embarrassment – to talk straight to our children about our heritage, about our past, and about aspects of life they may not fully understand. We need the courage to deny at some times and to give at others, so that structure, order, and meaning can be incorporated into the lives of our children, while restoring some structure in our own lives.

We can begin by acknowledging the justice in the demands of youth for meaning, and the terror implicit in our instant culture's destruction of meaning. Pascal described his era in terms that fit ours:

When I see the blindness and the wretchedness of man, when I regard the whole silent universe, and man without light, left to himself, and, as it were, lost in this corner of the universe, without knowing who has put him there, what he has come to do, what will become of him at death, and incapable of all knowledge, I become terrified, like a man who should be carried in his sleep to a dreadful desert island, and should awake without knowing where he is, and without means of escape. And thereupon I wonder how people in a condition so wretched do not fall into despair.

Pascal, writing in the closing days of an age of faith, gave effective voice to the sense of alienation. If even Pascal could be beset by doubts, blindness, confusion, and misery, how much greater and more intense must be the dread of those who come to consciousness in our own time. Are we not outrageously hostile to our youth if we fail to acknowledge their plight and ours with sympathy? For their plight is ours. Is it strange that in their blindness and confusion, denied explanations and honest answers, they should experiment? Are not the more sensitive forced by their anxiety to Faustian extremes?

Our youth can acknowledge the justice of the charge that they are at times ignorant, misdirected, confused, and foolish. But are they asking too much when they seek an *amicus curiae*, a helping hand? Is there not something amiss in our denunciation of those who effectively decry our false steps? Is it not reasonable that our children complain of the squalor of their lives in a spiritual wilderness, saying that their elders have neither vision nor hope of a promised land? Our youth articulate with remarkable clarity the blindness of our leadership. And their charge is not answered by our pointing out that their blindness is congenital, that it comes from us. If fault is to be found, surely greater fault belongs to the mature who lack vision than to youthful visionaries. Our children, estranged from us, suffer alone. We would have them back and share their suffering in the hope that we may heal each other.

BRIDGING THE GENERATION GAP

Of course there is a generation gap, but it is not unbridgeable. Under careful examination it is the ancient problem of generations. The generations have rarely understood each other. Why else should Moses have said, "Honor thy father and thy mother"? Not because mothers and fathers were being consistently honored at the time of Moses! The young and old will always be forced to carry the burden of transferring the vitality of civilization from one generation to the next. Physical vitality is transferred through the act of procreation, but the vitality of civilization is not so easily passed on. The heir must be readied for his or her patrimony, and the parents must be prepared to relinquish their estate.

Aristotle observed that "youth has a long time before it and a short past behind: on the first day of one's life one has nothing at all to remember and can only look forward." By contrast, the elderly "live by memory rather than by hope; for what is left to them of life is little as compared with the long past; and hope is of the future, memory of the past." The old must be taught to hope and live for a future even while little is left them; the young must be taught to look to the past of which they know almost nothing. The old must look forward in imagination to what youth can see; youth must look back to discover what the old have already seen. In this way a significant present comes into being for both young and old as the specious now is extended before and after to become a temporal matrix in which meaningful existence can flourish.

The problem of generations is hard, but not insoluble. We have seen a dramatic resolution in the way in which young and old each possesses Zeffirelli's film version of *Romeo and Juliet*. After 375 years, this tragedy of the generations still stirs and educates young and old, and may bring them to common ground.

I doubt that Shakespeare's lovers and friends have ever been presented more compellingly than in Zeffirelli's movie, with marvelously beautiful and vivid young men and women. And I was amused to observe my own children's resentment at the presence in the audience of older men and women, for they thought it their film – a celebration of youth at which the middle-aged or older were not welcome. Their feeling that the film was so peculiarly theirs that it should not be desecrated by older eyes was particularly touching, for clearly the play is about the tensions between the older and the younger generations and was written as much from the standpoint of the Montagues and the Capulets as that of Romeo and Juliet. So this film reflects the vitality of the problem and warns both young and old of the loss that attends misunderstanding. The film's success confirms the truth of this Shakespearean statement.

Zeffirelli's presentation was particularly effective in giving us a feeling for the difference between the old and the young. They are so radically different, so properly and wonderfully different, and it is important that we cherish those differences. When a fifteen-year-old girl and a seventeen-year-old boy awake from the night of their nuptials to argue about whether it is the lark or the nightingale that is rousing them from their sleep, it makes lovely, poignant sense. Before Zeffirelli, the argument was more likely to be between a thirty-five-year-old woman and a forty-five-year-old man. At those advanced years, they would have either known the answer or been less passionate about the question. Zeffirelli proved that older people cannot play those youthful roles convincingly.

Zeffirelli respected time, and in so doing gave us an example we may emulate and ponder. He understood that lyric poetry is virtually impossible for the old, just as it is natural for the young. How can an old man say that he will die of unrequited love, when he knows that he didn't? To suppose that one could requires the ignorance of youth. But this is the ignorance that, for a time, surpasses knowledge. The capacity to love with the intensity of the young, the capacity to cherish ideals with that absolute and intransigent commitment of youth, is one of the marvelous human traits. It is a quality that diminishes with age. And this is why longevity is not in all respects a blessing: not only the precious, delicate moments of youth, but the future of idealism might be eclipsed if the old ever substantially outnumbered the young. Youthful enthusiasm and idealism could then be overwhelmed by the multitude of persons who had lived long enough to know better.

Of course it would be no less an evil for the young substantially to outnumber the old. Both are needed. The old, with their wisdom and earthbound experience, are necessary correctives to the soaring fantasy, untested idealism, and despair of youth. But the intensity, idealism, and despair of youth are equally needed correctives to the pragmatism, cynicism, and pallor of age. It is important, desperately important, that we accept our youth for their idealism and that they accept us for our experience. Together, we are effective partners. Separate, we are murderous gangs – one intent on filicide, the other on parricide. To avoid the murder of our children, we must recognize them as our own. To avoid killing their fathers and mothers, the young must recognize the identity of their intended victims. Initially, their parents; eventually, themselves.

No failure in political leadership in recent years can compare in importance with the failure of all politicians and all parties to denounce those who exacerbate the difficulties between the generations and encourage a civil war between young and old that can only be the tragedy of Romeo and Juliet writ large.

The initial skirmishes of that war have been fought in Vietnam, where, for nine long years, the old have squandered the lives of 45,000 young men and bled the bodies and the spirits of millions of others to assert a right for the people of South Vietnam analogous to that rejected by Abraham Lincoln. When Robert E. Lee and Jefferson Davis claimed for the Confederacy the right of self-determination, they were told by President Lincoln and by force of Union arms that "a house divided against itself cannot stand." The house stood, and the Union prevailed, but American support of the right of self-determination for a part of an initially cohesive people was a casualty of the Great Rebellion. Can we tell the youth of America that on the sacred principle of the right of self-determination South Vietnam may demand or expect our support in separating from North Vietnam? The same claim was made by Jefferson Davis to elicit British intervention in our Civil War – another move stoutly resisted by Lincoln. By what illogic and what ignorance of our past is this right now proclaimed?

In Concord, Massachusetts, is a grave of British soldiers. Over that grave are written the following lines:

> They came three thousand miles, and died,
> To keep the Past upon its throne;
> Unheard, beyond the ocean tide,
> Their English mother made her moan.

The poetry is embarrassing, but the thought is tragic. After more lives are lost, after more of our youth are absorbed into the drug culture of Saigon, our engagement in Vietnam will cease. And somewhere in Vietnam an ironic survivor may adapt that poem for the graves of American soldiers left behind:

They came eleven thousand miles and died
To keep the past upon its throne.
Unheard beyond the ocean tide
Their American mother makes her moan.

Young and old, each guilty of rhetorical overkill, are participants in a culture on which none of us has had an effective influence – an instant, time-polluting culture that, after a 400-year gestation, caught us by surprise. For this perhaps unavoidable destruction of the meaningful order of time in the instant culture, we are neither individually nor collectively to blame. Nevertheless, we are moving rapidly toward our own destruction. But the process is not inevitable, and the rewards to be gained are of the highest value.

If we reorder time to celebrate youth and age and the gradual metamorphosis from one to the other, if we regain our sense of time and value our present differences in the recognition that each of us plays all the parts in sequence, we shall see that there is no salvation for the young or the old at the expense of either. Our fulfillment depends on collaboration in a time that is well ordered.

A Tribute to Martin Luther King Jr.

"The fad of the anti-hero should not blind us to the importance of genuine heroes and to the miracle of great individuals."

I accepted the presidency of Boston University on January 15, 1971, and quickly immersed myself in the history of that institution. Among other things, I discovered that Martin Luther King Jr. was our most famous alumnus. In the spring of that year, we took note of Doctor King's birthday with a two-day observation focusing on his work as America's foremost civil rights leader and the tragedy of his assassination and that of Robert Kennedy. I addressed our students on April 5 on the importance of celebrating the lives of our great leaders and urged them to remain undeterred and undiscouraged even though outraged and saddened by their untimely deaths.

A GENERATION OF HISTORIANS has debunked the theory of the great man, the importance of the individual person to the history of a nation or an age. But other historians and the facts of history, obvious to all with even a modest knowledge of their own times, prove the opposite. The history of the Weimar Republic and, hence, the recent history of Germany and Europe would have been profoundly different had it not been for the series of assassinations and heart attacks that removed all of their most effective and constructive democratic leaders.

More painful to us as Americans is the recognition that today our nation faces a crisis of political and spiritual leadership through loss by assassination and heart attack of Malcolm X, John F. Kennedy, Robert Kennedy, Whitney Young, and Martin Luther King Jr. We face the question: Can a nation survive the loss of so many of its finest leaders? All but the most Pollyanna must acknowledge that the answer to this question is not yet in.

Barring the emergence of new and as yet unrecognized sources of spiritual insight and imagination, of political sagacity and moral force, the pessimist's answer becomes increasingly persuasive.

The fad of the anti-hero – that current tendency to seize quickly, if briefly, on a virtual nonentity as the object of public acclaim or to write that nonentity into the leading character of a best seller – should not blind us to the importance of genuine heroes and to the miracle of great individuals.

To offset the anti-heroic craze, we might do well to designate special days of mourning and memorial services for all those recently fallen. But if we cannot spare the time to remember and to honor each of them, we do well in selecting Martin Luther King as representative of our loss. For while Malcolm X, John and Robert Kennedy, and Whitney Young fell in early- or mid-career, much of Martin Luther King's work had been accomplished. Though cut short, there was a completeness to his life that was denied the others.

Martin Luther King left behind not merely a strategy for social change that is being carried on by his followers, but also a body of philosophical and theological argument establishing the basis for change and the reasons for his strategy. And he bequeathed a dream of the future that has inspired all of us.

Between the first and the final attempt on Martin Luther King's life lay a decade of achievement in defining the moral and religious justification for courageous and assertive nonviolent resistance. From the day in 1958 when Martin Luther King was almost fatally stabbed while autographing books in a Harlem department store to that day three years ago when he was fatally shot, he wrote, among other things, his "Letter from a Birmingham Jail." This document has already found its place, along with the writings of Thomas Jefferson, Thoreau, Plato, and Gandhi, among the normative treatises on the Rights of Man.

In this work Martin Luther King drew upon Jesus, Socrates, Amos, Saint Augustine, Saint Thomas Aquinas, Martin Luther, Martin Buber, Paul Tillich, Thomas Jefferson, and the Negro Church to argue in favor of "nonviolent direct action [seeking] to create such a crisis and establish such creative tension that a community that has constantly refused to negotiate is forced to confront the issue."

In that document he set forth the four basis steps in any nonviolent campaign: "(1) Collection of the facts to determine whether injustices are alive; (2) Negotiation; (3) Self-purification, and (4) Direct action." In developing the concept of self-purification, Martin Luther King made one of his most original contributions. He prescribed workshops on nonviolence and insisted that those engaged in campaigns of nonviolence ask themselves, "Are you able to accept blows without retaliating?" and "Are you able to endure the ordeals of jail?"

In order to distinguish himself and his followers, who broke laws in a campaign of nonviolence, from those who violate the laws under other circumstances, Martin Luther King wrote:

I hope you can see the distinction I am trying to point out. In no sense do I advocate evading or defying the law as the rabid segregationist would do. This would lead to anarchy. One who breaks an unjust law must do it *openly, lovingly* (not hatefully as the white mothers did in New Orleans when they were seen on television screaming "nigger, nigger, nigger") and with a willingness to accept the penalty. I submit that an individual who breaks a law that conscience tells him is unjust, and willingly accepts the penalty by staying in jail to arouse the conscience of the community over its injustice, is in reality expressing the very highest respect for law.

In this we have a relevant restatement of Socrates' argument in the *Crito*, as he expressed his respect for lawfulness by accepting execution while preserving his integrity as the Gadfly of Athens who had aroused the conscience of his community.

The basic position developed by Martin Luther King Jr. in his "Letter from a Birmingham Jail" was reiterated on the steps of the Lincoln Memorial during the march on Washington on August 28, 1963, when he said:

We must not allow our creative protests to degenerate into physical violence. Again and again we must rise to the majestic heights of meeting physical force with soul force. The marvelous new militancy which has engulfed the Negro community must not lead us to distrust of all white people, for many of our white brothers, as evidenced by their presence here today, have come to realize that their destiny is tied up with our destiny.

They have come to realize that their freedom is inextricably bound to our freedom. We cannot walk alone. And as we walk we must make the pledge that we shall march ahead. We cannot turn back. There are those who are asking the devotees of civil rights, "When will you be satisfied?"...

... We will not be satisfied until "justice rolls down like waters and righteousness like a mighty stream."

In so speaking, Martin Luther King spoke not only for blacks; he spoke for all human beings in the range of his voice or his pen. He spoke for and to the conscience of all mankind.

The moral case of the Negro is overwhelming. It shames all fair-minded persons. Martin Luther King, as few others in history, could evoke that shame – first, through laying the moral and spiritual predicates for his indictment, and then by dramatizing the injustices suffered by the black community so grippingly that even the blind could see.

Martin Luther King reached the heights of the Prophet Nathan in his denunciation of King David, when he indicted the American people from his cell in Birmingham:

I guess it is easy for those who have never felt the stinging darts of segregation to say, "Wait." But when you have seen vicious mobs lynch your mothers and fathers at will and drown your sisters and brothers at whim; when you have seen hate-filled policemen curse, kick, brutalize and even kill your black brothers and sisters with impunity; when you see the vast majority of your twenty million Negro brothers smothering in an air-tight cage of poverty in the midst of an affluent society; when you suddenly find your tongue twisted and your speech stammering as you seek to explain to your six-year-old daughter why she can't go to the public amusement park that has just been advertised on television, and see tears welling up in her little eyes when she is told that Funtown is closed to colored children, and see the depressing clouds of inferiority begin to form in her little mental sky, and see her begin to distort her little personality by unconsciously developing a bitterness toward white people; when you have to concoct an answer for a five-year-old son asking in agonizing pathos: "Daddy, why do white people treat colored people so mean?"; when you take a cross-country drive and find it necessary to sleep night after night in the uncomfortable corners of your automobile because no motel will accept you; when you are humiliated day in and day out by nagging signs reading "white" and "colored"; when your first name becomes "nigger" and your middle name becomes "boy" (however old you are) and your last name becomes "John," and when your wife and mother are never given the respected title "Mrs."; when you are harried by day and haunted at night by the fact that you are a Negro, living constantly at tip-toe stance never quite knowing what to expect next, and plagued with inner fears and outer resentments; when you are forever fighting a degenerating sense of "nobodiness"; then you will understand why we find it difficult to wait.

The power of Martin Luther King's indictment was multiplied by the tactics of nonviolent resistance, for in the program of nonviolence he shattered the moral pretensions of those who would resist the claims of justice. He spoke not just for blacks but for us all in demanding, in the words of Amos, that "justice roll down like waters and righteousness as a mighty stream." He knew, as few people have, that moral and spiritual power may exceed mere physical strength. He knew that a person who would be callous and indifferent to a show of physical force that could easily be put down, could be shamed and transformed by a moral indictment lovingly presented.

The futility of trying to correct one wrong by committing another has been pointed out numerous times. The poet Yeats put the argument as follows in his four-line poem, "The Great Day," written on the eve of the Second World War:

> Hurrah for revolution and more cannon-shot!
> A beggar upon horseback lashes a beggar on foot.
> Hurrah for revolution and cannon come again!
> The beggars have changed places, but the lash goes on.

This insight was one of King's central concerns.

Martin Luther King, clear in his indictment of injustice, advocated nonviolence as the strategy for its correction. He knew that unless the oppressor is removed by love and the power of righteousness, the injustices of one oppressor will be replaced by the injustices of another – with no moral advantage to the world.

In closing, I am reminded of Yeats's poem, "In Memory of Major Robert Gregory," in which the poet reviewed in imagination his fallen friends and companions. As the faces of some returned to him in imagination, he wrote, "I am accustomed to their lack of breath." But when the face of his special friend appeared, Yeats was shocked that he "could share in that discourtesy of death."

We feel this shock and incongruity about Martin Luther King. Thinking of King, we might say with Yeats:

> Some burn damp faggots, others may consume
> The entire combustible world in one small room
> As though dried straw, and if we turn about
> The bare chimney is gone black out
> Because the work had finished in that flare.

And with Yeats we ask, "What made us dream that he could comb grey hair?"

Do we stop here? Or do we go on to remember and honor the other fallen heroes to whom I referred earlier? The last stanza of Yeats's poem has the answer:

> I had thought, seeing how bitter is that wind
> That shakes the shutter, to have brought to mind
> All those that manhood tried, or childhood loved
> Or boyish intellect approved,
> With some appropriate commentary on each;
> Until imagination brought
> A fitter welcome; but a thought
> Of that late death took all my heart for speech.

The Humanities, the Crucible of Higher Education

"If one cannot be knowledgeable in all things, the knowledge of Shakespeare may be more important than the knowledge of calculus."

In 1973, shortly after becoming president of Boston University, I was invited by an editor of the *New York Times* to write on the humanities for the *Times*'s annual education review. I chose to emphasize the fact that the humanities, while quite properly making use of the sciences, are not themselves to be understood simply as scientific in the usual sense, or as subordinate to the sciences; rather, it is in the humanistic context that the sciences themselves flourish.

IT WOULD BE CURIOUS if scientists did not study science, if artists did not practice the arts. Yet humanists need not and often do not specialize in the humanities. It would likewise be curious if those who work in science and the arts were not scientists and artists. Yet those who work in the humanities need not be and often are not humanists. This anomalous situation has a historical explanation.

Humanists were first recognized as men with secular concerns who studied human affairs, history and culture. Petrarch, for instance, is considered one of the founders of humanism and one of the inaugurators of the Renaissance. Humanists presumably had "the mental cultivation befitting a man," that is, a liberal education. When humanism developed, the essential content of education was literary and moral – the study of grammar, rhetoric, classical languages, poetry, and philosophy. These fields, which were then the substance of secular education, survive more narrowly today as the academic departments of the humanities.

But that liberal education befitting a human being can no longer be so confined. To answer questions central to human culture and affairs, humanists have been forced to move far beyond their traditional boundaries into the natural sciences, social sciences, and the arts. So it is no accident that among our greatest humanists we must count men like Michael Polanyi, Victor Weisskopf, René Dubos, Paul Samuelson, Paul Rosenstein-Rodan, and Paul Freund. And although there are distinguished humanists in literary studies, notably Jacques Barzun, Edmund Wilson, Lionel Trilling, and Harold Bloom, one finds no more humanists in the traditional humanities than outside them.

The alienation of humanists from the humanities is an established fact. Many of the successors of the traditional humanists are not humanistic at all; they have lost the enabling faith in human greatness.

Confronted with the triumphs of science, the humanistic disciplines have responded by becoming ever more "scientific." An almost religious scientism has captured the academic and public imagination. Scientific programs that are powerfully effective in understanding and controlling artificially isolated data have been applied crudely, reductively, and disastrously in the humanities and the social sciences. Discipline after discipline has succumbed to the dogma that only the quantifiable is true.

Classics departments have become covens of philological "scientists." Classicists who can do paleographical somersaults with every line of Euripides may understand less of the controlling moral terms of tragedy than the average tourist guide to Greece. Students who have been taught to run computer checks on textual variants in Shakespeare, to do exhaustive image counts, to analyze Tudor phrenology, and the like, are unable to expound the human meaning of "ripeness is all." Was it Shakespeare's point that we live in time, are therefore mortal, and that humans must think mortal thoughts? Or shall we count the stressed syllables per line, trace out alterations in the texts, and identify the Dark Lady of the sonnets? All these studies are respectable, polite, and possibly important, but they are of direct concern, not to humanists, but rather to other scholars, to linguists, biographers, prosodists, chiropractors, and detectives.

A major branch of linguistics, like cavalry, has been mechanized; by computer metamorphosis this Panzer division made of what was once a humanistic study has rolled over semantics and syntax and speeds towards translation with uninhibited hubris. Economists and sociologists who refuse to put their insights in the language of mathematics are increasingly ignored, and this despite grave warnings from first-rate theoreticians that a mathematical façade often conceals utter triviality. While clinical and phenomenological psychologists fight for their lives, Skinnerian behaviorism reduces human existence to the simplest non-meaningful levels of its dogmatic, although "scientifically" formulated, metaphysic.

Mathematical logic, semantics, and linguistic analysis have castrated philosophy: There are few major departments where the Socratic tradition and its preoccupation with justice and virtue, courage and wisdom is taught without apology or compromise. Many leading philosophers speak with open contempt of "wisdom philosophy," unaware that the philosopher who is ashamed of wisdom is no philosopher. The majority of philosophy departments have compromised themselves with scientific subjects which they teach amateurishly with trivialistic rigor and fatuous clarity.

The study of the past, once crucial to the humanities, is now, by edict of professional historians, a social science. Its justification as a science is as elusive as ever, but the opposition to literary and intellectual historians is hardening. Witness the current disdain for Macaulay, Duff Cooper, Carl Sandburg, and A. J. P. Taylor.

The reductionistic use of the methods of science by the traditional humanities and the social sciences may lead eventually to the overt reaction against science predicted by Polanyi. There are already signs of that reaction in flights to irrationality by student protesters. The true concerns of humanists are now largely unexplored by teachers in the traditional humanities and social sciences. The scientist, all too aware of the false extrapolations made from scientific methods, is now a likelier custodian of these concerns. The humanities therefore will not profit from any reaction against science. The scientist's respect for probable or reasonable answers to questions that can never be answered with certainty is an article of faith of every humanist. It frees us from the superstition that truth can be known with absolute certainty.

No one has contributed more to confusion about the humanities than C. P. Snow. There are not two cultures but at least three – the scientific, the artistic, and the literary. All must be mastered through the enlightened concerns of humanists or misunderstood through the distortions of reductionists. Instead of arguing that humanists and scientists should understand one another, Snow should have argued that all matters of human concern are the proper concern of humanists, and that knowledge is incomplete when science, letters, or art are studied exclusively.

If one cannot be knowledgeable in all things, the knowledge of Shakespeare may be more important than the knowledge of calculus. The more important point, however, is that the educated person should know both. If we must choose, we choose to fall back on those studies central to human existence and experience. It is possible to live reasonably well in ignorance of many scientific and mathematical discoveries; but no one, not even the most creative scientists, can be truly human without a generous sense of poetry and the human past.

The Norseman would have been impoverished without his sagas. Take from him his sagas and give him algebra, and he would lose in the trade. Poetry touches and reflects human experience more nearly than mathematics, although mathematics may be closer to pure rational being.

Of course, we must be mundane, professional, and parochial as we identify the order of the tales of Chaucer, examine the role of propinquity in the selection of marriage partners, and break the code of DNA – making our livings in the process. But we touch the core of our lives and those of our students as we contemplate and discuss the human verities, the mysteries of birth, love, suffering, joy, and death. These are the proper concern of the humanities and humanists, whether in science, social science, letters, or the arts. These are the issues that Jacques Barzun, the greatest humanist of our times, has examined in *The House of Intellect* and *Science: The Glorious Entertainment*.

The humanities have traditionally professed a faith in humanity and in human greatness, a faith that "the proper study of mankind is man" and that the crucial obligation of each individual is to know himself or herself. If this faith is kept alive, it will be nourished and cherished as often by physicists, chemists, and economists as by philosophers and classicists. If it is kept alive, it will be because the humanities have been rediscovered as concerns that motivate and shape all scholars, artists, teachers, and students. It will be because all academics come to recognize themselves as essentially humanists, obligated to hold human concerns foremost in their studies and teaching and to resist inhuman reductions wherever they occur.

The Tremble Factor

"Without the element of risk, the capacity for serious thought is lost."

In 1974, I was invited by The Colorado College to speak at their centennial program. I knew the college well through my friendship with its president, Lloyd Worner, and with Professor Glenn Gray, an important philosopher and the only one who, at that time, as far as I know, had written a book on war - this despite the overwhelming presence and importance of war in the twentieth century. My address was attended by most of the student body and faculty. I felt honored to receive this invitation until I was notified by both President Worner and Professor Gray that, to whatever criticism I might offer of education and the humanities, I was to make a constructive response. What follows is my attempt to meet these somewhat exacting demands.

THE PRESENT AGE in America and in most of the West is perhaps best described as an age of bewilderment: it is marked by a pervasive sense of loss, alienation, and indirection. In every age and in every society, men and women have known personal tragedy; many generations have witnessed the destruction of family, social class, or nation. But we, like the Greeks of the fifth century B.C., have witnessed the climax and accelerating deterioration of a culture. In the span of Socrates's life, Sophoclean order gave way to Euripidean chaos and Aristophanic derision; leadership passed from Pericles to Alcibiades, prosperity gave way to wretchedness, and power to ruin. In the span of our lives, change has been even more rapid and pervasive. Consequently, although we have not yet experienced general destruction and ruin - despite our Syracusan misadventure in Vietnam - we have suffered nevertheless a serious loss of meaning and direction.

It is not merely our cities that are changed before our eyes - historical and comforting old landmarks torn down to make room for the bastard offspring of the Bauhaus; it is not merely the general diaspora of families and ethnic groups by the nomadic forces of industrial technology; it is not merely the inherent instability of an economic system in which too many forces are variable; it is not merely a matter of displaced religious fervor consequent upon the secularization of the age; it is all of these and more. Change appears to have devoured the entire fabric of tradition on which the meaning and significance of our existence depends. As Sholem Aleichem has said, "It is tradition that tells us who we are and what we are to do." Now that tradition has been consumed by change, we must all endure a diminished identity until we find ourselves anew.

This diminished identity affects institutions no less than individuals, particularly liberal arts colleges for whom tradition has historically provided a core curriculum. Institutions and individuals must regain their sense of identity and direction by coming to terms with change. But coming to terms with change must not mean capitulating to change, learning to float in the flux of solutions offered by cultural opportunists. Instead, I suggest that we must reach an understanding of change: we must fathom it, measure it against those aspects that are constant; we must discriminate between that which is enduring, that which is inexorably in motion, and that which, though in flux, can be anchored by human resolve.

Among the things that endure are surely the realities of economics, even though a generation of affluence unprecedented in world history has resulted in avoidance or unawareness of economic reality. Consider a society in which artificially aged and worn blue jeans sell for more than new ones. The ragged blue jeans that a Depression generation wore with resignation and looked forward to replacing are the very blue jeans a subsequent generation deliberately goes out and buys. This is a straightforward consequence of excessive affluence and an additional verification of Adam Smith's law of supply and demand – a predictable market phenomenon in which abundance deflates while scarcity inflates. The younger generation finds a special value in the costumes of poverty and disarray simply because these aspects of life have become far scarcer for the children of the middle class than good clothes and comeliness. Just as French aristocrats at the time of the French Revolution took delight in dressing as peasants and in playing out bucolic roles, our affluent young people affect the costumes of poverty. In their horizon, the poor are little more than a romantic abstraction.

Avoidance of intellectual and mental reality reaches a climax in the drug culture. Andrew Weill, in his book *The Natural Mind*, advocates "stoned" as opposed to "straight" thinking. Weill argues that, in "stoned" thinking, under the influence of drugs used to enhance one's mental processes, things go better than when one is engaged in "straight" thinking. By "straight" thinking, he means the kind of thinking that "squares" do. The presumption and double-talk in Weill's writing is revealing: for example, he says, "The trouble with straight thinking is that straight thinking arises directly from the first characteristic of straight thinking – identification of the mind with the intellect, and the acceptance of intellectual descriptions of reality as truths without submitting them to the proof of trial by actual experiment." What is the basis for this idea? One of the chief characteristics of "straight" thinking has been the achievement of scientific method, in which the intellect deliberately devises techniques for asking nature questions and forcing nature, like a reluctant witness before the bar, to answer "yes" or "no" to a series of experiments before her. And the use of nature as a witness either to confirm or to discredit hypotheses of the intellect is, of course, at the very heart of scientific method and intellectual inquiry.

In a "stoned" experiment, moreover, who can test the content of this experiment against reality? By what actual experience is the content of the "stoned" intellect tested? The faculty available to make the test is a "stoned" intellect – an intellect after it has been disrupted by drugs and deprived of its evolutionarily derived correspondence with reality. Will this intellect be in a better position to assess, verify, and evaluate the content of the "stoned" experience than one not disrupted? The characteristic feature of "stoned" thinking is the withdrawal from all but idiosyncratic experience. If one could derive meaning in life from talking solely to oneself – and if we ignore the social dependence of talking – there might be a case for drug-induced thought. Yet the fascination with drugs and the question-begging character of their description as "psychedelic" are facts worthy of careful examination. They evidence further avoidance of reality.

We see a more general avoidance of personal reality in the development of encounter groups in which the concepts of privacy and personal dignity are either debased or rejected entirely as total strangers meet to reveal everything about themselves. As if there were no such thing as indecent exposure of the mind and the psyche; as if we could allow ourselves to be known by just anyone; as if we can be known by just anyone.

Note the difference in the theology and anthropology of the encounter group movement and the Christian Church. An ancient collect of the Church says in part, "Almighty God, unto Whom all hearts are open, all desires known, and from Whom no secrets are hid. . . ." It is one thing for a man or woman to reveal himself or herself openly and freely before an all-wise, all-good, and all-powerful God, if that is their belief. It is quite another to reveal oneself in the context of an encounter group openly and freely to just any old stranger whose name one does not even know. As a matter of fact, Caribbean cruises were designed for the same purpose. They are less expensive, at least as therapeutic, and far more dignified.

One of the worst encounter groups, of course, is the underwater school that practices therapy by total immersion. Participants find that by bathing together naked in warm water they can escape more effectively the reservations, hesitations, and aspects of self-control on which civilization has depended for at least 10,000 years. As if nothing were lost by losing the capacity for self-restraint; as if some repression were not a good thing.

It is interesting to note the encounter group movement's departure from Sigmund Freud without so much as an argument. Freud recognized civilization's dependence upon sublimation, upon inhibitions, upon the capacity to deny expression to a variety of human instincts. In *Civilization and Its Discontents*, Freud pointed out that mankind's capacity to sublimate its sexual drive motivated the development of civilization. If Freud is right, we should not expect many civilized advances from those who would rather make love than anything else. One of the most powerful sources of human motivation is the desire to provide both the means and context in which to realize sexual potentiality. When this potentiality can be expressed casually, with daily accessibility under any circumstances and without obligation, it is possible that some of the motivation crucial to personal achievement and civilization is lost. It is possible that a large part of Freud's hypothesis will be put to a test over the next generation.

The avoidance of reality in these various aspects – physical, social, economic, intellectual, and personal – alters substantially the role and responsibilities of the college. Its role is likewise altered by the change and decline of other institutions, most notably the decline of the home and the church. Rearing our children in affluence, we have left them in moral and spiritual ignorance. We reared our children to be happy, without making too many demands upon our time or theirs, and we reared them without interference from their grandparents. By "happy" we meant nothing more profound than personal, immediate pleasure. Suspicious or merely bored by the judgments of priests, rabbis, and ministers, we in effect turned our children over to television for their basic theological and moral education. Our children have not been corrupted by the teachings of the Old and New Testaments, but they have learned by heart to enjoy themselves. The view that you have the right to whatever you want and whatever you can get, provided it makes you happy, is the morality of Watergate. It is also the morality of many who commit mindless, pointless crimes of violence.

The college must not merely redirect the interest and concern of students to those aspects of physical, biological, social, economic, and personal reality from which in this cultural desert they have been encouraged to withdraw; it must assist the family and the church by providing instruction in ethics, civility, and parenthood.

The faculty and administration of our colleges must regain their sense of responsibility. The tremble factor – muted by tenure, senatorial courtesy, and long disuse – must be reactivated in the academic community.

The tremble factor is, of course, reality. The term "tremble factor" was first coined by the economist Paul Rosenstein-Rodan, a member of Boston University's faculty, to explain certain economic behavior. Its relevance is not restricted to economics but is applicable to all aspects of human life. It was used, for example, in the construction practices of ancient Rome. When the scaffolding was removed from a completed Roman arch, the engineer stood below. If, as a result of his own incompetence, the arch came crashing down, he was the first to know. The quality of his arch was an intensely personal consideration with him, and it is not surprising that so many Roman arches have survived.

Those of us within the walls of the academy too easily forget the serious purpose that brings us together and the responsibilities that are ours. We are trusted to work hard without the presence of time clocks, at salaries two and three times those of garbage collectors, store clerks, or factory workers. We are trusted with the lives of other people's children and given time to develop our own lives with virtually no interference. We are granted tenure in the trust that we will not let it become sinecure. At the same time, we are as prone as anyone else to laziness, loss of nerve, lack of passion, want of energy, and irresponsibility. Without careful attention we in the academy become a society of kept men and women – a society that has more in common with a resort than with a shoe factory or a coal mine from which the tremble factor is never absent. Like monks who have lost their faith in God and squabble over the keys to the wine cellar, we have lost our motivating faith in the transcendent goals that once gave meaning to our lives. Instead, we jockey for position in new schemes for university governance. In the last decade, we have witnessed a substantial loss of faith in and dedication to social, moral, and intellectual responsibility.

This faith must be regained. We must retain the clearest perception of those purposes that bring us together: the transformation of young people into mature, self-fulfilling, socially responsible human beings, capable of exercising clear, independent, rational judgment; the advancement of our knowledge and understanding of the physical world and human society and history; the achievements of perceptive and presentational imagination; the enthusiasm and excitement of discovery and the concern for teaching. Michael Polanyi, in his book *Personal Knowledge: Toward a Post-Critical Philosophy*, has aptly noted that:

Modern mathematics can be kept alive only by a large number of mathematicians cultivating different parts of the same system of values: a community which can be kept coherent only by the passionate vigilance of universities, journals, and meetings, fostering these values and imposing the same respect for them on all mathematicians. Such a far-flung structure is highly vulnerable and, once broken, impossible to restore.

Its ruins would bury modern mathematics in an oblivion more complete and lasting than that which enveloped Greek mathematics 22 centuries ago.

These goals properly bring people together in an academic community and give it meaning and purpose. Their intangibility is such, however, that faith in them is easily lost, and once the faith in these transcendent goals is lost, academic politics tend to become a major preoccupation. Woodrow Wilson correctly observed that the intensity of academic politics is a function of the triviality of its goals. When the transcendent ideals are forgotten, faculty members worry more about representation on a committee that, by its very size and constitution would be incapable of doing anything, than they do about solving the problems for which the committee was called into existence. Students, incidentally, can also lose sight of the goals that bring them to college and become mistakenly preoccupied in similar ways. They may suppose, for example, that instruction and practice in college administration are part of the approved curriculum.

The tremble factor – the return to reality – in higher education, of course, need not involve the threat of extinction that faced the Roman engineer or the threat of bankruptcy that faces the businessman or loss of election that faces the politician. When educators recognize that without the dedicated fulfillment of their responsibilities the arch of civilization will fall, they too experience the tremble factor. Those fit to hold academic positions are sufficiently sensitive to apprehend the tremble factor in imagination without physical or economic threats; their pride as teachers and scholars and their dedication to the values and insights that sustain the arch should be sufficient.

As faculty and administrators, we must also have the authority to call for excellence from students who work with us. The authority of the teacher is a direct function of his or her competence. The more competent the teacher, the more easily he or she can make claims on the time, attention, and effort of students.

We cannot sustain an effective teaching program unless it is staffed by persons who recognize themselves as mentors no less than as teachers. Students are concerned to know if there are living human beings who really care about the ideas and ideals professed in the academic community. If the intellectual program is merely a facade with no implications for the way anyone lives, this generation of bewildered and disadvantaged students is not going to be impressed.

Two years ago at Boston University, we hired a man named Brookshire who was amazingly crippled: he had a full-sized head and a body that was not more than eighteen inches long. He sat up in a wheelchair and smoked a very large pipe, taking small puffs of smoke that filled his fist-sized lungs. He had remarkable intellectual clarity, but he was little more than pure spirit. I doubt that we have ever hired a finer teacher. Imagine what it was like for a group of indulged students from Massachusetts, Long Island, and Connecticut to explain to Brookshire that they had problems! Imagine the effect on students who came face-to-face with the courage and vitality of this man. Did any dare complain about a grade?

The propensity to feel crushed or broken by trivial disappointment is to be expected from a generation whose priest and nanny is a television set. To dispel the false expectations of an ill-prepared generation, we must have teachers of competence and personal integrity – teachers like Brookshire. When a student discovers a teacher who spends his or her spare time in art galleries or theaters, who spends entire evenings reading books and writing, or who spends weekends in a laboratory, only then does that student take seriously the teacher's claim that such things have value. No teacher can affect the lives of students unless, like Brookshire, he or she gives meaning to courage and integrity and intellectual curiosity by the embodiment of these values in his or her own life.

Brookshire could not comb gray hair. Last February, our exemplary teacher died of influenza. Lungs as small as his succumb quickly to influenza. His life was short; his life was intense; his life was purposeful. There was no prayer or medication that could prevent Brookshire from dying; yet he had within himself the courage to be a happy man, the dignity and determination to be a fulfilled man.

Brookshire had the strength to stand beneath the arch of life without trembling. Without fear he affirmed life as it is and his fate as it was given. The way he lived sets the standard for us all.

The Thicket of Law and the Marsh of Conscience

"Mr. Ford has followed his conscience instead of subordinating it to the Constitution of the United States."

In 1974, the nation was deeply troubled by the scandal of Watergate and the fact that the highly competent president of the United States – who had not called for the Watergate break-in or had any responsibility for it – had nevertheless, out of misguided loyalty to his associates, defended them in ways that were criminal, compromising the integrity of his administration. I thought it necessary to speak out on this scandal and on its compounding by the pardon offered by President Nixon's successor. The issue, it seemed to me, was the threat posed to the rule of law on which our national polity is based.

The speech was an existential test for me because the vice chairman of our Board of Trustees was one of Nixon's key supporters and advisers. I had no idea what his reaction would be or whether my speaking and writing on this subject would jeopardize my position as president of the University. I can only conclude that my views must have been persuasive because I received no criticism from any member of the board.

I include a brief chronology which may help the reader to recall the situation in September of 1974.

A BRIEF CHRONOLOGY OF WATERGATE AND FORD'S PARDONING OF NIXON

On June 17, 1972, as Republican Richard Nixon is running for reelection to the presidency, five men are arrested attempting to bug offices of the Democratic National Committee at the Watergate hotel and office complex. The FBI and other sources gradually establish links between the operation and a large-scale illegal campaign against the Democrats conducted in the interest of Nixon's reelection. In November, Nixon is reelected.

On May 18, 1973, following conviction of two of the Watergate conspirators and the resignation or firing of top White House aides and the attorney general, a Senate committee begins nationally televised hearings into the Watergate affair. More evidence is uncovered.

On July 13, 1973, the Senate Watergate Committee learns that since 1971 Nixon has recorded all conversations and telephone calls in his offices. Edited transcripts of the tapes are eventually released. They include an unexplained eighteen-minute gap.

On October 10, 1973, Nixon's vice president, Spiro Agnew, resigns and pleads no contest to charges of income tax evasion stemming from charges of bribery and political corruption in a case pursued with the support of Attorney General Elliot Richardson. Once Agnew has resigned, Richardson argues for leniency. For the first time in history, the 25th Amendment is invoked: Republican Gerald Ford, House Minority Leader, is nominated for the vice presidency by Nixon and approved by majority vote of the House and Senate.

On July 24, 1974, the Supreme Court unanimously rejects Nixon's claim of executive privilege and rules that he must turn over tape recordings of White House conversations.

On July 27, 1974, the House Judiciary Committee passes the first of three articles of impeachment, charging obstruction of justice.

On August 8, 1974, Richard Nixon resigns the presidency and is succeeded by Vice President Ford. In his address after his swearing-in, Ford says, "Our long national nightmare is over.... Our Constitution works: our great Republic is a government of laws and not of men."

On September 8, 1974, President Ford grants "a full, free, and absolute pardon unto Richard Nixon for all offenses against the United States which he, Richard Nixon, has committed or may have committed or taken part in during the period from July (January) 20, 1969 through August 9, 1974."

"OUR CONSTITUTION WORKS: our great Republic is a government of laws and not of men." Thus Gerald Ford, succeeding to the office of president upon the resignation of Richard Nixon, began his administration by reasserting that enduring American value, the rule of law.

The importance of the rule of law is brilliantly set forth in Robert Bolt's play *A Man for All Seasons*, in a passage dealing with Sir Thomas More's impending confrontation with Henry VIII. More receives a visit from a devious and ambitious young man named Rich who appears to be spying on him in the guise of asking for a job. "Employ me," says Rich. "No," replies More. "Employ me!" says Rich desperately, and he turns to exit. Rich adds, "I would be steadfast!"

> MORE: Richard, you couldn't answer for yourself even so far as tonight.
> [Rich leaves and More takes counsel with his wife, Alice, his daughter, Margaret, and his prospective son-in-law, Roper.]
> ROPER: Arrest him.
> ALICE: Yes!
> MORE: For what?
> ALICE: He's dangerous!
> ROPER: For libel; he's a spy.
> ALICE: He is! Arrest him!
> MARGARET: Father, that man's bad.
> MORE: There is no law against that.
> ROPER: There is! God's law!
> MORE: Then God can arrest him.
> ROPER: Sophistication upon sophistication!
> MORE: No, sheer simplicity. The law, Roper, the law. I know what's legal, not what's right. And I'll stick to what's legal.
> ROPER: Then you set Man's law above God's!
> MORE: No, far below, but let me draw your attention to a fact – I'm not God. The currents and eddies of right and wrong, which you find such plain sailing, I can't navigate. I'm no voyager. But in the thickets of the law, oh, there I'm a forester. . . .
> ALICE: While you talk [Rich is] gone!
> MORE: And go he should if he was the Devil himself, until he broke the law!

ROPER: So now you'd give the Devil benefit of law!

MORE: Yes. What would you do? Cut a great road through the law to get after the Devil?

ROPER: I'd cut down every law in England to do that!

MORE: Oh? And when the last law was down, and the Devil turned round on you – where would you hide, Roper, the laws all being flat? If you cut them down – and you're just the man to do it – d'you really think you could stand upright in the winds that would blow then? Yes, I'd give the Devil benefit of law, for my own safety's sake.

Roper wants right to be done. He does not want to let the guilty go free; he seeks nothing less than the perfection demanded by the law of God. More is not insensitive to these higher demands, these loftier purposes. Like Roper, he prays, he reads the Bible, he understands theology, he is aware of the shortcomings of the law. But he would rather stand with human law and all its shortcomings than open wide the gates to the moral judgments of everyone, or anyone.

Without the constraint of law, not only Roper but anyone can decide what is right. He or she need not be deterred by what is legal. The imperative of conscience is a rationale open to any person, a guide to which everyone can lay claim. Conscience is therefore no better or wiser than the person to whom it speaks. Acutely aware of this, More recognizes that the voice of conscience is never backed by a Greek chorus authoritatively proclaiming, "This is the voice of God." By noting the advantages of a society grounded in law, More tries to convince his young friend of the need to transcend the subjectivity of individual opinion about what is right and wrong. It is More's point that without the law only contingencies may distinguish the idealist Roper from the scoundrel Rich.

The view that Bolt here puts into More's mouth is strikingly reminiscent of Justice Brandeis's celebrated dissent in the Olmstead case:

Decency, security, and liberty alike demand that government officials shall be subjected to the same rules of conduct that are commands to the citizen. In a government of laws, existence of the government will be imperiled if it fails to observe the law scrupulously. Our government is the potent, the omnipresent teacher. For good or ill, it teaches the whole people by its example. Crime is contagious. If the government becomes a lawbreaker, it breeds contempt for law; it invites every man to become a law unto himself, it invites anarchy.

On this issue the words of Brandeis are sage counsel for this nation. In the aftermath of Watergate we know that the president of the United States and some members of his staff, though not convicted in a court of law, were guilty by their own admission of precisely those actions that Brandeis condemns. The actions of Nixon's successor, while well intentioned, are also deeply troubling. As Roper wished to do, Mr. Ford, by his blanket pardon of Mr. Nixon, cut a path through the law in the name of God and conscience, thereby threatening to bring about the consequences outlined by Justice Brandeis. These consequences include a weakening of the balance of powers prescribed by our Constitution, as the executive power becomes less checked and balanced by the legislative and judicial branches.

During the late spring and summer of 1974, Congress, through the House Judiciary Committee, seemed to be shaking off the indolence of its last decade by faithfully fulfilling the duties inherent in its right of impeachment. Congress resisted Mr. Nixon's efforts to redefine an impeachable offense and otherwise to prescribe procedures of impeachment. These were steps toward the restoration of the balance of powers prescribed by the Constitution, but the process is far from completed. The authority and scope of the judicial branch have not yet been adequately reestablished.

Elementary legal traditions, such as that sanction should follow conviction of a crime, have not been observed. This part of the rule of law was clearly compromised in statements by former Attorney General Richardson at the time of former Vice President Agnew's resignation on charges of bribery. Richardson remarked, "I am fairly convinced that in all circumstances leniency was justified.... I am keenly aware of the historical magnitude of the penalties inherent in the vice president's resignation from his high office and his acceptance of a judgment of conviction for a felony.... Each individual will have to make up his or her mind about the justice of this result. I believe it is just, fair, and honorable."

Richardson's statement reveals the sharp decline of our expectations of our leaders. We are to be satisfied if a politician pays for his or her crime by removal from office and payment of a fine; that is, by denying him or her the opportunity to continue criminal activity and by taxing its proceeds. If the fox will wipe the feathers from his mouth, the fox may leave the chicken house with impunity. He has suffered enough by being asked to leave. This is perhaps adequate as a political solution to the political problem of removing a putative felon from the presidential succession. But Richardson confounds policy with justice and says of the arrangement, "I believe it is just, fair, and honorable." The national mood of cynicism was thus seen to erode even the sensibilities of the man who from the standpoint of personal integrity was one of the few redeeming members of the Nixon Administration. Fortunately, the Maryland Supreme Court resisted this cynicism. In disbarring Mr. Agnew, the court held, "It is difficult to feel compassion for an attorney who is so morally obtuse that he consciously cheats for his own pecuniary gain that government he has sworn to serve, completely disregards the words of the oath he uttered when he was first admitted to the bar, and absolutely fails to perceive his professional duty to act honestly in all matters." In this case, at long last, responsibility entailed consequence, and sanction followed conviction.

But the essential deficiency remained: it became increasingly apparent in the reluctance to move against President Nixon even after the House Judiciary Committee concluded that there was evidence of serious wrongdoing became unmistakable. This action was retarded not only by cynicism, but by a genuine, though ill-conceived, concern that no one should injure the office of the president of the United States. On this point we are all finally reassured. Subsequent events showed us that there is no way that anyone can injure or detract from the office of the president as long as we hold all incumbents to the very highest standards of moral, legal, and political rectitude. To hold the incumbents of this office to anything less would in fact have been the most serious way to impair if not destroy the office.

At last even Mr. Nixon's most loyal supporters realized that his conduct had been grotesquely incommensurate with the minimum demands of the office. Mr. Nixon himself was brought to understand that the Articles of Impeachment brought by the House Judiciary Committee were so well documented that he faced certain removal from office and that resignation was more advantageous to him than conviction following impeachment. With the accession of a new and unblemished president, the dignity of the office was instantly restored. The Ford Administration moved swiftly to regain the confidence and respect of the people by its explicit affirmation of the rule of law and the subordination of every citizen to it.

Regrettably, Mr. Ford held to this principle for no more than a month. Following the dictates of a conscience that although honest and sincere was far from wise, he pardoned a citizen who had neither been indicted for nor convicted of any crime. When Mr. Nixon went to bed on Saturday night, he was, in the eyes of the law, an innocent man. By Sunday evening, he was a pardoned criminal. The judgment that he had committed crimes was made by Mr. Ford alone, without benefit of any judicial proceedings. Such an act is an executive equivalent of a bill of attainder that our Constitution specifically prohibits Congress from passing.

Far from following the counsel of Brandeis and Sir Thomas More, the president impulsively and carelessly cut a great road through the law to "shut and seal this book [of Watergate]," to "write the end of it." With this laudable intent, President Ford laid flat every law that applied to Richard M. Nixon between January 20, 1969, and August 9, 1974. The winds of lawlessness now threaten Mr. Ford and the nation.

When Mr. Ford says that his conscience should be superior to the Constitution, he does no more than articulate the classical rationale for civil disobedience. But this may guide his personal and private behavior only. If citizen Ford finds that a higher law tells him to disobey the laws of human beings, and he is willing to take the legal consequences, a decent respect for the rights of conscience will allow citizen Ford to disobey the law and suffer the consequences. But President Ford must be bound to no law higher than the Constitution. He ought to have considered that restraint before accepting nomination as vice president.

Nor need he rely for an answer to legal questions on the subjectivity of his conscience. There are wise individuals on the Supreme Court who could have helped him understand his responsibilities to the

Constitution and the people. But Mr. Ford, in an unsettling revival of the habits of the Nixon White House, rejected all counsel and cut his own road through the laws.

The Supreme Court is the president's ultimate counsel on the Constitution. But President Ford has said of the Constitution that "the laws of God, which govern our consciences, are superior to it." There is in our polity no guarantee that the laws of God infallibly govern the conscience of the president of the United States. Nor is there in our polity any person or group of persons established to counsel the president on the laws of God. If Mr. Ford wishes to defend his act of conscience on the grounds that it faithfully expresses the laws of God, he would be well advised to consider that the Hebrew prophets and Jesus were unanimous in their opinion that God grants forgiveness only to the repentant sinner, that a prerequisite of forgiveness is a humble and a contrite heart. Mr. Nixon has not yet confessed to any criminal conduct for which pardon is required.

Only a lawless conscience, whether intentionally or not, counsels a course of action whose consequences involve obstruction of justice. Even if we believe Mr. Ford's reiterations of sincerity, we will not benefit from them if he pursues on principle the policy that Mr. Nixon pursued from expedience. Mr. Nixon's ruthless pursuit of self-interest and the misguided loyalty of some associates replaced the rule of law. President Ford's substitution of his individual conscience is little better. It is the essence of our agreement with Mr. Ford that he is to govern us according to the Constitution and the laws; we did not agree to be governed by his subjective conscience.

Despite the fact that Mr. Nixon's guilt was never proven in a court of law or by a Senate vote of impeachment, President Ford assumed Mr. Nixon's guilt and pardoned him from the charges of bribery; of burglary; of income-tax fraud; of the appropriation of public funds for personal use; of the misuse of the F.B.I., the C.I.A., and the I.R.S.; and of the obstruction of justice. In effect, President Ford first declared Mr. Nixon guilty without due process of law and then pardoned him. Instead of expecting more of those to whom much has been given, President Ford, following Richardson's unfortunate precedent, has held that far less shall be expected of a president of the United States than is expected from a Boston policeman. Following Richardson's rule, Ford concluded that merely to deny a person continuation in misconduct was sufficient punishment. Can this be the law of God? It is not the law of an enlightened community.

Mr. Ford told us that only he could write "The End" on what he called the American tragedy of Watergate. Mr. Ford is wrong, for only the law can put an end to Watergate. As things now stand, Mr. Nixon has gained what he sought so long in vain, what had been denied him by the Supreme Court itself: a special place in the legal system of the United States. President Ford has given Mr. Nixon what no other president ever gave to any alleged criminal: a blanket pardon for unspecified crimes without even the formality of an indictment, a confession of guilt, or a conviction. President Ford has overturned the precedent set by the Supreme Court in its decision that all Watergate tapes must be turned over to the House Judiciary Committee. He replaced it with a new one: no future president need worry about facing the legal consequences for any crimes he may wish to commit, if his vice president is willing to pardon him.

In cutting a road through the law, President Ford has used the power of his office in a highly irresponsible way, opening the door to an almost endless extension of pardons and commutations. Judges and juries who follow Mr. Ford's precedent cannot apply the standard of equal justice under law except by ignoring all violations of law. Mr. Ford can avoid these consequences only by recognizing and publicly acknowledging his mistakes. If he allows this one glaring injustice to stand, he should at least refuse to generalize his error. His error was not his desire to be merciful but his appeal to conscience and his failure to satisfy the formal requirements of justice before mercifully absolving Nixon of the penalties that would normally follow his conviction.

There is certainly nothing in Mr. Nixon's behavior to warrant special treatment. Despite his incessant attempts to blame Watergate on the press, to say he was hounded from office by his enemies, and to attribute his resignation to a loss of a political base in Congress, we must now see that he was personally responsible for what his successor has called the nightmare. Had he in fact been willing to get the story out in June 1972, or even following his reelection in November, there would have been a Watergate affair, but it would not have immobilized the government and distracted the people from the serious substantive problems at hand. It was Mr. Nixon's own formula to speak of Watergate getting in the way of the people's business.

Mr. Nixon has shown no contrition for what he has done to this country. He has not even shown any contrition for his contribution to the ruin of the lives of those involved in Watergate. Some of them were originally honest men too foolish to understand that not even the dictates of conscience allow the president of the United States to place himself or his subordinates above the law. His own insistence of his innocence and on treating the charges against him as mere errors of judgment shows how little Mr. Nixon at this point merits pardon. Only after Mr. Nixon acknowledges the claims of justice may mercy and pardon follow unrestrained.

Mr. Agnew has recently claimed that because he was not tried he is therefore in fact innocent of crimes. Mr. Nixon is likely to make similar good use of the fact that through the pardon process he has become, in the words of the Supreme Court decision that governs the granting of pardons, "a new man."

That the pardon process can be so grievously and easily exploited suggests the need for some reforms. President Ford should acknowledge his mistake, as President Kennedy acknowledged his mistake in the Bay of Pigs, and he should take all steps necessary to deny its force as precedent or example. There should also be a constitutional amendment placing some elementary limits on the use of pardons. A president should be barred from ever pardoning himself or his predecessor or successor, or from pardoning anyone prior to conviction. As it stands, the power of pardon has been open to grave abuse and remains open to worse: a president might enter into a corrupt bargain with his vice president, or with a prospective vice presidential nominee, and secure effective immunity for any crime he might commit. Even worse, a president might use the promise of pardon to procure the commission of crimes by others. As long as the power of pardon is unlimited, so is the range of crimes it can encourage. There is no sure way to prevent such abuses without limiting the power of pardon.

Mr. Ford appears to regard an ex-president as a royal personage, not affected by the precedents appropriate to mere subjects. In this he disagrees with Benjamin Franklin, who told the Philadelphia Convention, "In free governments the rulers are the servants and the people their superiors and sovereigns. For the former therefore to return among the latter is not to degrade them but to promote them." Mr. Ford's legal principles, inappropriate to the Founding Fathers, might have been appropriate in the Middle Ages when a new reign was frequently accompanied by the providing of blanket pardons.

Certainly these kinds of pardons serve no public end in a democracy and are in fact useful only to those who would abuse them. The Constitution of Massachusetts, adopted in 1780 and now the oldest written constitution in force, still contains its original provision that a pardon granted before conviction shall be of no avail. It is time the Constitution of the United States followed suit.

Before Governor Rockefeller is confirmed as vice president, he ought to be asked to renounce, in terms less ambiguous than those used by Mr. Ford last fall, any intention of granting pardons prior to conviction.

The government should now publish in full transcripts of all the Watergate-related tapes, without any deletion. The American people have a right to know exactly what has been done to them in the last five years. We are strong enough to bear the shock and to learn from it. If the president believes that we must be shielded from the truth, he will join his predecessor in believing that we are like children. Such contempt for the people is offensive under any government, and outrageous in a democracy.

In all of this President Ford has been quite sincere. He has responded faithfully to his conscience without recognizing the awful scope of his power and the range of responsibility that goes with that power. Instead of subordinating his conscience to the Constitution of the United States and a respect for the rule of law, he has, in a remarkably simplistic fashion, relied on his conscience alone. Apparently unaware of the web of consequences he has spun, Mr. Ford tries vainly to reassure us by saying, "I am certain in my own mind and conscience that it is the right thing to do." The people of the United States want and intend to be governed by the thicket of law rather than the marsh of conscience.

On his first night in the White House, John Adams wrote his wife, Abigail: "I pray Heaven to bestow the best blessing on this house and all that shall hereafter inhabit it. May none but honest and wise men ever rule under this roof."

The man who now lives under that roof is honest. While recent events raise doubts that he is always wise, a lapse of wisdom is perhaps easier to remedy than a lack of honesty. In his first speech as president, Mr. Ford affirmed his deep commitment to the rule of law. The American people, by frank criticism of Mr. Ford's actions, can help him to realize the magnitude of his error, avoid a repetition of it, and succeed in his great project of restoring the precious rule of law on which our nation is based.

Rabbi Joseph S. Shubow Memorial Lecture, Temple Bnai Moshe, Brighton, MA, September 11, 1974

Generations on Generations

"No generation can find meaning unless its present moment is informed by what it inherits and is accountable for what it bequeaths."

In "The Pollution of Time" I spoke on the generation gap and the problems we faced in overcoming it. On this occasion, I drew on examples from cultures ancient and modern, western and eastern, to establish and elaborate on the necessary and long-recognized interdependence of generations, and the crucial role of familial and mentoring relationships in personal fulfillment.

I was pleased to speak on this subject in Salt Lake City, the home of Mormonism, a religion that has emphasized these important interpersonal relationships.

THE INVITATION TO SPEAK to this conference is somewhat anomalous, considering that I have not published even one article on family life or even read extensively on this subject. Nor have I ever saved someone else's marriage or family. I suppose my only qualification for being invited here is that I have seven children and am still married to my first wife. The topic, however, is a matter on which all of us have to be concerned and on which some general statements can be made. A starting point are the eloquent words of John Quincy Adams, who thought of himself not as a founder, but as an inheritor of the American revolution and of the Constitution. Adams exhorted his fellow citizens to, "Think of your forefathers! Think of your posterity!" This is the position in which all responsible adults find themselves. If they want to have a life of their own, they must think of their forefathers and of their posterity.

These are the conditions on which continuity depends. The middle years together with the generations before and after are coextensive with human experience. They encompass the total range of all that human beings will ever administer or be concerned with. Our youth, our children, represent our future and posterity; the dead and the aged represent our past; and we face the problems of the present.

We must recognize the present as something that either does not exist – or that exists over time and hence is not merely present but a combination of present, past, and future. I regret the necessity to become philosophical, but there is no other way to discuss the present. What is the present? Is the present this year? This quarter of a century? Our generation? This century? The last 200 years of this great experiment in democracy? Is it the period since the Renaissance? Or is it now? If it is now, how much of now? The "n" of now or the "ow" of now? Is it a microsecond? A full second? The tenth of a second? An hour?

We must conclude that the present does not exist at all. It is, as philosophers have long claimed, specious. It is only as the present moment extends back into the past and prehends the future that it takes on any kind of endurance or significance. The same is true of our own lives. Our lives have no meaning, comprehension even of words like these is impossible, were it not for our capacity to live in a present thoroughly imbued with the past and in anticipation of the future. When I say "united," having already referred to John Quincy Adams, listeners will undoubtedly be thinking "United States." But if I had been talking about a banana republic and said "united," people might have been thinking "fruit company." Comprehension depends on our capacity to extend our understanding beyond the moment in which we exist to include a past and a future. The words "United States" would mean nothing if you could not remember part of our nation's history.

This is not a casual philosophical point, but one of fundamental, personal importance. In order to live in the present, we must recognize that our present lives and all meaning and coherence depend on our living simultaneously in the past and in the future. No generation can find meaning unless it be informed by what it inherits and accountable for what it bequeaths. It must, in the process of living in the time available to it, take into account what has been and what will be.

No child can live without parents, who existed before it did and brought it into being; therefore no child is without obligation to parents.

At the same time, all persons who have been reared by parents have an obligation to children (not necessarily their own) who will survive them; and this obligation is equal to the obligation that each person's parents had toward him or her; otherwise one does not account for the conditions of his or her existence.

Like individuals, a society does not exist in day, but from a past into a future. And it is only when those in the prime of existence, in the "now" of a nation's life, learn from the past, refine the past, receive its fruits, and do something to bequeath the advantages of that society to posterity – it is only then that the society has a present. The Third Reich had almost no present, almost no existence, because it arose through a rupture with the past, and no seeds were sown for its posterity. Hitler's ambition was Ragnarok, a day of destruction after which nothing could survive.

Continuity is required for meaningful existence in the present both for individuals and for society, and families provide the continuity that sustains generation on generation. When I think of families, I do not think of them in the way in which Kipling satirized the exclusive family:

> Father, Mother, and Me,
> Sister and Auntie say
> All the people like us are We,
> And every one else is They.

Not do I have in mind the kind of family described by Disraeli when he said, in his novel Lothair: "Every day when he looked into the glass, and gave the last touch to his consummate toilette, he offered his grateful thanks to Providence that his family was not unworthy of him." The smugness of the Victorian family is not what I have in mind either. Rather, I have in mind the family as it appears in the works of an individual such as Marcus Aurelius.

Marcus Aurelius, writing his *Meditations* among the Quadi on the River Gran, acknowledges his indebtedness to others by saying (I use the Arrowsmith translation):

To my grandfather Verus for his example: Integrity and sweetness of temper.

To my father as I remember him and heard him spoken of: Respect for self and others; manliness.

To my mother for her example: The sense of reverence; generosity. Freedom from malice in thought and action alike. The simplicity of her life, in marked contrast to the typical life of the wealthy.

To my great-grandfather: ... The knowledge that for education it is one's duty to spend liberally.

To my childhood tutor who taught me: ... To endure physical hardship and to keep my wants to a minimum. To work with my own hands; to mind my own business. To turn my back on slander.

To my teacher Diognetus: My aversion for frivolous pastimes.... That I was made to write essays in my childhood. For my passionate apprenticeship to the discipline of the Greek schools and their regime – the hard pallets, the blankets of hide, etc.

To Rusticus: For impressing upon me the urgency of moral discipline and reform.... To write unaffected letters (like the letters he wrote to my mother from Sinuessa). To be conciliatory toward those who have angered or offended me....

To Apollonius: Moral freedom. The determination to leave nothing in one's power to the caprice of chance.... Equanimity: in severe pain, in the loss of a child, in long illness. The opportunity of observing from a living example how the same man can be at once completely serious and yet relaxed too.

To Sextus, for his example: Kindliness. The pattern of a household governed by a father. The idea of a life lived according to Nature. True dignity. His intuitive consideration for his friends.... His grasp and method in discovering and ordering the crucial principles of human existence. Great learning without pedantry.

To Catulus who taught me: To be unstinting in praise of [one's] teachers.... Genuine love of children.

To my adoptive father, Antoninus Pius, for his example: Gentleness. Unalterable resolution in decisions reached after due deliberation. Indifference to official honors. Love of work and the habit of perseverance.

To the gods for their gifts: Good grandparents, a good father and mother, good teachers, good associates, good relatives, good friends – almost without exception.

That I had so good a brother, whose character stimulated me to concern about my own, while his respect and affection gave me encouragement....

That I have been granted clear and frequent perceptions of a life according to Nature so that – insofar as the blessing, assistance, and inspiration of the gods are concerned – nothing prevents me from living in accord with Nature.

That my mother, though doomed to die young, spent the last years of her life with me.

Marcus Aurelius expresses the purposes for which families exist: the provision of continuity and a structure of meaning, both in individual life and in the life of the state.

It is this concept of family that we need to keep in mind when we examine such treatises as the recent *Centuries of Childhood* by Philippe Aries and some other recent writing on the family, including those of R. D. Laing, and David Cooper's *The Death of the Family*.

When we examine Aries's work, the argument and methodology defy comprehension. I would caution every reader that in this age of revisionist history it is very important to examine not merely the results of a study but how one has arrived at those results. For instance, Aries concludes that "The density of [medieval] society left no room for the family," but in the next sentence says, "Not that the family did not exist as a reality: it would be paradoxical to deny that it did." But if the family exists, there must be room for it. Aries tries to avoid this contradiction by adding, "But it did not exist as a concept."

What does it mean to say that a society left no room for the family, when all one means is that the society had no concept of the family? If we had no concept of the horse, that would not mean that there was no horse. If the Medieval people had no concept of the family, it would not mean that there were none.

When asked for evidence of his claims, Aries relies on portraits that were done by artists of children from the eleventh to the thirteenth century. The artists made children appear to be little men and women. But beginning in the fifteenth century, by contrast, portraits included husband and wife, the dates of their marriages, and the dates of their children's birthdays. Children were shown sitting on their parents' knees or standing beside them, with formal trappings that indicated a self-conscious recognition of the family.

Aries's reasoning from the history of portraiture ignores the fact that there are changes of style in painting. The baby Jesus was portrayed, in earlier works, as a little man. This was only a matter of style and not the denial of the infant Jesus. How does the absence in Romanesque times of accurate portraiture of children lead us to any conclusion about the existence of families? What would we say today if we tried to describe horses by the way in which Picasso draws them? Or women by how he drew them in *Les Arlesiennes*? We would have to conclude that horses look more like dragons, that women have many-sided faces, one eye lower than the other, and noses pointing in two directions. What would we conclude about the conception of human beings in the twentieth century by looking at the works of Henry Moore?

We are living in a no-fault age. When one abandons requirements of draftsmanship and representation, one cannot be faulted for the absence of likeness. And this is, of course, characteristic of most painting and sculpture of our time. Back in Romanesque days, spatial perspective was not yet understood as it was in the Renaissance. Yet there was such a thing as space. We would be mistaken to conclude that there were no children in the Middle Ages because they were not portrayed as children. There are no records to suggest that women gave birth to dwarfs who looked like little men and women and later grew up to be full-grown adults, even though artists portrayed children in that way.

It would also be a mistake to suppose that the way in which the artist drew children was an accurate reflection of the role they had in society. That children worked with adults in the Middle Ages is undoubtedly true. But that there was no such thing as affectionate family relationships in the Middle Ages is a conjecture for which evidence is not available.

When R. D. Laing says that the initial act of brutality against the average child is the mother's first kiss, he introduces a very curious, indeed, in my judgment, a pathological view of the family and the mother's kiss. He finds it hurtful that a child is completely at the mercy of its family even to being forced to accept affection. While Laing may think it is a damned shame that the child is dependent upon his family for food and shelter, this is the way it is. It is fortunate that the child receives the affection of his parents along with warm clothing and food. Were it not for the emotional tie between parent and child, it is doubtful that our species would have survived. The affectionate bond that binds parent and child together is manifest in many animals lower on the evolutionary scale than humans. It contributes to their survival and to their pleasure in being alive. Only an age that prizes specious principles – revisionism for its own sake – over an objective search for truth will take seriously the idea that the family is a form of tyranny that subjects the child to an initial act of brutality by being loved and kissed by its parent. That view is simply pathological.

When I go back many hundreds of years in many different cultures, I find a vastly different account. Never a culture whose literature is without substantial evidence of a family; never a family without bonds of affection; never a family without interrelationships and interdependencies between young and old; never a family lacking in concern for and delight in children. We may recognize deficient families just as we recognize deficient human beings. There are parents who are cruel to their children even to the extreme of infanticide, just as there is matricide and parricide. These are all deficient modes of the normative mode of affection and concern.

I know of no scholar who dates Homer's *Odyssey* later than 800 B.C. Some parts are probably as old as 1200 B.C. The entire structure of the *Odyssey* revolves around Odysseus's quest to return home to his wife, his son, his father, and his household.

Or consider Oedipus, when he addresses the people of Thebes:

> Poor children! You may be sure I know
> All that you longed for in your coming here.
> I know that you are deathly sick; and yet,
> Sick as you are, not one is as sick as I.
> Each of you suffers in himself alone
> His anguish, not another's; but my spirit
> Groans for the city, for myself, for you.

This is the metaphor of the state as family, the same that was suggested by Marcus Aurelius. In the *Oedipus* it refers to a time hundreds of years before Marcus Aurelius, a time at which the concept of the father of the family and the father of the state were identified. We also find familial examples in *Antigone*.

In Confucian scriptures from 600 B.C. we hear a widow lament:

> O mother, O heaven,
> Why will you not understand me?
> It floats about, that boat of cypress wood,
> There by the side of the Ho.
> With his two tufts of hair falling over his forehead,
> He was my only one;
> And I swear that till death I will not do the evil thing.
> O mother, O heaven,
> Why will you not understand me?

Another passage from Confucian scriptures of the same period refers to affection in the family:

> *Brothers Are Best*
>
> Brothers may quarrel inside the walls,
> But they will oppose insult from without,
> When friends, however good they may be,
> Will not afford help.
> When death and disorder are past,
> And there are tranquility and rest,
> Although they have brothers,
> Some reckon them not equal to friends.
> They are mistaken.
> Loving union with wife and children
> Is like the music of lutes;
> But it is the accord of brothers
> Which makes the harmony and happiness lasting.
> For the ordering of your family,
> For your joy in your wife and children,
> Examine this and study it;
> Will you not find that it is truly so?

If we move to India, between 1000 B.C. and 600 B.C., we find in Hindu scriptures:

Now next, the father-and-son ceremony or the transmission, as they call it. A father, when about to decease, summons his son. Having strewn the house with new grass, having built up the fire, having set down near it a vessel of water together with a dish, the father, wrapped around with a fresh garment, remains lying. The father says:
Father: "My speech in you I would place!"
Son: "Your speech in me I take."
Father: "My breath in you I would place!"
Son: "Your breath in me I take."

And then it goes on, "My eye in you ...," "My ear in you ...," "My tastes in you ... ," "My deeds in you ... ," "My pleasure and pain in you ...," "My bliss, delight, and procreation in you I would place!" And so, the father bequeaths to his son the responsibilities of being the master and father of the house.

We have in Plato and in Lucretius the examination of the family at the most basic levels of mankind, as contemplated 2,500 and 2,000 years ago.

We find that Lady MacBeth, as cruel and heartless as any person portrayed in Shakespeare, confesses to her husband:

... Had he not [speaking of Duncan] resembled
My father as he slept, I had done't.

She could not kill Duncan because he looked too much like her father. This bond of filial piety stands out in almost any literature one examines.

It is no accident, I would suppose, that the entire Greek Pantheon is a large family. It is no accident that in Christianity there is a Father, a Son, and a Holy Spirit – and then, with the rise of devotion to Mary, a Father, a Mother, and a Son. The familial relationship is relied on to make sense of and symbolize the Godhead in Christianity.

In Proverbs 4 and 5 of the Hebrew Bible, we have concern for the love of one's mother and the importance of fidelity to the wife of one's youth.

While Proverbs notes the foolish delights of a strange woman, it speaks there also of the delight in restricting oneself to the love of the wife of one's youth – whose breasts, it says, will satisfy him and who will be a ravishment to him all of his years.

In these passages there is no denial of the importance of sex in marriage or the importance of full intimacy, but only an insistence on responsibility and continuity on which a meaningful sexual relationship depends.

The Book of Genesis tells the story of Jacob and his sons, or of Joseph and his brothers, with especial attention to Joseph and Benjamin. The bond between brothers and between them and their father is beautiful and emotionally powerful.

I have reviewed not a handful of contemporary observations but a quick sampling of world literature. We have found over and over clear expressions of the family as a constant, as a basic social structure grounded emotionally and biologically in human nature. That constant provides the continuity on which human society and life depends.

Despite its great importance, that continuity is severely threatened at the present time. Change makes continuity in families difficult no matter how well established they may be. As social continuity breaks down, the continuity of the family itself is threatened. The damaging aspect of change is its embrace of the instantaneous. In pursuit of immediate gratification, our culture has abandoned the obligations, responsibilities, and forbearance of an earlier period. For at least sixty years the Gospel of our TV broadcasters and their sponsors has made immediate gratification the dominant preoccupation of our society.

The intellectual seeds of this preoccupation were sown with the development and popularization of utilitarianism. When the good is defined simply as pleasure and the absence of pain, momentary sensations govern our lives. That Plato had refuted the doctrine of utilitarianism 2,000 years ago did not inhibit its revival.

Dostoevsky warned that, if there were no God, there would be no structure on which morals and moral obligation would depend. During the Enlightenment, a time of waning belief in God among intellectuals, Diderot and others sought to establish a rational foundation for morals in order to sustain morality without divine sanction. The Enlightenment was remarkably capable of sustaining its moral foundations and convictions despite waning religious belief. Kant offers an excellent example: reared as a Pietist, Kant came to adulthood, shook off his belief in pietism, and then tried to establish by means of reason alone the basic ideas that he had learned in a pietistic school. He sought to establish through reason alone a secular version of Christian ethics.

This seemed to work rather well until a generation arose that had never been reared in pietism or any religious tradition. Two World Wars effectively ended confidence in a religiously ordered world. I think Saul Bellow is correct now to speak of a post-Christian society. We live now, in the words of Paul Tillich, at a time "when the religious substance of humanism [has] disappeared, [and] the mere form [is] left, abundant but empty.... [I]ndifference, cynicism, despair, mental disturbances, early crimes and disgust of life [follow]."

Pleasure seems to be our answer to this situation. Hedonism, of course, seems to be wonderful advice. It promises pleasure and the avoidance of pain. Pleasure is certainly a good, pain certainly something bad, but pleasure and the avoidance of pain cannot be the ultimate goal of human life.

Pleasure is nonreferential: I cannot have your pleasure; you cannot have my pleasure. Unless we contrive our pleasures very carefully, through conversation or through a relationship of sex between individuals who know one another in a genuinely intimate sense, the notion of sharing pleasure becomes very tenuous indeed. Hedonism essentially leads to solipsism, to the isolation of the individual within his or her own sensorium. And solipsism faces the serious difficulty that it leads to meaninglessness. No one can make meaning merely out of his or her own private existence. As one seeks to escape the natural basis of continuity, the fundamental meaninglessness that follows creates an even greater need for continuity.

A young man from a college in New Mexico told me, "There is nothing wrong with sex unless something bad happens." I asked, "What would that be?" He replied, "Oh, having a baby." The young man was shocked when I asked him, "So the bad event was your birth?" When the creation of human life is "something bad happening," the hedonistic exploitation of sex is revealed. Sex bereft of its procreative function – not merely freed from it on occasion, but essentially detached – is reduced to mere pleasure. One of the most meaningful aspects of our life, one on which continuity of generations depends, is degraded into mere immediate gratification with no thought for past or future.

The pursuit of pleasure and the avoidance of pain, both for ourselves and for our children, leads to the lowering of standards in our schools and in behavior that might be difficult or unpleasant to learn. Playing with toys – playschool toys, drugs, sex, cars, and all varieties of adult toys – becomes the goal of life. We will not expect, or even allow, our parents, grandparents, or great grandparents to assume responsibility in the home, to cook, to do some of the babysitting, or provide moral instruction for the young. Rather, we map out for them that second childhood of which Shakespeare's Jacques speaks with such telling effect. They belong in the old folks home, playing shuffleboard, playing dominoes, playing croquet. Life ideally progresses from children's toys to adult toys.

If anything is to be done in this situation, we in the middle between our ancestors and our posterity, are going to have to do it. We will have to reestablish networks of interdependence and responsibility between our parents and our children. Just as surely as Lear needed his daughter Cordelia, as surely as his banishment of his loving daughter led to tragedy, our grandparents and our parents need us and need our children. Gorki, in his autobiography, devotes the first section largely to the discussion of himself and his grandmother. This is the finest portrait I know of the crucial interdependence of the old and the young. Polonius, tendentious as he is, something of an ass, nonetheless offers sound advice to his son Laertes, advice that a callow youth needs to hear.

The reestablishment of the web of responsible interdependencies is our major responsibility. Only in this way will the present be truly present. Let me offer an example from the wine industry. In the Eduard Schuster Weingut in Karlstadt, Germany, I met with the owner who had inherited the winery from his father who had inherited it from his grandfather. The grandfather built the first vault for the wines; the father built the second large vault; the son improved the business by adding new machinery and replacing horses with tractors and the mechanical winepresses with electric ones.

The present owner pointed out to me that 25 percent of his life is devoted to posterity. A grapevine can last twenty-five years, but at twenty years every vine is uprooted and a new vine is planted. Five years of production are sacrificed in order that new stock may be started. Twenty-five percent of his life, the man told me, he worked as an apprentice to his father, a master vintner, learning the process, learning the business, his main job being to supply the needs of his father. That accounts for 50 percent of his life. Approximately 25 percent of his life was spent in modernizing and maintaining the equipment, the machinery, and the building. About 75 percent of this winegrower's life, then, was involved in acquiring the right to inherit the family property and in being sure that he was bequeathing this great property to his posterity. The remaining 25 percent was gloriously his own. This is an example of living responsibly in the present.

In restoring the interdependency of the family we must also recognize the importance of the homemaker, be that a man or a woman. Feminism is irrelevant here. Whether a man or woman, there needs to be a homemaker if there is to be anything like a decent quality of life in the American home or in any other. The rearing of the young is the most important task there is for human continuity and flourishing. Even if we wish to think merely in financial terms, the work done by a first-class homemaker is easily worth the salary of an executive or highly skilled technician.

There is a stage, of course, at which a woman is required: we have no male substitute for the conceiving and bearing of children, or for the nursing of a child. But beyond that physiological dependency, either male or female will do, and either can become the teacher, the confidant, the chef, the maker, interior decorator, and one of the lovers in an effective home.

Most basic of all must be the concern to develop within the home a system of personal nurture that promotes the principle of nonparasitism, the dependency principle, that each must contribute to the life of the community even as each will profit by that life. In this way the continuation of human life, of generations on generations, is possible. The increasing pressure on both parents to work outside the home is one of the most counterproductive phenomena of our time.

Can we reverse the trends of our society and strengthen the family? I think we can, but as A. E. Housman remarked:

... since the world has still
Much good, but much less good than ill,
And while the sun and moon endure
Luck's a chance, but trouble's sure,
I'd face it as a wise man would,
And train for ill and not for good.

That may be sound doctrine, but I do not believe it is the last word. Even in this secular age, I believe that the truth of Stoicism offers us a more positive and optimistic conclusion. We can say with the Stoics that:

Whatever is in harmony with you, O Universe, is in harmony with me. Nothing which is in its time for you comes too soon or too late for me. O Nature, whatever your seasons bring is fruit for me. All things come from you; in you all things are; everything returns to you.

Confidence in Nature, when our lives are lived in accordance with Nature, is possible for us even in a secular age. Those with a theological bent may be able to go farther. But it can be enough for many of us if the family, on which continuity depends, is deeply in harmony with nature. When we do all we can to strengthen the network of relationships between generations, such that we have a posterity and that we bring dignity and joy to our forefathers, namely our parents and grandparents, the meaning and fulfillment of our lives is in harmony with nature.

The burden is on us in the middle years. With nature's help, there will be fruits of that burden. Can we guarantee that it will all be happy and pleasant? No, but we would be well advised to curb our obsessive pursuit of immediate pleasure in favor of a pursuit of those natural values that make life truly worth living.

National Council on Family Relations, Salt Lake City, Utah, August 23, 1975

The Myth of Overqualification

"The only question to ask on graduation is,
'Are you underqualified or overqualified for the human race?'"

It was my practice, two weeks before graduation, to address the senior class. I found as a rule that the first requirement of the occasion was to find some common ground in laughter. This proved always to be the means by which I could reach the seniors in a nonconfrontational way.

In 1971, when I came to Boston University, students were so hostile that they used the occasion to propose refusing to wear caps and gowns at commencement, and I had to remind them, using both laughter and logic, of the historic and symbolic importance of caps and gowns as the only means of differentiating graduation from other large assemblies. I also suggested it was a duty they owed parents, grandparents, and relatives whose financial support and guidance enabled them to complete their education.

Hostile relations between students and the administration continued but were substantially reduced after 1974 when the OPEC oil embargo introduced to students some realism about the uncertainty of their futures and put an end to participation in the costume party and the wild hairdos that characterized their earlier expressions of liberation.

In 1976, the year in which I gave this talk, a small group of trustees of Boston University decided that the tensions between the administration and the students were largely caused by the president. This handful of trustees moved publicly for my dismissal. The outcome was touch-and-go for a few weeks until the April meeting of the board at which I was given a vote of confidence by a large majority. Prior to that, the issue was in doubt, so that when I met with seniors in 1976, uncertainty was still in the air.

In this speech I reminded seniors that education is not merely vocational training but prepares one for life.

IT IS MY PLEASURE to welcome you to this Senior Breakfast of 1976 and to have this occasion to speak to you.

Ordinarily we anticipate that only the graduating class will be leaving the University. This morning, however, there is some anticipation that we may all be leaving. Your parents will be very disappointed if you do not depart; and my mother will be very disappointed if I do. It may have surprised some of you that I have a mother. Those of you who majored in biology know that all mammals have mothers.

I thought it might be best if I used this last chance to speak to you before Commencement itself to engage in a belated act of self-disclosure. It would be a pity if you were to graduate without getting to know your president a little better. On the other hand, it seems to me that all of you know me far better than I know you, and not merely because there are more of you than there are of me but because my life has, after all, been something of an open book, described repetitively and assiduously in the local press. In that way I think you have come to know me perhaps in a reasonably satisfactory fashion. I am abrasive, acerbic, ambitious, angry, arrogant, and autocratic. And that is just the a's.

I have for some time tried to understand why I am perceived in this way. I did not have a clue about how to answer this public relations problem until I was in the car one day, turned the radio on, and there was Mac Davis singing. He had a song that fit my situation perfectly and would give you some understanding of the problem that I face, and I hope, though I have no license to practice singing, that you will let me try.

> Oh, Lord, it's hard to be humble,
> When you're perfect in every way.
> I can't wait to look in the mirror,
> 'Cause I get better looking each day.
> To know me is to love me.
> I must be a hell of a man.
> Oh, Lord, it's hard to be humble,
> But I'm doin' the best that I can.

Now that I have exhausted that subject, I would like to turn to what is really on my mind this morning. And that is to talk to you briefly about what has happened in the last four years and what is likely to face you in the years ahead. Through no fault of your own, and contrary to some opinion, certainly through no fault of mine, you did not find yourself born into the happiest era of humankind. It would have been a lot more convenient for most of you had you been born about 1930, young enough to have experienced only a very few years of the Great Depression, avoided the Second World War, but were then old enough to have enjoyed the twenty-five-year period of unprecedented affluence that followed that war. This was a lovely time to be born. It will go down in history as a golden age, in which Americans enjoyed a standard of living of a sort never known before. It is very unlikely that this standard of living will ever be repeated on such a large scale. Before you reach the thirty-fifth anniversary of your graduation, you will live in a world of widespread hunger, if not a world decimated by war. The wisdom of your having gone to college will be determined largely by your own courage and your own ability to cope with the uncertainties that lie ahead.

Courage is very often misunderstood as a capacity to suppress emotions of fear. Plato had a far more important and profound understanding of courage. He said that courage was not to be understood in terms of the emotions, but rather as the knowledge of what is or is not to be feared.

Consider, for example, the case of a babysitter. Let us suppose the babysitter comes in to take care of a youngster and has a powerful urge to torture the child. Now are we supposed to believe that if this babysitter has a great moral character, somehow the babysitter will be able to repress these emotions and resist the temptations, and by a great struggle of the spirit manage to care for the child properly? This would not be an example of a fitting and suitable babysitter, but of a potential criminal.

Plato believed that anyone whose life is torn apart by conflicting emotions, by emotions that strive to control the human psyche, is lacking in wisdom and knowledge, and most especially in courage. He believed that if one knew what was or was not to be feared, these kinds of emotional turmoil could not occur.

If one is a student and knows it is more shameful to cheat than to earn a lower grade, one will be under no temptation to cheat. A bank teller who understands that it is more disgraceful to steal than it is to be poor would not be under any temptation to steal. There is no reason to be torn apart by emotion.

My second example is from what is sometimes called the "real world." I am sure all of you have heard the idea that college is not the real world but that the real world is the one that, on graduation, you are about to enter. Let me assure you, however, there is no world as real as the one in which you reside now and from which you are about to depart. It is almost the only place in our society where ideas – such as the idea of courage – are taken seriously and experience is structured by them. The world into which you are moving is, if anything, less real than this one because it is less structured by ideas and more dependent on random impressions and mere appearances.

Reality depends not merely on what we can feel with our fingers or see with our eyes or hear with our ears but on a structure of coherence in which isolated facts and experience can be integrated and understood, so that wise decisions can be made. The most real world is the world in which you have been living for the past four years, surrounded not only by knowledgeable faculty but by wise mentors. Your ability to make sense of the world which you now enter will depend upon your determination to hold on to all that you have heard and learned – through the teaching and especially the example – of your wisest teachers.

Through the difficult task of integrating all that you have experienced in these four years, you will forge your own structure of coherence that is at the core of your own integrity. If you do that, the rest will follow. Yours, because of surprises that lie ahead, may not be what is called a happy life. It may be a life battered by adversity. But, happy or not, it will be a good life, for it will be a life of purpose, a life of dignity, of meaning and of service to others. All of that is within your power and your control.

Those of you who understand that you are going to die, and understand that thoroughly, can enjoy a freedom to live in a way that is very difficult for people who are not sure about their own mortality. It is insights of this sort that are the purpose of going to the university: to find out the importance of the knowledge of what is or is not to be feared; to understand the conditions of courage; to discover those elements of understanding on which a mature and satisfactory human life can be built.

Newsweek has just been considering the question, "Why go to college?" It points out that nowadays there is no reason for students to anticipate earning more than 6 percent of the income they would have earned had they not gone to college. In terms of what college costs, that is not much of a bargain. But it is only because college has been falsely merchandized that anybody thinks that one goes to college in order to earn more money or in order to have a better job.

Consider the current talk about "overqualification." A PhD may work as a welder, or a B.A. as a janitor. Does this constitute overqualification? A PhD might make a very inadequate welder. Far from being overqualified, such a person might not be qualified at all. I think of Socrates, an average sculptor, who was one of the world's greatest philosophers. There is nothing recorded to suggest that Socrates was overqualified for the rather simple sculpting that he did. Nor did the sculpting disqualify him to pursue a life of philosophy. Spinoza, another great philosopher, made his living by grinding lenses. This gave him the livelihood so that at night and on weekends he could work on his philosophy. How did that constitute overqualification for lens grinding or underqualification for philosophy? St. Augustine managed to be a saint after having lived a prodigiously romantic youth, and having written major books and served a distinguished career as a bishop. But was he overqualified for sainthood? St. Sebastian managed to be sainted only by being struck appropriately by arrows in a good cause. Consider the difference in preparation for sainthood. Wallace Stevens made his career in insurance, or did he make his career in writing poetry? Was he overqualified to be an insurance executive, or was he underqualified to be a poet, or did things work out just fine as he received his education in one area and practiced a more important vocation outside the area of his employment? The same question might be asked about T. S. Eliot.

The only question that you really have to ask on graduation is, "Are you overqualified for the human race, or are you underqualified?" And if you are underqualified, can you find remedial education in the process of continuing education? Your education, I hope you understand from your four years at Boston University, has not ended; it is only begun. The quality of your life is the issue at stake. It is not what job you are going to have, it is not how much money you are going to make. It is the quality of your existence and the kind of human being that you are to become.

It is whether you will find yourself significantly and meaningfully involved in a community where your life takes its place as a part of the human adventure. The question is this: When you graduate from Boston University, have you begun to understand what Edgar in *King Lear* has in mind when, toward the end of that play, he says, "Ripeness is all." If that is no more than a dark saying to you, then a large part of your education lies ahead. If that saying is beginning to take on meaning for you, then Boston University has made a major contribution to your education.

Whether you have learned as much as you hoped to learn, or whether you have only discovered that learning is a lifetime process, I hope you will look back on the years at Boston University with pleasure, with a realization that these were good years, and with a recollection of several professors and many students whom you came to know and whose knowing has enhanced your life. I hope you will see that your years here were well spent and that we can welcome you here again as alumni.

Democracy: Its Counterfeits and Its Promise

"Democracy is counterfeited by the claim that every institution in a democracy ought to be democratic. An effective democracy is essentially elitist, and flourishes when led by persons of virtue and talent."

For the national bicentenary, I was asked by the mayor of Boston, the Honorable Kevin H. White, to offer the municipal oration at historic Faneuil Hall. Considering the occasion, and considering also the trends of our nation's educational and political systems as they appeared in 1976, I thought it appropriate to examine the state of our democracy. I spoke from a philosophic point of view, not only of the great strengths and virtues of our democratic nation, but also of the dangers it was facing and the false paths a democracy can take when it succumbs to illusions and misunderstanding.

THE BEST WAY for us to celebrate the bicentenary of the Declaration of Independence is to renew our dedication to the proposition that all men are created equal and to our historic national goals of the protection of life, liberty, and the pursuit of happiness.

We must regain the clearsighted sense of purpose that inspired the people of Revolutionary Boston. We must retain the distinctions our ancestors made between political appearances and political realities. "To be, rather than to seem" – the motto of North Carolina – is a crucial motto for this bicentenary and reminds us to distinguish democracy from its counterfeits.

To give greater meaning and substance to the concept of equal opportunity has been a continuing concern of our government and our society over the last 200 years. Whatever our shortcoming in attaining these ideals, there can be no doubt about their increasing realization.

But while we have been remarkably successful in extending opportunity through education, we have debased the coinage of educational competence in the process and deprived our educational programs of their central core of moral instruction. "All value judgments are relative and of equal validity." "Anyone's opinion is as good as that of any other." These slogans are dominant in our educational institutions. They are counterfeits of the legitimate democratic principle that each person has a right to his or her own opinion. They obliterate the differences between right and wrong and good and evil.

The difference between saying that anyone's opinion is as good as any other's and that everyone has a right to one's own opinion is neither obscure nor difficult. Persons have a right to their own opinions no matter how wrong, how ignorant, or even how stupid they may be. Persons have the right to express their opinions, but not every opinion is right.

Neither Adams nor Jefferson ever suggested that the average citizen is a person equal in judgment, discernment, or knowledge to those competent to serve the people in government. "That all men are born to equal rights is true," said John Adams.

> Every being has a right to his own, as clear, as moral, as sacred as any other being has.... But to teach that all men are born with equal powers and faculties ... is as gross a fraud, as glaring an imposition on the credulity of people as ever was practiced by monks, by Druids, [or] by Brahmins.

As Jefferson recognized, "There is a natural aristocracy among men. The grounds of this are virtue and talents." To which Jefferson contrasted "an artificial aristocracy, founded on wealth and birth, without either virtue or talents." A natural aristocracy, Jefferson believed, was "the most precious gift of nature." "May we not even say," Jefferson continued, "that that form of government is the best which provides most effectively for a pure selection of these natural *aristoi* into the offices of government?"

Democracy freed from a counterfeit and ultimately destructive egalitarianism provides a society in which the wisest, the best, and the most dedicated assume positions of leadership. The members of a legislature, of a city council, or of a school board, ought to be chosen by democratic process and no other way. We should be prepared to die in defense of this principle. But the persons elected to these offices should be better than average. Ideally they should be the best qualified to hold office. They ought to be better in their intellectual capacity and in their commitment to hard work. This does not mean that they should be males, college graduates, middle class, white, or members of any group other than Jefferson's natural aristocrats. Lawmakers, as Benjamin Franklin said, are "the servants of the people" – and for the people nothing can be too good.

Democracy is also counterfeited by the claim that every institution in a democracy ought to be democratic. That the government must be democratic follows from the principle that it derives its authority from the consent of the governed. This is the principle for which 200 years ago our forebears mutually pledged their lives, their fortunes, and their sacred honor. We should be willing to do no less. But it does not follow that every institution within a democracy should be organized democratically. In fact, most institutions should be run on an elitist basis – that is, decisions within them should be made by those most qualified to make them. Elitism, like aristocracy, has its proper and improper forms. Elitism is improper only when the qualifications for inclusion in the elite are irrelevant. Among the irrelevant qualifications often imposed are those of wealth, gender, and race. Whenever an unqualified man or woman is given a job merely because *he* is a male or *she* is white, the principle being followed is not elitism, but its counterfeit. The elite thus created is artificial rather than natural. That ours is not now a truly elitist society is shown clearly by the existence of serious discrimination against women and minorities. In a society whose elite were selected on the basis of their qualifications, the proportion of women physicians and corporate executives could conceivably approach 51 percent. The proportion of blacks in these positions could be as high as 11 percent. That is what a real elitism could mean for this country; we fall short of it through the continuing scandal of our denial of equal opportunity in education and employment.

Through this denial we create a bogus "elite": many of the people in it are less qualified than many who are not. Those who are excluded and deserve to be included have everything to gain from true elitism. It is notable that one rarely finds black educators and black students arguing against high educational standards; rather, they ask for a fair chance to meet the standards required of everyone else. By and large, the opposition within higher education to a maintenance of standards comes from that group that has the most to lose from a genuine elitism – middle-class whites.

Rightly understood, there is nothing wrong with elitism. It is essential to the quality of life. Indeed, life itself may depend upon it. All would agree that the practice of surgery should be restricted to persons of extraordinary knowledge and skill. The term "butcher" is used to describe a surgeon who fails to meet this genuinely elitist standard. No one would consent to be operated on by a surgeon who polled those in the operating room before deciding on a procedure. We recognize that the surgeon's opinion should prevail without any plebiscite because it is better than the opinion of the nurse, the medical student, the intern, or the patient.

As long as intelligence is better than stupidity and knowledge than ignorance, no university can be run except on an elitist basis. A university that strives for the commonplace and is content with mediocrity is roughly comparable to a Supreme Court on which seats were reserved for the mediocre. Thus handicapped, these institutions could not fulfill their missions.

In order to develop a natural aristocracy, our forebears placed great emphasis on education. Writing in 1717, John Wise, minister of Ipswich, Massachusetts, quoted Plutarch: "Those persons who live in obedience to reason are worthy to be accounted free: They alone live as they will, who have learned what they ought to will." The writings of Madison, Jefferson, and Adams abound in detailed expositions of this principle. They insisted that the value of education could not be exaggerated because it is the condition on which effective self-government, whether of the state or the individual, depends. "If a nation expects to be ignorant and free … it expects what never was and never will be," said Jefferson. Adams wrote, "Laws for the liberal education of youth, especially of the lower class of people, are so extremely wise and useful that to a humane and generous mind no expense for this purpose would be thought extravagant." So great was the concern of Adams and Jefferson for education that the former wrote a provision for it into the Constitution of the Commonwealth of Massachusetts, and the latter drafted and commented on a law to establish education in Virginia.

The education they had in mind was a liberal education rich not merely in the study of the sciences, but also in the study of morals. Adams wrote, "It shall be the duty of legislators and magistrates in all future periods of this Commonwealth to cherish the interests of literature and sciences" and to establish institutions that would "countenance and inculcate the principles of humanity and general benevolence, public and private charity, industry and frugality, honesty, and punctuality in their dealings, sincerity, good humor, and all social affections and generous sentiments among the people."

These concerns were advanced dramatically and effectively not merely in Massachusetts but throughout the nation by Horace Mann, who explained what our schools should have been and should yet become. "In them," he said,

> the principles of morality should have been ... intermingled with the principles of science .... The multiplication tables should not have been more familiar, nor more frequently applied, than the rule, to do to others as we would that they should do unto us. The lives of great and good men should have been held up for admiration and example....

Horace Mann prescribed a system of education for the whole child that would lead to each one's personal, economic, and social fulfillment.

Education that is not excellent is a counterfeit and a betrayal of a truly democratic society whose existence depends on education. A democratic society cannot function effectively unless the curricula of primary and secondary schools and of colleges and universities are designed to prepare citizens for the tasks that lie before them. But it is idle to speak of values and the inculcation of values as if the term "value" in isolation had any significance. A pornographic bookstore exhibits and encourages values. The problem is: What values should we inculcate? We should not be concerned to inculcate values in general; rather, we should encourage knowledge of and respect for truth, courage, sincerity, justice, and wisdom. We must, for example, establish in the consciousness of our children the hard-fought-for distinction between right and power and the rational basis for preferring right to power. Although it is rarely articulated, the rational derivation of that distinction is quite as objective as any scientific demonstration. It is a part of our historical legacy, though often forgotten.

According to a more recently minted counterfeit, individuals must define themselves not as Americans but in terms of their ethnic group, with a consequent rejection of the historical ideal of the melting pot. The national motto, "*E Pluribus Unum*," one out of many, is replaced by an exaggerated ethnicity. This can be seen in the current assumption – illustrated in attempts to require bilingual ballots – that citizens need not be literate in the national language so long as they are literate in the language of their ethnic group. I do not mean to decry worthy bilingual programs that accelerate the acquisition of the English language by children from non-English-speaking homes. Such programs can contribute to the provision of equality of opportunity and the realization of full democratic rights – for citizens must speak their national language if they are to participate fully in the rights of citizenship.

When we emphasize ethnic culture to the extent of substituting it for the national culture, we utterly mistake its relation to American citizenship. Ours is an amalgam of imported cultures: one out of many. This explains our extraordinary diversity and strength. But ours has been *one* culture. Never before in the history of mankind has one culture been shared in and contributed to by so many people from such diverse origins and inhabiting so vast a territory. It is remarkable that a nation of such ethnic diversity has lived in freedom without being torn apart by intercommunal violence. This is the blessing conferred by the melting pot, and we would be foolish to exchange it for the anarchy of the Tower of Babel.

But we do not have to choose between the melting pot on the one hand or the Tower of Babel on the other. A more useful metaphor might be a symphony orchestra or a Dixieland band: our basic concern should be to ensure an essential harmony amid the multiplicity of notes and timbres.

A particularly ignoble counterfeit is the substitution of the goal of equal achievement for that of equal opportunity. This nation and its citizens can never fulfill their destinies if achievement is reduced to the lowest common denominator. Liberty must include the freedom to excel for all who have the energy, motivation, and capacity to do so. Abilities – physical, intellectual, artistic, motivational – are unearned talents. They are to be used for personal development and the development of that society on which each always depends. We must not allow those who start out life with extraordinary advantages of wealth or position to erect either barricades that deny upward mobility to others or guardrails to protect themselves from downward mobility.

When white, middle-class students began demanding to take courses on a pass/fail basis, they had discovered an ingenious means of protecting themselves from downward mobility and of denying social and economic advancement to the ambitious new classes of blacks, disadvantaged whites, and other minorities. The determination of minorities to join the middle class threatens middle-class whites who lack either the energy or the ability for the invigorating life of personal fulfillment. The freedom to excel is the genuine coin debased by the doctrine of equal achievement.

It is not only life and liberty that are diminished through the counterfeiting of democracy. The pursuit of happiness is also diminished when it is confused with the pursuit of pleasure. The distinction between the two is fundamental and must be maintained; since it is largely lost, it must be recovered. In the midst of prosperity more accurately described as luxury on a scale unprecedented in the history of mankind, we have come to believe that the pursuit of happiness can be reduced to the pursuit of pleasure. Concurrently, we have mindlessly pursued immediate gratification, willingly forfeiting health, human dignity, and national security.

Our age has developed the ultimate defense of pleasure as a guide to the moral life. Four years ago, a young Californian explained to an audience how she knew that certain of her actions had been right. She said, "I knew it was right because it felt good when I was doing it." She was not explaining her justification for taking some new drug or for performing a new sexual act. This was the justification offered by Susan Atkins, a member of the Manson family, for her savage murder of seven people. The criterion of pleasure cannot differentiate between higher and lower pleasures or between good and bad ones. Once it is agreed that the criterion of right is pleasure, one can no longer distinguish right from wrong.

This is the extreme pathology of the pursuit of pleasure. For the past twenty-five years the television industry and its advertisers have, in less extreme forms, promoted the pursuit of pleasure, substituting this counterfeit for the pursuit of happiness. In this they have been enormously successful. It is doubtful that those in attendance at the Continental Congress would have voted for the phrase "the pursuit of happiness" had they known how their descendants would debase it.

The promulgation of this counterfeit has resulted less from the abdication of moral instruction in our schools than from the usurpation of moral instruction by cynical television advertisers. Television advertising has a philosophical, and sometimes a theological content. Schlitz, a firm with a license to brew but none to preach, intones, "You only go around once in life; so you've got to grab for all the gusto you can!" These are not statements about beer, but a theological claim and moral injunction for which no justification has been made. The current moral injunction from Schlitz is one that Susan Atkins would probably applaud: "When it's right, you know it!" The child watching Schlitz advertising learns that ethical decisions – among the most difficult and important that he or she will ever make – are a simple matter of intuition, no more difficult than the assessment of one's pleasure while drinking a can of beer.

Dedicated to the pursuit of pleasure rather than happiness, television has reduced the pursuit of nutrition to the pursuit of sweetness. Wholesome cereals with high nutritional content, like oatmeal, are increasingly replaced by trashy concoctions designed to please rather than to nourish. Professor Jean Mayer, distinguished nutritionist and president of Tufts University, has said that popular cereals have a sugar content of as much as 50 percent and that many have less protein than a candy bar. By constant reiteration of the idea that the sweeter the breakfast cereal, the better, television has educated a generation in self-destructive eating habits. It has successfully instilled the idea that the first meal of the day should be dessert.

But perverse theologizing is not limited to the advertising breaks. The presence on television of a lovable, racist bigot like Archie Bunker – an oxymoronic character made plausible only through the acting genius of Carroll O'Connor – is frequently applauded on the grounds that it does the country good to see itself as it is – even to the point of indecent exposure. We are asked to believe that this will be a better nation if, following Archie's example, instead of suppressing our vices, we sincerely avow them. In sordid truth, Archie gives us pleasure by indulging gloriously in our vices. We indulge vicariously through him, with no feeling of guilt: without responsibility or guilt, we achieve no-fault participation.

It would be far better for us to attempt, with whatever degree of hypocrisy, to live a virtuous life that is not fully habitual in the hope that it will become habitual and finally an essential part of ourselves, than to express ourselves in fun-loving, pleasure-giving racism, violence, and overindulgence. Shakespeare was well aware of this principle, for Hamlet tells his errant mother, "Assume a virtue, if you have it not.... For use almost can change the stamp of nature...."

These counterfeits of democracy detract from our sense of national purpose. They weaken our nation as they weaken each individual citizen. Our democracy does not need the competition of so many counterfeits. It may well be subject to Gresham's Law: the counterfeit may expel the genuine. Counterfeited democracy is destructive; it weakens the ability of the people to rule themselves wisely and, in the absence of wise government, attenuates those bonds of affection and patriotism on which our survival depends.

Thus far we have addressed internal threats to our survival as a democracy. But we must not overlook the external threats to democracy. In 1949, a sanguine President Truman predicted increasing international security and growing prosperity:

> [A]s more and more nations come to know the benefits of democracy and to participate in growing abundance, I believe those countries which now oppose us will abandon their delusions and join with the free nations of the world in a just settlement of international differences.

This reasonable expectation has, unfortunately, been shattered by the conflicting purposes and vaulting ambitions of nations we sustained through the Second World War.

Aleksandr Solzhenitsyn, deeply appreciative of the "shining strongholds of western freedom," has felt compelled to note the continuing encroachment of totalitarianism on the free world. And he has iden-tified, correctly, I believe, the cause of this trend in the democracies themselves:

> If the region of free social systems in the world keeps shrinking, and if huge continents only recently obtaining freedom are being drawn off into the zone of tyranny, then the fault lies not just with totalitarian-ism – which devours freedom as a function of its natural growth – but, obviously, also with the free systems themselves which have lost some-thing of their inner strength and stability.

Acutely aware of the dangers, Solzhenitsyn does not despair of our capacity to face them with the strength and purpose that animated the delegates to the Continental Congress. "I believe profoundly," he said,

> in the soundness, the healthiness of the roots, of the great-spirited pow-erful American nation – with the insistent honesty of its youth, and its alert moral sense. With my own eyes I have seen the American country, and precisely because of that I have spoken today with steadfast hope.

Our ability to preserve our freedom in the face of devouring totalitari-anism depends not so much on our material strengths as on our moral determination. If, confusing pleasure with happiness, we say with Ber-trand Russell, "Better Red than dead," we must face this withering reply from Solzhenitsyn:

> In this horrible expression of Bertrand Russell, there is an absence of all moral criteria. Looked at from a short distance, these words allow one to maneuver and to continue to enjoy life; but from a long-term view, it will undoubtedly destroy those people who think like that.

We may pursue détente as a matter of national policy, but it will be a policy of national suicide unless we use all our skills as Yankee traders and demand a concession in return for every concession. Solzhenitsyn has perceptively insisted:

Détente is necessary, but détente with open hands. Show that there is no stone in your hands. But your partners with whom you are conducting détente have a stone in theirs, and it is so heavy that it could kill you with one single blow. Détente becomes self-deception.

On the 200th anniversary of the birth of our Republic, we face dangers at home and abroad. We may feel oppressed by the magnitude of our problems, but let us take pride in and draw courage from the fact that men and women the world over, like Solzhenitsyn, still look to America as the last best hope for freedom in the world.

Despite our weakness, we are very strong. Despite our uncertainty, we are capable of great resolve. Whatever our faults, we have also our virtues, and the former do not eclipse the latter.

Today our gravest internal problem is the problem of race. But in Jefferson's day it was the odium of slavery itself. Reflecting on that cruel estate, both he and Adams despaired of our nation's future, and Jefferson feared for his country when he remembered that God is just. As a nation we took our first steps toward atoning for the crime of slavery in a bloody war by which slaves were emancipated and the Union preserved. And in the 200th year of our independence, after remarkable progress in achieving the ideals and goals of our revolution, there is no excuse for further delay in removing the last vestiges of slavery.

We stand between a past glorious and unequaled in human history for the fulfillment of freedom, and a future dark and uncertain, perhaps as frightening as that faced by the members of the Continental Congress. Even as they debated the question of independence, it became clear that the British government had decided to retain the American Colonies even at the cost of making war on them. Informed that General Howe had begun concentrating his forces for the invasion of the city of New York, the delegates nevertheless adopted the Declaration of Independence.

"Think of your forefathers and of your posterity!" This was John Quincy Adams's perceptive injunction in his inaugural address. On this occasion we express our gratitude to earlier generations for our national legacy, which each succeeding generation has made its own. And we pledge to our posterity that we shall do our part in passing on the

Republic whole and worthy. Our forebears, like ourselves, were bound to this country by a patriotism that was both instinctive and reflective. Instinctive, as a feeling that connects one with one's birthplace, a fondness for customs and traditions, a love of one's country like one's love for one's home; and reflective, as an appreciation of self-government, sound laws, and the opportunity to flourish in an atmosphere of freedom. Our patriotism, hereditary and rational, ties us to the land where our fathers died, the land of the pilgrims' pride, the land where freedom rings.

Samuel Adams told his fellow Bostonians:

> The liberties of our country, the freedoms of our civil constitution, are worth defending at all hazards; and it is our duty to defend them against all attacks. We have received them as a fair inheritance from our worthy ancestors: They purchased them for us with toil and danger and expense of treasure and blood; and transmitted them to us with care and diligence. It will bring an everlasting mark of infamy on the present generation, enlightened as it is, if we should suffer them to be wrested from us by violence without a struggle; or be cheated out of them by the artifices of false and designing men.... Our contest is not only whether we ourselves shall be free, but whether there shall be left to mankind an asylum for civil and religious liberty.

Samuel Adams's fellow Bostonians took him seriously and had the courage to act on his advice. They gave birth to a new nation and subsequent generations sustained it. If we would earn our heritage, we must do no less.

By the Rivers of Babylon:
The Mission of the University

"The university has so thoroughly accommodated itself to life in Babylon that it has now renamed it Jerusalem and does not even know it is captive."

On rare occasions, I considered speaking at the university's annual baccalaureate, a non-denominational service held in the university chapel prior to graduation and attended primarily by parents and relatives who usually outnumbered the students, and by a small group of faculty and administrators, including a fair representation of the Board of Trustees. During my long tenure at Boston University, only once did I have the sense of a message worthy of the occasion. My topic, in 1981, was what I considered to be the responsibilities of the university to its students and so, indirectly, to their parents and other mentors.

First Scripture Lesson: Psalm 137:1–6

By the rivers of Babylon, there we sat down, yea, we wept,
when we remembered Zion.
We hanged our harps upon the willows in the midst thereof.
For there they that carried us away captive required of us
a song; and they that wasted us required of us mirth, saying,
Sing us one of the songs of Zion.
How shall we sing the Lord's song in a strange land?
If I forget thee, O Jerusalem, let my right hand forget her cunning.
If I do not remember thee, let my tongue cleave to the roof
of my mouth; if I prefer not Jerusalem above my chief joy.

Second Scripture Lesson: Matthew 5:17–20, 14–16

Think not that I am come to destroy the law, or the prophets:
I am not come to destroy, but to fulfil.
For verily I say unto you, Till heaven and earth pass, one jot
or one tittle shall in no wise pass from the law, till all be fulfilled.
Whosoever therefore shall break one of these least commandments,
and shall teach men so, he shall be called the least in the
kingdom of heaven: but whosoever shall do and teach them, the
same shall be called great in the kingdom of heaven.
For I say unto you, That except your righteousness shall exceed
the righteousness of the scribes and Pharisees, ye shall in no
case enter into the kingdom of heaven.
Ye are the light of the world. A city that is set on an hill cannot be hid.
Neither do men light a candle, and put it under a bushel,
but on a candlestick; and it giveth light unto all that are in the house.
Let your light so shine before men, that they may see your
good works, and glorify your Father which is in heaven.

It is a commonplace that the university is in crisis. Critics outside the university blame the faculty or the students for the crisis; students and faculty blame the administration; the administration blames a world it never made. But the crisis of the university derives from more complex and profound origins. It is not immune from the crises afflicting the society about it. Taking its life from the individuals who participate in it, it changes as they change.

Individuals, institutions, and nations are all in crisis. Following the suffering and loss of the Second World War, men and women in the industrial nations turned to peaceful and productive work and began to prosper to a degree and an extent unprecedented. The nations of the West were in a position for the first time in world history to test, on a grand scale, mankind's capacity to resist the temptations of materialism and, delivered from the yoke of necessity, were free to choose a spiritually meaningful life.

In the industrialized West, we have observed a decline of the Church, a deterioration of the family, and a lowered respect for institutions.

Shortly after World War II as our physical needs for food, clothing, and shelter were satisfied, our primary concerns became blurred. The enemy against whom we could focus in World War II was gone. The need to put our lives in order economically and financially was satisfied to a reasonable degree, and in the absence of specific threats and dangers, we gave way to anxiety.

As affluence increased to levels of luxury and excess and extended beyond America to Europe, upwards of one-half billion men and women found themselves free from the constraints that normally structure human life and free to decide voluntarily what they would do with their leisure time and surplus income.

Men and women became increasingly preoccupied with the exploration of the outside limits of choice itself. They became devoted to the pursuit of choice for its own sake and in the process carried it to cancerous extremes, to experimentation in hallucinogenic drugs, to experimentation in social roles through insistence upon alternative lifestyles, even to the extreme of putative sexual transformation through surgical operations. In the absence of social, religious, and economic constraints, individuals claimed that "doing their own thing" – arbitrary willfulness – was its own justification and the normative way of life. "Doing it my way" was the right way, whatever the effects on others. Increasingly we came to reserve to ourselves the right to do virtually as we pleased and to interfere with others to the extent that we could.

Liberation became the watchword: liberation of students from the oppression of teachers; gay liberation; women's liberation, child liberation, animal liberation – whatever the individual merits of each cause, they combined to reduce our age to one of confusion bordering on chaos.

In this position, it is essential that individuals, institutions, and nations stop to reflect on themselves, on who they are, where they are, and on where they are going. It is a time to examine moorings and check compasses, to take readings of the stars or make use of whatever guidance systems are available. Where are we? Where are we going?

In earlier ages it would have been natural to turn to the churches, if not the universities, for an answer to the questions that face us. But the institutions of church, family, and university are subject to the pervasive influences of our time and to the general lack of direction and sense of identity. I could point my finger at religious institutions and note with accuracy that society finds itself with very few teachers in the important sense in which a rabbi should be a teacher, a minister should be a teacher, or a priest should be a teacher. I could point to reduction in the quality of educational programs in church schools. Or I could point directly at universities and note the way in which the cultural malaise has become reflected in the disappearance of coherent curricular programs.

A recent curriculum proposal at a great university says, "We do not think there is a single set of great books that every educated person must master and we do not think an inevitably thin survey of the conventional areas – humanities, social sciences, natural sciences – is any longer useful." That last part may be harmless; the first part is a cultural statement of the greatest importance: "we do not think there is a single set of great books every educated person must master." This means that a person may be thought to be educated without ever having read the Bible, or Homer, or Aeschylus, or any of Shakespeare or Plato or Aquinas.

We are in danger of losing our way. This is no fault of ours, nor our fathers, nor our predecessors, nor the previous president of our institution, nor some board of trustees. The fault lies neither in our stars nor in ourselves, but in the cultural disarray that marks our age.

By now the reason I have chosen as my text Psalm 137, "By the Rivers of Babylon," should be clear. It is a psalm which voices the despair of a people captive to all that is alien, and separated from all they hold dear – a situation characteristic of the university at the present time. In the midst of a largely secular, materialistic, and madly hedonistic society, the university has become captive. Upon secular demand it hangs up its harp and sings the songs it is asked to sing. It makes mirth when mirth is demanded, and it forgets Jerusalem. But the writer of Psalm 137 had not forgotten Jerusalem. "If I forget thee, O Jerusalem," he sings, "let my right hand forget her skill. Let my tongue cleave to the roof of my mouth if I remember thee not, if I prefer not Jerusalem above my chief joy."

The writer sings passionately of his refusal to forget Jerusalem. And he knows that he is captive to Babylon and far removed from Zion.

Unlike the writer of this psalm, the university has so thoroughly accommodated itself to life in Babylon that it has now renamed it *Jerusalem* and does not even know it is captive! As you know, of course,

"Jerusalem" and "Babylon" are not geographical locations merely, but rather symbols vital to the Judeo-Christian tradition: the former, the symbol of all that is sacred to the Jewish, Christian, and Islamic communities; the latter, of all that is foreign. Although the writer of Psalm 137 was painfully aware of his captivity and remembered Zion with longing, the university has so thoroughly adjusted itself to life in Babylon that it now calls it home and thinks of itself as free. It has forgotten Jerusalem.

In forgetting Jerusalem, what precisely have we forgotten? First, by cutting ourselves off from the guidance and insights of the religious worldview bequeathed to us by the religions of the Book, our society delivers to the university students who are ignorant of the Bible and of the history of the major religions it supports.

One can no longer speak of the faithfulness of Ruth. One can no longer talk of the courage of Esther, of the cunning of Judith. One cannot talk about the importance of selecting one's soldiers on the principles of Gideon. There are no archetypal moments on which one can depend unless they have appeared as media entertainment. When, last year, I asked a group of Boston University freshmen, "What did David and Jonathan have in common with Achilles and Patroclus?" few knew who David and Jonathan were, and only a couple of classics students had heard of Achilles and Patroclus. As an experiment, I then added Starsky and Hutch to the pairs and everyone knew the answer. One can measure the decline of a civilization by noting that this generation finds its archetype of friendship not in David and Jonathan or Achilles and Patroclus, but in the confused television images of Starsky and Hutch.

Second, as a consequence of this ignorance of the religious worldview, we have cut ourselves off from an understanding of those ethical distinctions essential to the education of the young. The distinction between right and power, for example, was made abundantly clear in the Old Testament story of King David's refusal to take the ark of the covenant into battle against his own son, Absalom. David's refusal to co-opt God's blessing in a less than worthy cause provides an example worthy of thoughtful reflection in our own day. We have also the denunciation of King David, at the height of his power, by the prophet Nathan who condemned him for killing Uriah and taking Uriah's wife Bathsheba. The fact that a prophet could denounce a king with impunity is an indication of how clearly the people of Ancient Israel understood the distinction between right and power. Although David had power, he recognized the limitations on the legitimate exercise of his power. Nathan had right on his side despite the fact that his power was limited to moral suasion.

In addition to such ethical distinctions, the higher religions all deal with the inevitable problem of suffering. The proper understanding of the role of suffering in human life is – almost – the beginning of wisdom. Yet we have greatly diminished the possibility of achieving this understanding by cutting ourselves off from our religious heritage.

Perhaps the most exceptional and significant fact about the religions of the Book – Judaism, Christianity, and Islam – is that, although they agree with many other religions and with common experience about the nature, origin, and cessation of suffering, they radically disagree with other religions about how life should be lived in the face of these facts. The facts about suffering have been beautifully and succinctly described in Buddhist literature. The Buddha enumerated the Four Noble Truths: The first, that to live is to suffer; the second, that suffering has its origin in desire; the third, that release from suffering requires giving up desire; and fourth, that the Eight-Fold Path to Nirvana leads to the cessation of suffering.

Even Bertolt Brecht, in the *Threepenny Opera*, presents a dramatic statement of this doctrine in the "Solomon-Song," which I have translated.

You saw the wise Solomon
You know what became of him.
To him was everything clear as day.
Yet he cursed the hour of his birth
And said that all was vanity.
How great and wise was Solomon.
And see it was not yet night
When the outcome was plain to see.
Wisdom brought him to this plight.
Envy those who are free of it.

You saw the beautiful Cleopatra
And you know what became of her.

She plundered two great emperors,
Then whored herself to death,
Withered away and now is dust.
How beautiful and great was Babylon.
And see before darkness fell
The world could see the outcome.
Beauty brought them to this knell.
Envy those who are free of it.

You saw the daring Caesar then
And you know what became of him.
He reigned like a god upon an altar,
And was murdered, as you have learned,
And at the height of his greatness.
Oh how he cried: "You too, my son."
And see it was not yet night.
But the outcome could be seen by all.
Boldness brought him to this plight.
Envy those who are free of it.

And now look at Macheath and me
God knows what will become of us.
So powerful was our passion;
Where did we go astray
So that he is now on the gallows' way?
You see the wages of our sins!
And you see it is not yet night
Yet the outcome is plain to see.
Our passion brought us to this plight.
Envy those who are free of it.

It is true that beauty is vain, that wisdom is vain, that boldness is vain.
But, parting company with Buddhism, Ecclesiastes, and Brecht, the Jew
and Christian insist that passion and love are not vain. Rather, they are
life! They are value. Confirming the fact that to live is to desire or to
love, and that to love is to suffer, and hence that to live is to suffer, the

Christian and Jew affirm both life and suffering. The Christian takes up his or her cross and carries it. The Jew, despite what suffering he or she may endure, sings the traditional song of affirmation, "*Ani Ma'amin*," and gets on with life.

What parent, husband, or wife does not know this? Those who bring children into the world are not unmindful that anxiety, loss, and suffering are born with their children. The cross, or suffering, is the burden of intense living. This is a hard doctrine, and rarely preached. The Christian and Jewish communities, when they have not abandoned themselves to the dominant secular culture, find renewal of their faith not in prosperity but in suffering. Christianity and Judaism are phoenix religions, renewed eternally from the ashes of living.

If the university is to be faithful to its mission, it must also affirm this truth. Otherwise, we abandon our students to the mindless Babylonian pursuit of pleasure or to an essentially lifeless Buddhist passivity. If we are not to forget Jerusalem, but to remember Zion in the midst of Babylon, the university must make use of its religious tradition. And it must include in that tradition the insights of Homer and the Greek dramatists no less than the insights of the Book. Those who teach in the university must not obscure the fact bequeathed to us by religious tradition and the tradition of the classics that all human beings are losers, for this insight does much to enlarge the imagination and insight of our students. When they recognize that all humans face essentially the same end – that all humans die – and that the problem posed by higher religions and by ethical systems has been one of seeing how defeat can be transformed into victory through a variety of spiritual and moral movements, they will confront religion and ethics in a profoundly different light.

Precisely because we live in a time of accelerating change with its derivative confusion, uncertainty, and anxiety, precisely because we are trying to cope with a world we no longer understand, our few precious and invidious verities – birth, love, suffering, joy, and death – span the whole range of the university's concern. Our educational task is to understand and transmit these verities in their full richness, in their ecstasy and tragedy. Education, even as it includes the mundane, the professional, the parochial, has no other end.

A university that does not consciously view its students in this light, a university unconcerned to develop these insights in its students, and to bring them, through study of poetry, drama, music, art, history, and philosophy, to awareness of themselves and of their human potential, is clearly in Babylonian captivity. Although the university cannot leave Babylon, the secular culture of which it is inescapably part, it can still sing the songs of Zion, and it must sing them by the rivers of Babylon. It must not forget Jerusalem.

The university succeeds when, through the humanities, understood in their fullness, it confronts the student with his or her approaching death and, eliciting the dread appropriate to this thought, encourages him or her – in celebration of life – to invest with passionate seriousness in enterprises and in an existence that will not endure. Individuals, the humanities, and the university flourish in this way and no other. It is their purpose, their relevance, and their necessity.

Students today, as they depart from the university, enter the stream of life in Babylon at flood tide. If they retain these insights and allow their lives to be guided by them, they will hold fast to their true heritage. They may still sing the songs of Zion. They need not forget Jerusalem.

The Next Parish Over

"The Irish have shown immigrant groups how to make the system work."

Although most of the chapters in this book are addressed to general audiences, one was addressed to a particular group of individuals – the Boston Irish. I include this speech to exemplify the importance of ethnicity as it gives meaning and dynamism to the lives of individuals. While ethnicity is sometimes divisive, the ethnicity of the Irish has given added significance to the lives of individuals and encouraged, strengthened, and facilitated their participation in the political and social life of our nation.

The Irish citizens of Boston are far more passionate in the display of their Irishness than the inhabitants of the Emerald Isle itself. As a person of German and English background, I was particularly honored to be invited in 1987 to address the Clover Club, an association of successful Irishmen, many of them affluent and influential in politics and in civic affairs. It was a time when politics in Massachusetts was dominated by Speaker of the House Thomas P. O'Neill, Chairman of the Rules Committee John Joseph Moakley, and Senator Edward Kennedy. The roster also included local dignitaries such as Massachusetts Senate President William Bulger, who led a spirited St. Patrick's Day breakfast in which nearly all of the political figures of Boston participated.

There was a substantial consumption of alcohol on this occasion along with humorous commentary on the leadership of the club and a continual roasting of those in attendance. It was about 11 o'clock when I was finally called upon to speak. Recognizing the difficulty of holding this audience at so late an hour, I thought it best to engage in shameless flattery of the Irish. This seemed to work: My speech was sufficiently well received that Congressman Moakley had it placed in the Congressional Record. The membership found it interesting enough to ask me to give it again in 1994.

I MUST BEGIN WITH a confession: I was not born Irish. But then, neither was St. Patrick, an Englishman who was kidnapped and taken to Ireland, where he sensibly decided to remedy the accident of his birth and made himself not merely an Irishman, but the greatest Irishman. As a matter of fact, there are three ways of being Irish. Some are born Irish, a happy condition that is enjoyed by most of us here tonight. Others, like St. Patrick, achieve Irishness. And finally, some have Irishness thrust upon them, as I have by being invited to address the Clover Club even though my name is Silber.

Far from being from Galway or Mayo, the Silbers were Germans. Nor did my mother or her people come from Ireland, but from a large land mass just to the east of Ireland which tonight it would be unseemly, perhaps imprudent, to name.

Now, I am also a philosopher, and so in preparing to speak as a German before an audience of Irishmen at their annual high revel, I naturally consulted a philosophic text. I could expect no help from my mentor Immanuel Kant, because he too was German. And of course Plato and Aristotle were Greek and St. Thomas was Italian.

I turned naturally to the most distinguished Irish-American philosopher – the late Martin Dooley, saloon-keeper in Archey Road in the Sixth Ward of Chicago. I was not disappointed, for I quickly learned that in 1898, Mr. Dooley was deeply engrossed in the question of fraternal relations between the Irish and the Germans. Relations between the two groups had not, to be frank, always been the best in the Sixth Ward. A gentle feud existed between Mr. Dooley and his professional colleague Schwartzmeister, who kept a saloon down the road. Mr. Schwartzmeister committed aggression upon Mr. Dooley by installing a pool table. One thing led to another. Mr. Schwartzmeister claimed that a friend had been poisoned by Mr. Dooley's beer, and Mr. Dooley said that he would sooner go for whiskey to a harness-shop than to Schwartzmeister's.

This feud festered until relations between Great Britain and Germany took a sudden downturn. Now it dawned on Mr. Schwartzmeister that the enemy of his enemy was his friend, and Mr. Dooley concluded that if the Kaiser was on the verge of war with the English, there was much to be said for Schwartzmeister. This is the account of the reconciliation in Mr. Dooley's own words:

... I heard a man singing' "The Wearing of the Green" down the Street, and in come Schwartzmeister. "Erin go brag," says he, meanin' to be polite. "Lieb vaterland," says I. And we had a drink together.

"Vell," says he (and you know the murderin' way he has of speaking), "here we are," he says, "friends at last." "True for ye," says I. "Tooley," he says, for he calls me that, "we're one tonight, alretty," he says. "We are that," says I. But glory be, who ever thought the Irish'd live to see the day when they'd be freed by the Dutch? "Schwartz, me lieber friend," I says, "here's a health to the Emperor. Hock!" says I. "Slanthu," says he; and we had one.

Mr. Dooley quickly realized the implications of this détente for the Sixth Ward:

" '[T]would be a great combination," says I. "We'd carry the ward be the biggest majority ever heard of," I says. "We would so," says he. "I'd be alderman." "After me," says I. " 'Tis my turn first." "I don't know about that," says he.

At this point, the détente seemed in danger, but Mr. Dooley won Mr. Schwartzmeister over by an act of typical Irish magnanimity.

"We're both patriots," I says. "We have a common cause," I says. "You're a Dutchman and I'm of the other sort," I says. "And in the interests of the freedom of Ireland," I says, "I forgive you the pool table." Well, sir, he wept like a child. "Tooley," he says, "we'll march side be side. Alderman Tooley and Alderman Schwartzmeister, to free Ireland," he says. "But where does Germany come in?" he says. "Germany!" says I. "Germany! Well, we'll take care of Germany, all right. We'll let Germans into the primaries," I says. And there and then we formed the Sarsfield and Goeethee camp.... We shook dice to see which nam'd come first. Ireland won. They was my dice.

And so I come here tonight in the spirit of my compatriot Schwartzmeister, like him rejoicing in having Irishness thrust upon me. But if it comes to dice, I've brought my own.

In the days of Brian Boru, on great feasts, the high king and those in vassalage to him were entertained by poets called *fili*. The greatest of the *fili* – the man who knew every story and all laws, the man versed in every trick of rhyme, meter, and music, the man expert in every mode of flattery and truthtelling – in short, a man almost proficient enough to enter the Boston political arena – this man was called an *ollam*. It is said that with one rhyme an *ollam* could kill a hundred rats – imagine what such a man could accomplish today in politics. And that with two rhymes, an *ollam* could create a cloak out of a sunbeam.

If his entertainment went well, a performer was permitted to beg a boon of the high king. Sometimes it was money, sometimes honor, sometimes it had to do with love. Occasionally the *ollam* would ask Brian Boru to turn his mind to some important matter.

Although I am no *ollam*, I may, tonight, touch briefly on important matters. If one is to praise the Irish – and if that's not why I was invited, then why am I here? – one must speak of such matters as the love of beauty, the struggle for freedom, the drive to learn and to educate. Education is in large part the assimilation of what is foreign so as to transform oneself. Through the centuries the Irish genius for assimilation and transformation waxed so great that Ireland became the repository of western civilization when Europe and England lapsed into barbarism.

Much of what we now think of as European culture has been transmitted and transfigured by Irish learning and Irish imagination. Even before St. Patrick's time, as barbarian hordes were overrunning Europe, scholars from the Continent were emigrating to Ireland to escape them. Welcoming these exiles, who brought with them priceless Greek and Latin manuscripts, Ireland became the last outpost of western culture, preserving the works and developing the traditions which Europe had lost. Without the labors of generations of Irish scholars, writers, and ecclesiastics, much of the world's literature would have been lost. The Irish missionaries who brought their glowing faith back to Europe later in the Dark Ages were more than evangelists – they were Europe's only remaining humanists.

The splendors of Ireland during Europe's dark ages are revealed in a myth told about King Alfred, called "the Great" for his valor, learning, political genius, and encouragement of civilization in a savage time.

Alfred, who in the late ninth century ruled much of what is now England, was the prototype of a great English king. But although he was undoubtedly English, the Irish recognized in him the ideal of an Irish High King. A myth grew up in Ireland that Alfred had been educated there. It survives in a medieval Irish poem in which Alfred is made to speak with wonder and admiration of the civilization he found in Ireland. Alfred says:

> I found in Innisfail the fair,
> In Ireland, while in exile there,
> God's people rich in pity,
> Found many a feast and many a city.
>
> I found in Munster unfettered of any,
> Kings, and queens, and poets a many –
> I found in Connaught the just, and fame,
> Hospitality, vigor, heroic name.
>
> I found in Ulster, from hill to glen,
> Hardy warriors, resolute men;
> Beauty that bloomed when youth was gone,
> And strength transmitted from sire to son.
>
> I found besides, from Ara to Glea,
> In the broad rich country of Ossorie,
> Sweet fruits, good laws for all and each,
> Great chess-players and truthful speech.
>
> I found strict morals in age and youth,
> I found historians recording truth:
> The things I sing of in verse unsmooth,
> I found them all – I have written sooth.

This myth about Alfred reflects the truth that the English were civilized by the Irish. When the Anglo-Saxon barbarians – cousins of my German ancestors – arrived in England, they had made only one halting step on the road to literacy: They had developed a runic alphabet which they carved on monumental stones. Needless to say, this earliest Anglo-Saxon literature was characterized by its exceeding brevity. From the flat surface of the stone to a sheet of paper may seem only a step, but it was one apparently beyond the abilities of the Anglo-Saxons. The Irish took the English by the hand and taught them the Roman alphabet and the use of pen and ink: That is, the Irish taught the English to read and write, making thereby a mistake they have regretted ever since!

The gift of literacy was the first transformation of the English by the Irish. Once so equipped, the English eventually developed the strategic capabilities which allowed them to turn on their benefactors and occupy Ireland. England oppressed the Irish; yet so powerful was the Irish spirit, its love of beauty, its expansiveness and liveliness, that it captured the foreigner's tongue and made it a well-tuned instrument, expanding its range to embrace harmonies and follow after melodies never heard before.

The Irish transformed the English language, and in so doing transformed themselves into masters and shapers of one of the world's great tongues. One of the greatest poets of the twentieth century, admired throughout the civilized world, William Butler Yeats, is an Irishman writing in English. In fact many of the greatest authors known as English were Irishmen – Jonathan Swift, Richard Brinsley Sheridan, Oscar Wilde, and George Bernard Shaw, who illumined and transformed the English stage.

The Irish quality that made this possible is summed up in an old bit of poetic wisdom quoted by Matthew Arnold:

> For acuteness and valor, the Greeks,
> For excessive pride, the Romans,
> For dulness, the creeping Saxons,
> For love of beauty, the Gaels.

In America, the Irish have shown a similar power of assimilation and transformation. Many of them came to America and found their condition little better than indenture – and in some ways worse. There is mute evidence of this in the houses on Commonwealth Avenue where the top floor – on which the Irish servants lived – was originally unheated.

But the Irish took the American system and made it their own.

How they were able to do this has been described by Lord Macaulay in his *History of England*. Distinguishing between the Scots and the Irish, Macaulay first notes that both rank high in natural courage and intelligence. But while the Scots, he says, have certain peculiar virtues designed to make men prosperous,

> The Irish [are] distinguished by qualities which tend to make men interesting rather than prosperous.... Alone among the nations of Northern Europe they have the susceptibility, the vivacity, the natural turn for acting and rhetoric.

The very existence of the Clover Club demonstrates that Macaulay underestimated the relationship between being interesting and being prosperous. But Macaulay correctly noted that the Irish have been given the qualities designed to make men charming. With those gifts, which are the stuff of politics, the Irish made their way in America.

It is one of the great triumphs of modern history that the Irish, denied self-government in their own island, proved themselves masters of the democratic process as soon as they landed in America. Nor should anyone be surprised that once Ireland won her independence and suffered a brief civil war, she should rapidly have become one of the most stable democracies. The Irish had already proven their genius for self-government in the New World.

The Irish in America are the model of intelligent ethnicity in a democracy; while retaining their heritage, they embrace the values and the system of this great land, expanding it and fulfilling it. They are, in short, the embodiment of the American dream.

The Irish who fled their country in the famine years and came to Boston and New York and Chicago found their political situation transformed. In the Ireland they had left, the right to vote was limited to the prosperous, and the vote could only elect an outnumbered delegation to a distant parliament at Westminster. In the America to which the immigrants came, every white male could vote, and the Irish were not shy in seizing political opportunities.

They voted and they organized. They took up their positions in the essential public services of the great cities. Soon they provided mayors and governors. One of the greatest of these, Al Smith, found himself barred from the highest office by his religion, but in the next generation, John Fitzgerald Kennedy, by his forthright demonstration that there was no conflict between being a Catholic and being an American, became the first Irish president. And one of the greatest of our politicians born Irish is here with us: the distinguished and beloved Speaker of the House of Representatives, Tip O'Neill.

The Irish provided an example for all immigrant groups of how to make the system work, leading them to learn English and enter the political system. As the Germans, Italians, Jews and other eastern Europeans emulated the success of the Irish, the result was the melting pot. It was the Irish led the way. American blacks are increasingly devoting themselves to the political process and in consequence accelerating their integration into the political and economic system.

In recent years it has, unfortunately, become fashionable to question the validity of the melting pot and to encourage groups of what Theodore Roosevelt called "hyphenated Americans," who perpetuate their ethnic particularism at the expense of their integration into American society. When some ethnic groups resist the learning of English and urge bilingualism as a national program, they propose a program that, were it to succeed, could undermine the unity essential to American freedom. We can with realism urge them to reconsider the wisdom of the Irish model which, judged by its consequences, can scarcely be wrong.

Although only the Irish of later immigrant groups enjoyed the advantage of speaking English when they arrived at Ellis Island, their success once ashore demonstrated to all other immigrants that knowing English was not merely advantageous but essential. The spectacular success of Southeast Asians is only the most recent confirmation of the lesson the Irish taught us.

The Irish have done more than show a country of immigrants how to achieve unity and make the system work. They brought the Irish soul from their island, and have made it live in the New World. The celebration of St. Patrick's Day by Americans of all ethnic backgrounds and religions is a unique cultural phenomenon. As my colleague at Boston University, former ambassador to Ireland Bill Shannon has pointed out, nowhere in Ireland is the Saint's day honored as intensely and widely as it is in any American city. The Irish provide the critical mass for a proper St. Pat's Day parade, but the marching and watching is done by Americans of all backgrounds. This is not, I think, a matter of mere sentiment, for in a profound sense, we are all Irish.

Wallace Stevens, one of the greatest American poets, has movingly spoken of this essentially Irish quality of America: "Our Stars Come from Ireland," Stevens wrote,

> Our nights [are] full of the green stars of Ireland.
> The whole habit of the mind is changed by them,
> These Gaeled and fitful-fangled darknesses,
> Made suddenly luminous, . . .
> An east in their compelling westwardness.

Irishmen used to stand on the edge of Boston harbor under the westward-moving stars and say, "The next parish over is Dingle." When Americans of German, of Swedish, of Jewish, of African, of Cambodian, of whatever ancestry, don the shamrock and march in the parade, they are recognizing, however unconsciously, that Irish east in the westwardness of the moving stars. For all of us Dingle is the next parish over.

The University and the Defense of Freedom

"Those who beat the sword of truth into the plowshare of ideology can neither fight nor farm – neither defend their freedom nor feed themselves."

In recent years, it has been the concern of some of our leading universities to take great care not to be caught in service to their nation. Thus they have banned ROTC from the campus or failed to discipline faculty and students who harassed units of the ROTC to the point that these organizations withdrew from prior association. It also became fashionable to assert the doctrine of value-neutrality and the claim that the unfettered search for truth is simply one more ideology, equal in its claims to any other, but no more than that.

It seemed to me, and seems still, that a university engaged in the search for truth and enjoying the benefits of a free society has an obligation to that society on whose existence it clearly depends. With this in mind, I addressed a group of faculty and students at the Center for Defense Journalism of the College of Communications of Boston University in 1988 on the subject of the university and the defense of freedom.

EDUCATION AND A FREE SOCIETY

Democracy and free enterprise, this combination – with all its potential weaknesses and problems – has proved itself the most just and beneficial mode of government and economic development. South Korea, to take a single example, is a nation that has been transformed by free enterprise. As the practice of free enterprise has created literally tens of thousands of centers of economic power – from major industries to individual shops and small service enterprises – it has enabled millions of South Koreans to achieve a spectacular degree of economic independence. As a consequence, South Koreans have demanded fuller participation in the political process, and their leaders, following the lead of President Chung, have presented for their ratification a new constitution. In accordance with that constitution, free elections with genuinely competing political parties will now take place.

These developments would have been impossible apart from the education of the South Koreans in the democratic process; and if they are to fulfill responsibly their obligations as citizens of democracy, their education will have to be continued and further extended.

Citizens in a democratic society must be able to evaluate doctrines of all kinds – economic, social, political, religious – and they must be able to do so for themselves. To be genuine, this evaluation must be rational, that is, based on an understanding of the relevant facts. It cannot be derived from experience that diminishes not only rationality but also the very sense of reality. Rationality and respect for facts are absolutely indispensable to a democratic education.

The distinction between education in democratic and nondemocratic societies is critical and profound. In a society without respect for individual rights, true education is impossible. In an unfree society, the educator's only sanctioned role is to deceive, to indoctrinate, to intimidate. Such an educator's role is merely to train, to shape each student into a functional part of the great machine of state. Such a person *trains*; he or she does not *educate*.

In a free society, on the other hand, the educator's role is far more complex and demanding. It is to awaken in students the love of freedom and an understanding of the nature and conditions of freedom. The educator must also encourage in students that self-restraint essential to a free society: that restraint which recognizes and truly respects the rights of others as the condition of one's own rights. The educator does not seek to produce human machine-parts or components, no matter how complex, but seeks to guide each student toward an ideal defined by the philosopher Immanuel Kant: the ideal of the *autonomous* individual whose freedom lies not in doing whatever he or she pleases, regardless of the consequences, but rather in the ability, by means of reason, to exercise freedom in accordance with moral and social laws that define the conditions of fulfillment for oneself and all other members of one's society.

Many today wonder whether there are such laws. Autonomy, today, is too often misunderstood as "doing one's thing." On the other hand, individuals are encouraged by governments, by organizations, and by charismatic leaders to believe their autonomy is compatible with a political ideology or religious cult. In a free society, it is the educator's duty to oppose and demonstrate the limitation and falsehood of these counterfeit notions of autonomy.

COUNTERFEITS OF EDUCATION:
RELATIVISM AND VALUE-NEUTRALITY

The ideal of truth has become increasingly unfashionable in intellectual and political circles and has been replaced in the minds of many of our most influential scholars, writers, newsmen, and politicians by a relativism guided by an ideology. In literary theory no less than in political science, intellectuals have increasingly adopted the notion that one's thoughts and opinions are not to be grounded in fact or sustained by argument as more or less adequate expressions of the truth. Rather, outside the sciences, there is a prevalent tendency among intellectuals to denigrate as hopelessly naive or confused any teacher who practices the Socratic search for truth, who seeks through diligent study and investigation the likeliest account of the nature of things. The Socratic quest has been replaced by the relativism of Sophists. "Whirl is king, having cast out Zeus," as Aristophanes once put it; we again hear Protagoras' assertion that mankind is the measure of all things – indeed that there are as many different standards of measure as there are classes or even individuals.

The notion that all truth is relative, and that there are no values worth defending, is often confused with the notion of academic freedom. In reality, the two are very different, and indeed contradictory.

Every university depends on academic freedom, a concept implicit in the life of the mind going back to the days of Socrates. As an explicit concept, academic freedom can be traced back to the principles of *Lehrfreiheit* and *Lernfreiheit* – freedom to teach and freedom to learn – embodied in Humboldt's reforms at the University of Berlin in the early nineteenth century.

Today, unfortunately, it is taken for granted by many that freedom to teach and learn involves freedom from values. But no university can be value-neutral. Its very being presupposes a commitment to the search for truth. It is committed to logical thought and scientific method. The work of the university cannot be done unless the individuals who do it are humble before facts and logic, willing to test their experience against the experience of others, and assiduous in avoiding or correcting for prejudice and irrationality. Freedom to teach and freedom to learn do not exist in a vacuum. They exist, as Kant correctly observed, in a moral context in which practical reason is primary. Scientists and scholars are obligated to subordinate themselves to the rules and procedures of rational thought. Unlimited freedom is an oxymoron, for there can be no freedom unless we observe the conditions that make freedom possible.

The university, in committing itself to the search for truth, beauty, and goodness – those transcendentals articulated as its goals by the medieval philosophers and theologians – commits itself to academic freedom: freedom to teach and freedom to learn. Therefore it cannot be value-neutral or indifferent with respect to the conditions by which academic freedom may be attained. The myth of value-neutrality is a tenet of positivism, a philosophical theory of science advanced in the late-nineteenth and early-twentieth centuries. Positivism promoted the doctrine of value-neutrality despite the fact that the myth had been exposed and laid to rest centuries before the positivists rediscovered it.

Plato understood the interdependence of facts and values. How, Plato asked, can you know what a thing is until you know its value? How can you define a knife without knowing what a knife is good for? Only when you know its purpose, its value as a cutting instrument, can you know what a knife is. How could one understand the nature of water, if one did not know the essential relationship of water to life – the dependency of all life, plant, animal, and human, on water? To define water simply in terms of the formula H_2O, in the absence of any knowledge of the relationships to reality entailed by this formula – as, for instance, its interconnectedness with other substances described by other formulae, and the relationship of all of these to human life – would ensure that one remained profoundly ignorant of the nature of water.

COUNTERFEITS OF EDUCATION: IDEOLOGY

Once adrift on the sea of relativism, having accepted the idea that there is no truth, one can only offer one's allegiance to one or another of the ideologies. Ideology accepts in principle and inevitably demands in practice that we overrule reason, ignore method, falsify facts, and constrain the freedom of others in the projection and defense of preestablished objectives void of any rational legitimation.

An ideology cannot be refuted by a counter-ideology. It must be exposed by those who are committed not to conformity to one ideology or another, but to the search for truth. Within an ideological framework, there is no truth or reality or history – except the "truth," "reality," and "history" generated by the ideology itself. In order, therefore, to refute an ideology, one must subject all its claims to rigorous tests for truth independent of any and all prior ideological commitments.

To describe, for example, our relationship to the Soviet Union as a war between ideologies is, in effect, to declare the epistemological equivalence of the United States and the USSR. If we grant their epistemological equivalence, their moral equivalence follows in easy steps. But anyone remotely knowledgeable in the history of the twentieth century will recall Stalin's reversal of his assessment of Adolf Hitler and Nazi Germany at the time of the Molotov–Ribbentrop pact establishing an alliance with the Nazis whom the Soviets had previously denounced. This total reversal in the factual description of Nazi Germany and in the moral position taken toward it would be impossible in a society committed to the truth. It is totally consistent, however, with the Leninist ideology that the truth is whatever supports the revolution whose success – at whatever cost in human lives and human suffering – is the only unalterable goal. In this instance, the alliance with Hitler gave Stalin additional time in which to prepare for war with Germany, and the opportunity to take Finland and one-half of Poland.

The substitution of talk about ideology for a discussion of the facts and of truth has been the source of widespread confusion and has led to the intellectual disarmament of the democracies. Those who beat the sword of truth into the plowshare of ideology can neither fight nor farm – neither defend their freedom nor feed themselves.

No university can be neutral or indifferent with regard to those nations that have imposed serious restraints on freedom of thought, freedom of inquiry, and freedom of expression. By its very nature, the university is committed to the development of free inquiry for the highest of human purposes; and because of its commitment to the realization of human values, the university is also committed to a few limited political objectives. By its very nature the university is committed to a democratic society, to that form of government that recognizes and defends fundamental human rights of freedom of thought and freedom of expression.

From the dependency of universities on that form of government which protects and ensures the exercise of human freedom, it follows that no university worthy of the name can pretend to be value-neutral in the assessment of the United States and totalitarian governments. A university that promotes the doctrine of moral equivalence between these two, presenting them as two equally valid systems of government or as two equally guilty parties in the political realities of our time, repudiates the conditions for its very existence. Whether we realize it or not, the doctrine of moral equivalence becomes a weapon in the hands of the enemies not only of the United States, but of freedom. It turns the goodwill and openness of Americans – their honesty, their willingness to acknowledge their shortcomings and make amends for all faults large and small, real or imagined – into a weapon for use by our enemies.

A university, committed to freedom, is concerned with the defense of the free world. Universities, in whatever nation they may exist, must align themselves with principles observed always in theory, and generally in practice, by the free democracies. This is a matter both of survival and of moral obligation. While universities should treasure their status as ivory towers, they do not exist in a vacuum but are in fact highly dependent on the community and the nation in which they exist.

There are many ways in which the obligations which follow from this dependency can be met. One is through support of ROTC units to provide officers for the armed forces. The quality of officers produced by ROTC is measured in their achievements. In 1989, Colin Powell, an ROTC graduate, was appointed to the nation's highest military rank: Chairman of the Joint Chiefs of Staff.

Boston University first explicitly honored its obligation to educate officers for the nation's fighting services in 1919, with the founding of its first ROTC program. It has continued to honor that obligation ever since.

This statement is not compromised by the fact that in 1970, after several years of vociferous protest, the Army and Air Force units (then the only ones on campus) were withdrawn. In the late '60s and early '70s, a minority of students and faculty challenged the idea that the university should in any way support the nation. This demand voiced throughout the country developed a social pressure to which many universities bowed.

By the time I arrived at Boston University, the Chairman of the House Armed Services committee, Representative F. Edward Hebert, had essentially blacklisted us as one of thirteen universities that he considered to have thrown ROTC off campus. One of my first actions as president, taken at the urging of the Dean of Students, Staton Curtis, was to poll the faculty as to its opinion about ROTC. We discovered what both of us had guessed would be the case: two-thirds of the faculty supported the return of ROTC. I and most faculty members believed that civilian control of the military is better ensured when a significant percentage of officers are civilian in orientation and educated in civilian institutions rather than in military academies. We also believed that our students in financial need had the right to be eligible for ROTC scholarships.

Dean Curtis urged me to attempt a restoration and prepared applications for reinstatement. Arthur Metcalf, Chairman of the Board of Trustees, and I took his message to Washington and presented his plan to Congressman Hebert, asking for his assistance. Working behind the scenes with his contacts in the Department of Defense, Staton Curtis persevered until, in 1981, Army and Air Force ROTC were restored to the campus. In 1982, Dean Curtis was able to bring Naval ROTC to the campus. For the first time in our history, Boston University had on campus all three branches of the military service. In 1986, a Marine ROTC unit was also established.

Being willing in this way to take up our obligation to the nation does not mean that we fail to recognize the deficiencies of the United States. It means rather that we, free to pursue the truth, are obligated to recognize them and to call attention to them. If our universities contribute to the education of journalists in such a way that they recognize and prefer the success of the United States to its defeat by its enemies, we will be doing no more than our job – not only as patriots, and certainly not as chauvinists, but as educators. We will be meeting a fundamental obligation placed on the university: to put the highest value on human freedom as a *sine qua non* of human fulfillment.

GOALS OF THE FREE UNIVERSITY

The knowledge to which we ultimately aspire is knowledge of the goal of human life and the conditions for human fulfillment. In the past, the belief that there were transcendent principles by which we should guide our lives helped give society a goal and an understanding of the human condition. Writing in 1830, Alexis de Tocqueville noted that in ages of faith, people concerned themselves always with a distant supreme goal beyond this life. In doing so, Tocqueville wrote,

> [T]hey learn by imperceptible degrees to repress a crowd of petty passing desires in order ultimately to best satisfy the one great permanent longing which obsesses them. When these same men engage in worldly affairs, such habits influence their conduct.
>
> That is why religious nations have often accomplished such lasting achievements. For in thinking of the other world, they have found out the great secret of success in this. But in skeptical ages the vision of the life to come is lost, a problem that is exacerbated in democracies, where people are set free to compete with each other to improve their situations. In such a combination of circumstances, the present looms large and hides the future, so that men do not want to think beyond tomorrow.

Tocqueville thought it especially important that the philosophers and rulers in skeptical democracies should always, as he says, "strive to set a distant aim as the object of human efforts; that is their most important business."

Tocqueville did not specify the nature of the goals which need to be set in such ages – of which ours is one – but we can hardly doubt that such goals, if they are to have sufficient transcendence to give direction and meaning to life, must presuppose a decent respect for truth and a concern for the advancement of human fulfillment both for individuals and for society as a whole. Any lesser objectives would by their immediacy and triviality leave individuals so immersed in day-to-day affairs that they would fail to note and strive to ensure the conditions on which theirs and their children's future depend. That is, in a secular age in which few believe in a life to come, and in which for many God is, if not dead, at best indifferent, a vision of transcendent purpose in which individuals may find their fulfillment is essential. It is difficult in a secular age to believe that such a vision of purpose can be found in anything other than free pursuit of truth and the free examination of all theories and views pretending to truth.

TEACHERS IN OUR DEMOCRATIC SOCIETY

Tocqueville wrote in an age when philosophers were occasionally listened to, and in which television advertisers had not replaced philosophers, teachers, politicians, and businessmen as the primary instructors in ethics and the goals of society. Today our knowledge falters in the kaleidoscopic confrontation with incompatible claims of facticity. Rarely if ever does our knowledge reach the level of wisdom, which depends on the coherent assimilation of large bodies of facts and knowledge rather than sound bites which can be understood, if that is the right word, in ninety seconds.

Consider the effects of the television media on our understanding of world issues and matters of grave national import. Instead of presenting the news coherently, they have reduced the news not to a search for facts and truth but to the ideology of entertainment – the "miniseries of reality."

News treated as entertainment is a form of censorship. Let us suppose that the president of the United States gives a major speech. What happens? A commentator precedes the speech in order to "prep" the public by telling it in predigested form what the president is about to say. After the speech, a panel of commentators tells the public what the president has just said. In doing so, no commentator merely reports the president's words – that would be repetitive and therefore lack entertainment value. Instead, each commentator adds his or her own spin. Next, politicians from the opposing party add their slant. But this is still not enough. Even more remote commentators are called upon: experts from other nations are summoned to tell us not only what our president said, but what it means and whether he is sincere. Can one imagine that during the Battle of Britain the BBC would have followed Churchill's speech, "we shall fight on the beaches, we shall fight on the landing grounds, we shall fight in the fields and in the streets, we shall fight in the hills. . . ." by switching to Berlin for a comment by Dr. Goebbels? Would the radio have followed FDR's fireside chats with a commentary by Herbert Hoover? Would our country have started to revive and rebuild if, following FDR's statement that "we have nothing to fear but fear itself," a series of pundits had come on to say how many different things there were to fear – such as jobless-ness, want of food, hunger, disease, and so on?

Journalists, like all of us, are subject to the temptations of power. Power tends to corrupt them no less than it corrupts politicians. And as the fourth estate has become vastly more powerful through television, jour-nalists in the electronic media should be aware of their increasing vul-nerability to corruption. Many journalists come to think of themselves not so much as objective reporters but as the loyal opposition. But this is not their proper function. The adversarial relationship is not a relation-ship of objectivity. To be in opposition may be the duty of a politician or a party, but it is a violation of the responsibility of the journalist, which is to report on what happens as objectively and as dispassionately as possible.

The reporter's work should be like a pane of glass, flawlessly clear and unspotted, through which the reader may view the important events of the day. Today, the practice of "personal" journalism in reporting the news has sacrificed objectivity for entertainment and for the personal gratification and popularity of the reporters who consider themselves makers of the news. Too often we see and read not what happened or what was said, but the entertaining views of the fourth estate. Spasmodic journalists, those who offer an opinion every half hour in a context of incoherence, stand in stark contrast to journalists like Tom Wolfe who, building from a coherent understanding, with shocking accuracy hold the mirror up to nature. In short commentaries, in book-length studies and in novels, Wolfe does not pick out a statement here or there, but reveals out of many particulars the generalities that define with precision and without ideological slant the way we are. In his novels he has become the Charles Dickens of our time, setting forth without bias the character and characters of our nation. Those who practice such journalism may entertain, but their important contribution lies in their ability to see to the heart of the matter – that is, to educate. Such journalism is a service to our nation.

If by shortening the attention span, we create persons incapable of complex analysis and responsible judgment; if we distort events of the day, garble the words of our leaders, simplify the character of nations, positing a false equivalence between democratic and totalitarian governments – there can be only one result. A dictatorship may survive by virtue of the strength of one man and his army, but the survival of democracy depends upon the moral virtue and reasoning power of its people and on their participation in government as responsible, understanding citizens. If the media fail to assume responsibility to pursue the truest account, free from ideology and self-promotion, how will democracy survive the onslaught of counterfeit facts and ideologies? Since the media – not the primary and secondary schools, not the colleges and universities – have now become the chief educators of the American people, those working in television should assume the duties and responsibilities of educators in addition to those of journalists and entertainers.

Some of the problems of our age are perhaps unprecedented, but educating people for autonomy has never been easy. It can only be done by teachers who are themselves autonomous – teachers capable of ruling themselves in accordance with their intellectual and moral responsibilities. Good teachers do not succumb to the ideology of entertainment, telling their students what the students want to hear, what will amuse, titillate, or distract them. Good teachers accept the responsibility of doing the extremely hard work that is required to discover the truth and to make that truth known to students.

We are called upon to resist the entertaining but largely chaotic present and to teach that human knowledge and rational action must have a vector – that is, a direction and a velocity. To know enough to live decently as human beings we must live in an atmosphere of freedom, free to follow evidence wherever it takes us. The true educator cannot be value-neutral with respect to truth. He or she must reject both relativism and ideology.

By its commitment to a free society, to autonomy, to the search for truth and a rejection of ideology, any university should be a defender of freedom and proud to be found in service to its country.

Stretching the Envelope

"A university should encourage students not only to discover what course of study is appropriate for them, but also to discover what their individual capacities and limits may be."

Norwich University in Vermont, the nation's first private military college and the birthplace of the ROTC, enrolls both cadets and civilian students. Having recently read *The Right Stuff*, Tom Wolfe's excellent book on the astronauts, I thought it appropriate to center my commencement address in 1991 on taking knowledgeable risks in order to discover one's capabilities and one's limits. I was very pleased that in attendance were the university's president, W. Russell Todd, a retired general who had served in Korea and Vietnam, and the Army's Chief of Staff and member of the Joint Chiefs, General Gordon Russell Sullivan.

COMMENCEMENT is supposed to celebrate the achievement of students, but anyone who has walked through a post-commencement crowd knows that in most cases the achievements are a collaboration between the generations. The graduates have labored in their classes, their laboratories, and studios, and many have also labored at jobs that have helped to pay for their education. Their parents, in addition to having spent eighteen years in child-rearing, have made massive financial contributions usually requiring genuine sacrifice.

I suspect that many of you, both students and parents, have read Tom Wolfe's excellent book *The Right Stuff* about the NASA astronauts. In it, one hears test pilots use the expression, "He stretched the envelope." Let me recall what this means. In designing an aircraft, engineers develop a series of specifications that define a new plane's desired performance. They express this in a family of mathematical equations that are known as "the envelope." They then design an aircraft that will meet these expectations. In the process, as specifications are tested by the realities of physics and metallurgy, the design of the original envelope may have to be modified. The next step is to build a model of the aircraft and put it through a series of tests in wind tunnels. Here on a small scale the envelope is tested for aerodynamic performance, and once again modifications may have to be made to decrease drag, to improve the effectiveness of control surfaces or to increase the thrust of the engine. When the necessary modifications have been made and the model has finally passed all the wind tunnel tests, a prototype of the actual aircraft is built and turned over to the test pilot. We then discover for the first time whether the theoretical envelope matches the actual envelope of the real airplane.

It is the obligation of the test pilot to put the aircraft through its paces, to determine if it can not only reach the limits of its theoretical envelope but perhaps even exceed them. The test pilots who are most successful at stretching the envelope are said to have "the right stuff."

Any university worthy of the name proposes a variety of alternative designs to fit the individual abilities of the students who attend it. It also tries to encourage students to stretch their envelopes – not only to discover what course of study is appropriate to them, but also to discover what their individual capacities and limits may be. Those who refuse to take risks or who merely sit back and wait for things to happen will never exercise those abilities that might fully engage their capacities at the outermost limits. If a person does not try, for example, to run faster in a series of track trials, that person will never know just how fast he or she can run.

Every athlete knows that testing the envelope, stretching oneself to the outer limits, is necessary. Most of us accept the notion that this is what athletes are about. But it is also what students are about. Students have the obligation, if they are to get the most out of their education, to select the most demanding professors, the ones who give not the easiest but the hardest assignments; and to work as hard as they can in their laboratories and classrooms, in the library and elsewhere; to take advantage of the extracurricular activities available to them in lectures, plays, and concerts; and to push to the outer limits of their capacity to learn, to absorb, to assimilate.

When we strive to excel, there is always the risk of failure, of trying to go beyond one's capacity. One of the great experiences of my life was a summer spent at Northwestern's School of Music. At that time I planned to be a professional musician and was studying the trumpet. But during that summer, I was in daily contact with very talented young musicians who showed me that I was actually an amateur. I was good, perhaps, but certainly not good enough. It was through stretching the envelope in competition with people more talented than I that I came to this important piece of self-knowledge.

Knowledge of the range of our abilities is one of the gifts of a college education. It is just as valuable to learn what one cannot do as to learn what one can. All of this is part of the lessons to be learned by stretching the envelope.

Institutions of learning owe their students the knowledge not only of what they can do, but also of their proper limitations. At the University of Vermont, for example, the students who for three weeks occupied the president's office undoubtedly wished to stretch the envelope of their powers to determine the affairs of the University. Unfortunately, the administration, by allowing them to occupy that building for three weeks, failed to assert the limits that are defined by the laws of criminal trespass and encouraged these students in a false belief regarding their rights and their competence. Overstretching the envelope, the students had a small seductive experience of anarchy that could not finally be sustained. And, of course, the president of the institution stretched not only his envelope but his britches in climbing up a ladder to his office when students blocked the stairway. The university has the duty not to pander to or flatter its students, but through a program of contrived adversity to guide them in discovering the limits of student power and responsibility.

As some of you know, I engaged last year in an envelope-stretching endeavor otherwise known as a political campaign. There was no way that a person who had spent most of his sabbaticals engaged in research could have enlarged his horizons more thoroughly than I did by running for public office. I stretched my personal envelope, and I also tried to stretch the envelope of political discourse by the introduction of the so-called Silber shockers. I did stretch it, but not quite far enough. I came up short by 38,000 votes.

Some years ago, a young and callow assistant professor – and most assistant professors are young and callow – gossiped about a senior professor who, despite modest abilities, had achieved a far-reaching reputation. The callow assistant professor said, "He is the living refutation of Aristotle, having more than actualized his potentialities." This was intended as a witty sneer, but was actually a magnificent compliment. By hard work and determination to be the best he could possibly be, this senior professor had stretched his envelope beyond what anyone would have dreamed possible.

Now, how does this analysis relate to you as individual members of the Class of 1991? First of all, you have inherited a genetic makeup that establishes certain abilities, qualities of body, mind and spirit, that form your potentialities and your limitations. This is your envelope. But your Creator has not revealed the details of that envelope. You do not have a blueprint that defines it. You cannot learn its specifications except by trying to exceed them. You are, in effect, both the aircraft and its test pilot.

Of course, you are no longer totally ignorant of your envelope, nor have you been flying alone. Growing up with the guidance of your family, in your education in primary and secondary schools and most recently here at Norwich University, you have been put through a series of tests and challenges of contrived adversity not unlike those posed by a wind tunnel. Through these educational experiences you have come to know yourself better as you have pressed towards the limits of your ability.

This has been a nondestructive form of testing in which to fail is not to be destroyed or even injured. You have been able to take remedial steps or to abandon lines of exploration that were clearly fruitless. You can also be very grateful for a faculty and an administration at Norwich University that know their own objectives and their obligations to direct you, both with regard to your development and to the limits that are imposed by a responsible democratic society.

Now, on graduation, each of you is on your own. You are your own test pilot and must commence testing yourself in free flight. The goals will no longer be set by your parents and teachers but by yourselves. Some few may be content to live within limits of performance already demonstrated; but others, those who have the right stuff, will push farther and will attempt not only to reach the outer limits of their potential but to stretch their envelope. Those, the best of you, will live up to the motto of this great university, "I will try."

In the process, you may demonstrate superior performance as scientists, as artists, as teachers, as public servants, as parents. Some may redefine an area of knowledge, or through moral insight and action attain the heights of nobility. I hope that each of you is determined to seek and to stretch the limits of your envelope. Let us hope that this is a graduating class about which it can be said that every member has the right stuff.

Seeking the North Star

"If Nietzsche is right, if truth is merely a matter of perspective, we find ourselves transported into a bizarre universe in which there can be no certainty about values, or even about cause and effect."

The 1992 Atwood Lecture that follows was given not only to students, faculty, and administrators at Salve Regina University, but to the general public, who were also invited. I chose to consider the way in which ideologies and misguided intellectual fads such as deconstructionism have not only made higher education suspect in the public mind but have threatened the very purpose of the university – the unfettered search for truth and for meaning in our lives. I spoke not only of why many of our intellectuals have embraced what seems evidently a form of nonsense but also how universities and our society might recover their true sense of direction.

DURING THE 1960S AND 1970S, higher education went through a highly publicized convulsion that devastated public confidence. Citizens understandably wondered why the college campus, in theory a haven of rationality and civility, should have collapsed into instability, irrationality, disruption, and violence.

In recent decades, campuses have settled down. Some 1960s radicals, nostalgic for turbulence, decry what they call the "apathy" of the contemporary student. But most people on campus recognize this "apathy" for what it truly is, a deep concern for learning, or at least a concern for gainful employment after graduation.

Although college students on the whole are far less politicized now than they were thirty years ago, the same cannot be said for faculties and administrations. Until recently, academic liberals generally regarded the Constitution as protecting even very offensive speech; indeed, the more unpopular a position, the more it needed constitutional protection. Faculties did not, at least in theory, distinguish between different types of offensive speech, or between different political orientations supporting that speech. But now leftist radical opinions are not merely protected on campus but are, on many campuses, dominant. Many of those who once argued for free speech now support regulations that restrict it.

Across the country, many colleges and universities have adopted the Orwellian policy that although everyone ought to have free speech, some people ought to have more free speech than others. For example, in 1988 the University of Michigan adopted regulations which prohibited speech that "victimizes" anyone on the basis of sexual orientation. When a student remarked that he believed homosexuality to be a disease treatable by therapy, he was summoned to a disciplinary hearing and accused of violating the regulations. He was not expelled, but this was not because Michigan came to its senses. A federal court held that the Michigan rules patently violated the First Amendment guarantee of free speech.

At the University of Connecticut, a speech code actually forbade "inappropriately directed laughter." This risible regulation was finally withdrawn by the university itself without judicial intervention.

Academic freedom was a hard-won right, and many members of the public to this day barely understand its necessity. The public have seen faculty and administrators make a 180-degree turn on this issue, attempting to deny academic freedom and mandate political correctness. They understandably doubt the integrity of higher education and question the need to support it.

The rise of the Thought Police on campus is not so serious from the point of view of public support as is the rise of the critical folly generally known as "deconstructionism." This is an import from France, where literary theory has for a long time been exceedingly faddish and the last redoubt of Marxism. In the former communist world, we witnessed the destructive power of Marxism when applied to national economies; it is just as destructive to the understanding of literature.

The flag under which the current fashion for literary nihilism has chosen to sail is itself a metaphor: deconstruction. After all, these critics do not literally "deconstruct" the books or articles they review. I suspect that the authors of the books that are delivered to their mercies might prefer a literal burning of their works to the figurative shredding they receive at the hands of deconstructionists.

In his illuminating new book, *The Pleasures of Reading in an Ideological Age*, Robert Alter quotes the following passage from a deconstructionist essay on the Argentinean literary giant Jorge Luis Borges:

> What seems to me important are the correspondences between Borges and midrash in the idea of intertextuality, in the concept of reading not as lineality but as a configuration of textual space, in the notion of destructurization of the text as a condition for deciphering it, and in the arch principle, as I have said, of interpretative metatextuality as the basis of decentralization.

Alter's judicious comment on this passage is both devastating and understated: "[T]his single sprawling sentence is a veritable anthology of jargon and voguish imprecisions." Yet this passage is unusual only in its compression. Whole forests have been deconstructed in order to accommodate the printing of similar assaults on literature.

How are we to account for this phenomenon, in which men and women who have freely chosen the study of literature as their life's work decide instead to gnaw at their own vitals?

The answer, I think, is to be found in one of the psychological corollaries of the perspectival view of the world that we have inherited from Nietzsche. If Nietzsche is right, if truth is merely a matter of perspective, if there are no principles by which the welter of impressions that impinge upon our sensoria can be sorted and ordered, we find ourselves transported into that bizarre universe described by Hume, in which there can be no certainty about cause and effect. The inhabitants of such a universe – that is, a large and influential fragment of our contemporary intelligentsia – are thus thrown back on an unending series of inductive experiments unassisted by even the principle of induction. That is, if they stick to the limits of their theories, they lose the ability to know anything. Or, to put it in more precise technical language, when they go to McDonald's, they might deposit their paychecks, and even if, with Kierkegaard's leap of faith, they assume that it is a restaurant rather than a bank, they dare not order a Big Mac, because they appear to remember that trucks are not edible.

The metaphor of deconstruction is, of course, characteristically equivocal, for it assumes that there is something out there capable of being deconstructed. Peter Shaw, in *War Against the Intellect*, has made this point in a particularly telling way:

> But [deconstructionists] do assume that they know the nature of literature: they are certain that it is reflexive. When they proclaim that the novel is 'a self-consciously fictive construction,' they are themselves assuming knowledge of a certain version of reality, albeit a putatively confusing one; and when they assert that the novel reflects the world's unknowableness they are actually positing the oldest literary theory of all: Aristotle's mimesis, or imitation. As it turns out, then, they both know reality and believe that literature imitates it, so that they live with a more serene confidence about the way things are than most people do.

A basic tenet of deconstructionism is that a literary work has no meaning other than that which the reader brings to it. This is, in a perverse way, an immensely liberating concept that would be a blessing to most students who would like more freedom in getting things wrong. If the literary work has no meaning, then there is nothing whatever against which to compare a piece of criticism. One cannot say that Professor Boggs has utterly mistaken the meaning of *War and Peace*, because *War and Peace* has no meaning except that given it by Professor Boggs. Professor Stanley Fish of Duke University, a high priest of modern critical theory, once put this very well: critical theory, he said, "relieves me of the obligation to be right ... and demands only that I be interesting." Professor Fish later "retracted" this statement, but as a description of deconstructionism he got it right the first time.

This rejection of meaning leads to dreadful excesses of critical folly, as critics insert into books whatever most interests them at the moment – which, to judge from much of what they write, is largely sex, preferably of a deviant variety. In one year, the MLA had papers on such topics as "The Muse and Masturbation" and "Desublimating the Sublime: Autoerotics, Anal Erotics, and Corporeal Violence in Melville and William Burroughs."

Peter Mullen summed up the current scene in a poem called "Deconstruction":

> D'ya wanna know the creed'a
> Jacques Derrida
> Dere ain't no reada
> Dere ain't no wrider
> Eider.

The public may be offended by the prurient obsessions of contemporary criticism, but it is more likely to be outraged by its rejection of meaning. The tenets of critical theory are not limited to literature: it flourishes, for example, even in Harvard's Critical Legal Studies Program. George Orwell recognized such ideas as, "the sort of nonsense so bad that only an intellectual could believe it." When taxpayers see such nonsense being promulgated, they become increasingly doubtful that it ought to be done at their expense. And parents who are paying the tuition of their children are doubtful that they ought to spend their money that way.

The best way to secure adequate support for education from taxpayers and parents is to ensure education *worthy* of support. We need not succumb to cultural disarray. It is the result of a confrontation not with a superior culture, but rather with the antithesis of culture, with nihilism. That is the basis of fashionable critical theory and dominant strands of thought. Because nihilism has no independent force of its own, there is only one way it can flourish. And that is, if we embrace it.

The present crisis of higher education in America constitutes a special opportunity for church-related colleges and universities. Amid cultural decline, disillusionment and uncertainty, many students and their parents are eager for what church-related colleges might give them. They are eager for education that sees students in their full complexity as human beings with ethical and spiritual needs as well as intellectual and physical needs. They are looking for colleges and universities that are not embarrassed to hire professors who, beyond their competence in their specialties are also competent moral beings – professors committed to mentoring their students. They are eager for academic institutions that enforce the highest standards of scholarly excellence and the highest standards of civility. In theory, church-related colleges believe in these things. If they do not provide them, it is their failure and not their students'.

In the *Apocalypse*, the church at Laodicea is told:

> I know thy works, that thou art neither cold nor hot: I would thou wert cold or hot. So then because thou art lukewarm, and neither cold nor hot, I will spew thee out of my mouth.   (Revelation 3:15–16)

In some parts of higher education it is difficult to avoid being lukewarm. In state colleges and universities, for example, the inculcation of ethical principles explicitly based on theological tenets would be unconstitutional. But if church-related colleges and universities are lukewarm, it is because they have chosen to conform to current trends rather than offer an education solidly grounded in morals and in truth.

The hunger of students and parents for the recovery of both ethical and academic standards is unmistakable. A steady diet of hedonism, like a steady diet of candy, quickly leads to satiety and malnutrition. Most Americans increasingly sense that the unprecedented affluence of the past thirty years is unlikely to continue much longer. Parents, though seldom able to articulate their fears, believe that they will be doing their children a disservice if they educate them only for pleasure and prosperity. All colleges and universities, especially those that are church-related, ill serve their students by preparing them for a life of pleasure that is not likely to endure. They had better prepare them for reality, for a reality that is structured by moral law no less than physical law, a reality in which there is no consumption without production, in which there is no freedom without well-disciplined persons who subordinate their desires long enough to ensure survival. Church-related colleges and universities have the advantage of being rooted in a tradition of teaching these lessons and the behavior that derives from them.

I do not suggest that it will be easy. We live, whether we like it or not, in a secular society. We must be realistic enough to understand that in a secular culture we are all prepared to settle for a lot less than we might have been some years ago. But this does not mean that the religious or spiritual atmosphere that we create on our campuses, however ecumenical it may be, must be the theology of consensus, that is, theology at the lowest common denominator.

If church-related colleges set some minimum standard of religious and ethical belief and practice, be it ever so unsatisfactory to the saints among us, it will be vastly superior, more elevated, high minded, and civilized than that of the suicidal cult of the People's Temple in Jonestown, of the Moonies, the Maharishi, the Krishna cults, Jimmy Swaggart, Tammy Faye, and the rest of the Bakker's dozen. If we can manage to achieve a common core of our curriculum that is focused on personal integrity, we will have deserved the gratitude of our students and their parents. We will have fulfilled the central mission of education: to offer our students a sighting of the moral North Star. Just as the North Star is a fixed point in the northern sky, a point by which we gain our sense of direction, so the moral North Star guides us as we seek the way to live. Philosophers and religious leaders in many different cultures have located the moral North Star that each of us recognizes as authoritative in determining ethical conduct.

In the next few years, American colleges and universities will have to choose their course. Some students will embrace secularism and choose to worship Mammon in secular institutions. Some students may choose religiously oriented colleges that are known by the articles of faith for which they stand. Still others may choose colleges without religious ties that nevertheless have principles and are prepared to stick by them.

Colleges and universities that have a cultural center, a core of principle, a North Star, will certainly survive. It will be no disgrace if some modicum of piety animates that cultural center: after all, at his death Socrates's last words to his student, Crito, were, "[W]e owe a cock to Aesculapius; pay it, therefore, and do not neglect it."

By virtue of the traditions of our civilization, by virtue of the obligation we undertook when we became teachers, scholars, administrators, we, too, owe a cock to Aesculapius.

Parents' Convocation

"As you leave your son or daughter at college, you should remember the importance of maintaining the closest possible ties to them. When families break up, our students break down."

It was always my practice at the beginning of each school year to hold a special convocation for the parents of incoming freshmen. I used this occasion to thank them for their trust, to introduce them to some of what Boston University and the city of Boston has to offer (and some things to watch out for), to make clear the standards by which we operate, and to express our high hopes for their sons and daughters.

At the close of the first of these occasions, I was asked by many parents to give the same talk to their freshmen, and I began to do this on a regular basis at our freshman convocation. Thus parents and students each knew what I had said to the other. The talk that follows was delivered in September 1992.

LADIES AND GENTLEMEN, it is my great pleasure to welcome you to Boston University at the beginning of this academic year. We know that this is a busy and exciting time for your sons and daughters who are coming to Boston University; I am very pleased for a number of reasons to meet with you, their parents.

First of all, because of the importance of parents in the education of their children up to the time that they come to college; second, because it gives me an opportunity to speak to you on some important matters; and third, because your presence here is essential to our survival. I cannot tell you how grateful we are for your vote of confidence that has once again brought to Boston University a large and highly qualified freshman class. We stand for election every fall because there is nothing that guarantees our enrollment. We have no state agencies that provide grants to the University; we have to earn our way, as they say, the hard way.

We believe that your confidence is well deserved. The recruitment and retention of outstanding faculty has been our highest priority and our single greatest investment over the past twenty-two years. We have reached the point where each student at Boston University has the opportunity to work with truly outstanding scholar/teachers – and every student should take advantage of this by selecting the most demanding professors they can find in their fields of interest.

Although 28 percent of our tenured faculty are women, not a single one was appointed because she was a woman. We have never made an appointment on the basis of quotas, but always and only on the basis of outstanding qualifications. As those who know the history of the University are aware, Boston University from the time of its chartering opened all programs to all students without regard to sex, race, or religious affiliation. We have had women in every program at Boston University from its inception and have appointed women to our faculty from the very beginning. We now have the largest percentage of female faculty of any major research university in the country. If women continue to be more ambitious and hardworking than men, our faculty could be predominantly female. Nothing in our regulations or practices stands in the way.

Among the qualifications we seek in our faculty appointees is ability as a teacher and not just as a scholar. You did not send your students here simply to hobnob but to study with great scholars and researchers who are interested both in advancing knowledge and in developing the abilities of your children.

Our students, by the way, have as one of their basic rights – they assume many rights that they don't have, but this is one they do – the right to visit their professors in office hours or by scheduled appointments. This is absolutely imperative, first of all for the good counsel and advice that professors can give your sons and daughters in assessing their progress in their courses. More important, they can offer an assessment of their students' talents and abilities and can advise them on their future development. And just in terms of sheer practicality, if our students do not get to know some of their professors well, there will be no one to write letters of recommendation on their behalf.

I know that many of you are concerned about the major that your son or daughter may select. Perhaps you are worried that your son or daughter does not know what he or she wants to do. I understand, being a parent myself and having seen my children through college, just how anxious a parent can become when a child seems to be wandering, not able to find himself or herself.

I think this is not only acceptable but, in the great majority of cases, healthy. I say this because self-discovery is the primary function of undergraduate education. We do not anticipate that every or perhaps even most freshmen entering Boston University will know what they want to major in. There are many fields of inquiry about which your sons and daughters may know nothing. They might become most interested in an area about which they are at present completely ignorant. The possibility of their finding themselves might be cut short were they to decide prematurely on their major. We hope they will see these four years as a period of experimentation, of exploration, of coming to a better knowledge of who they are, of what interests them the most, and what they can do best. If they can answer these questions, they will have the greatest opportunity for making a contribution to the next generation.

If your son or daughter does not have a major by the junior year, then I think you might begin to worry. Some beginning students, perhaps 30 percent, will know precisely what they are here for and what they want to do – and they may be wrong. But some of them may be right. Mozart, by the time he was four or five years of age, knew he was going to be a musician. He was an accomplished musician by the time he was eight or nine. Since there was no other area in which he so clearly excelled, his decision about what to do in life was made for him. That situation is very rare, however, and you should not worry if even after graduation your son or daughter has not yet decided what they want to do in life.

Of course you are concerned about the financial future of your children. Many of you may be sending them to college for the purpose of equipping them to hold a job. This is not the best or even a sound reason for sending your children to college. I hope that does not come as too great a shock. If you simply want a quick fix for their financial future, you may be able to do better in one of the vocational or training programs that are offered in almost every city or town in this country.

For instance, it is relatively easy to become a computer technologist and to find a job paying good wages with a computer company or a firm that uses computers. It is a quick fix, however, because when the technology changes and when the equipment used by the company employing your child changes, then they may have to drop out for retraining.

When one is educated, however, as opposed to being merely trained, one begins to learn the fundamental principles of a field. In computer science one begins with mathematics and with the logic on which computers have been designed; one learns how mathematics has been applied to this interesting field of technology. One also begins to discover how one can imaginatively employ the computer in a variety of endeavors: in mathematics, yes, but also in accounting, in economics, in social science research, in many other forms of writing or architectural drawing. When one is educated as a computer scientist, he or she need not worry about subsequent changes in the technology. To keep up-to-date is well within the grasp of such a person. It is a part of that continuing self-education which is, for an educated individual, simply a part of life.

Computer science is only one example. Someone who has a true education, whether in a field of the sciences or even in a field such as English or history – the liberal arts in their most liberal and non-practical form – such a person will be employable.

If your sons or daughters become literate in the English language, they are going to be able to hold a job, because English is an endangered species in this country. Those who graduate from college thoroughly capable of speaking, writing, and reading the English language are in such short supply that they are going to be in demand for good jobs. If they can add some reasonable level of skills in computer science and in the handling of computer hardware and software, they will be in very good shape for getting a job, even if they have not gone into one of the pre-professional programs or do not intend to go to graduate or professional school.

But I come back to our primary obligation, to what seems to me the most important opportunity offered by college to a young person – self-discovery. Our faculty, as I said, have the obligation not only to do research and to keep themselves abreast of the latest knowledge so that they are fully competent in the instruction of your sons and daughters – they have also the obligation to fulfill the role of teacher as it was defined by the philosopher Nietzsche in an essay on "Schopenhauer as

Educator." In Nietzsche's opinion, Schopenhauer was the exemplary teacher, and in this essay, Nietzsche, as translated by William Arrowsmith, has this to say about what constitutes great teaching:

> Your true teachers, the men who formed you and educated you, revealed to you what is the true original sense and basic stuff of your nature, something absolutely uneducable and unformable, but something difficult of access, fettered, and paralyzed. They are your true teachers. And that is the secret of all education and culture; it does not give artificial limbs, wax noses, or corrective lenses – rather, that which can give those gifts is merely a caricature of education. Education, on the contrary, is liberation, the clearing of all weeds, rubble and vermin that might harm the delicate shoots, a radiance of light and warmth, a loving, falling rustle of rain by night. Your teachers can be nothing but your liberators. It is the imitation and adoration of nature where nature is motherly and mercifully minded.

That is the conception of the teacher that we hold before the faculty of Boston University. We expect them to participate in the process by which we liberate your sons and daughters, by which we free them from the restraints that hold them back, so that they can fulfill themselves in the unique way appropriate to each one's basic nature. With regard to that basic nature, it is as Nietzsche said: it is not educable. It is not formable. It is already there, to be developed, to be liberated, to unfold like a flower. It is not something that we can put there; we can only assist in its development.

At Boston University we are committed to equality of opportunity. We open our doors in a variety of special programs. We encourage, through scholarships and through tutorial programs, persons who have the native ability to succeed but who have not had a fully adequate preparation for study at Boston University. We recognize our social responsibility for certain students.

But while we believe in equality of opportunity, we do not believe in equality of achievement. To give everyone a chance is necessary in the name of justice; but it is totally unjust to suppose that everyone will achieve at the same level. Some people run faster than others, some play tennis better than others, some are finer musicians than others. In America, it is only in the intellectual world that elitism is condemned.

We encourage all students at Boston University to achieve all that is within their potential. That means, of course, that your sons' or daughters' achievement will depend more on their character, determination, and self-discipline than on anything else. It will depend on their hard work.

It is my opinion that Boston University does not require too much of our students – perhaps not even enough. Our education is far from blood, sweat, and tears. Any student who studies about seventy hours a week ought to do very well at Boston University.

It is interesting that many of you find that remark amusing. When we think about it: there are twenty-four hours in every day. If one studies ten hours every day, that is seventy hours a week. If we have used ten hours a day in study, that leaves another eight hours for sleep, so all together that is eighteen hours. There are still six hours left for having fun, and six hours of fun each day is about all that a reasonable person can stand. To the extent that students fail to study ten hours each day, they had better be able to compensate by a superior ability to learn.

As all of you know, Boston University is located in one of the major cities of the United States. It has many of the advantages and disadvantages associated with a large urban setting. The risks that your children run in coming to Boston University are not likely to include being butted by a cow or being run over by a tractor. On the other hand, we have trolleys that are serious risks to anyone who does not watch carefully. When a trolley and a student are in a race for the crossing, the score will too often be trolley, one, student, zip. We remind our students of this risk every year; but every year, at least one student is hit by a trolley.

It is also important to know that there is no logical association nor empirical correlation between the color of lights and the behavior of automobiles in Boston. Consequently, every year we warn the freshmen not to walk defensively but to run defensively whenever they cross streets.

In any urban setting in the United States today, there is the risk of drugs and crime. These risks are indigenous to American society, and you cannot go anywhere and be free of them. But most of the bad outcomes require the cooperation of your son or daughter. There is very little risk of drugs if your son or daughter does not use them. There is no risk of being killed in a single-car accident as a result of driving while intoxicated unless your child drives while intoxicated or agrees to be a passenger in a car being driven by someone who is intoxicated. Many of these risks can be substantially reduced simply by good common sense, intelligence, and moral responsibility.

With regard to drugs and alcohol, we have very strict policies on this campus. You should know about them, and our orientation programs will fully inform your sons and daughters. We have rules prohibiting bringing alcohol into the dormitories. There is a prohibition against the sale or use of drugs. We do not countenance any exceptions to those rules. Freshmen are informed that we will cooperate fully with the police with regard to the prohibition of these illegal substances. We will expel any student who uses or sells drugs or has them in his or her possession, whether or not he or she intends to use them or sell them.

We will not offer any sanctuary in these matters. We will not offer any protection against the search of a student's room. We are not interested in becoming a center for drug rehabilitation. If a student has a drug problem, we are going to separate that student from Boston University.

On the other hand, there are wonderful opportunities here. We have the Museum of Fine Arts, the New England Aquarium, the Boston Symphony Orchestra, the Huntington Theatre, the Boston Ballet, and the Red Sox. There are endless cultural opportunities here in Boston, and we hope our students will take advantage of them. We give all our students a membership in the Museum of Fine Arts, and tens of thousands of them use that membership every year. I engaged in a euphemism there. We give them that membership, but you pay for it.

One of the attractions of Boston as opposed to, let us say, Chicago, New York, Los Angeles, or other major cities in America, is that this is a city on a human scale. If you walk two and a half miles east, you will be in the Atlantic Ocean. A five-mile walk can take you all around Boston and back here in about an hour and a half, and you will have had a fairly thorough tour of Boston.

Finally, I would like to talk to you quite seriously about what this moment involves and what it means to you. I certainly recall the first time that we dropped our oldest child off at college and then, one by one, our other children. This moment is one of the central rites of passage, similar in a way to birth and marriage. It is a deeply moving experience for most families. It establishes a new and quite different relationship between parent and child, a difference of ultimate importance. You are leaving a child who is now on his or her own, moving toward becoming an adult. Once you say good-bye, you must know that your son or daughter is living apart from you, learning independence. Their success or failure is going to depend in large measure on how much they have internalized your guidance and example as they assume individual responsibility.

This is true. But it is not the whole story. You do not, by setting your son or daughter on the road to independence, become irrelevant. Far from it. As you leave your son or daughter at Boston University and return home, it is crucial that you remember the importance of maintaining the closest possible ties to your children. Your communication with them is still the most important single factor in their motivation. When families break up, our students break down. That is a law just as sure as the law of gravity.

For many parents, their parting words are likely to be, "Telephone if you need anything. Telephone us whether you need us or not. Telephone frequently."

I would like to suggest a better alternative. On separating from your sons and daughters, why not say, "Unless there is an emergency, don't ever telephone us. Instead we want a letter from you once a week. If we are willing to pay the tuition to keep you in this school, you ought at the very least to be able to find time to write us two or three pages every week about what you are doing, what is going on, how things are going. And we will promise that every time you write to us, we will write you back."

If you make this decision, and insist on it as a reasonable expectation of your children, and if you fulfill your part of the bargain by writing back, you will find at the end of four years that you have a large collection of priceless correspondence. You will know your children far better than you would know them otherwise. After they get over the initial embarrassment and awkwardness, they will say in writing things to you that they would never say face-to-face. You will hear of your students' discoveries and their hopes and their fears. You will begin to know them in a much better, more rounded way than you know them now. You will see them grow, and you will have for the rest of your lives a record of that growth. You may find that you are able to confide in them things that are of concern to you that you would feel embarrassed or awkward in trying to tell them face-to-face.

It will take time and it will be an intrusion on your ordinary way of living, but you will eventually have a lot to show for it. All parents who have followed this exercise have been most gratified by the results.

You will also be able to check on us. The first letters you get may not be well written. By the second or third year, the words may be better spelled, the syntax may be improved. Your children may express ideas of greater complexity. By reading these letters, you will find out whether we are making any improvements in the education of your children.

I will not see most of you again for about four years, when your sons and daughters graduate from Boston University at ceremonies held in May. In the meantime, I hope they find their experience here happy, challenging, and rewarding. I hope they will be inspired and ennobled by the values that were once expressed by Justice Oliver Wendell Holmes Jr. Writing late in life, he said,

> Through the great good fortune of our youth, our hearts were touched by fire. It was given to us to learn at the outset that life is a profound and passionate thing. And we were permitted to scorn nothing but indifference.

It is my hope that your sons and daughters will likewise be touched by fire and will learn to scorn nothing but indifference; that they will proceed with passionate intensity toward that self-discovery and self-fulfillment which is the purpose of education.

Multiculturalism True and False

"If in the name of multiculturalism we accept the idea that there is a Western physics or an Eastern justice, that mathematics is different in China and Uganda, we commit ourselves to a self-refuting relativism that reduces all knowledge to illusion."

When one thinks of the West Indies, I'm sure for most of us the name of Harry Belafonte and his wonderful songs of those islands come to mind. Those were certainly my first thoughts when I received an invitation to participate in the graduation ceremonies at the University of the West Indies in Jamaica in 1994. As I read up on the university, its history, its place among educational institutions of the Caribbean, its home on an island in which so many cultures are present with intermingling influence, I thought this was the right venue to speak on the issue of multiculturalism.

LADIES AND GENTLEMEN, GRADUATES: It is good to come to the islands of the English-speaking Caribbean, the Commonwealth Caribbean, and breathe the air of freedom. Here, in the states that developed from the British colonial experience, democracy is honored not only in precept but in practice. The traditions of the Caribbean are diverse indeed, embracing the heritage of many peoples. But politically speaking, the area is unified by the heritage of the English language and of self-government that descends from the barons at Runnymede through Magna Carta and the English common law, handed down to your countries and mine when we were British colonies. Goethe remarks that in order to possess our inheritance, we must first make it our own. The peoples of the Commonwealth Caribbean have truly made their British inheritance of freedom and law their own.

The University of the West Indies is remarkable – I am tempted to say unique – for it transcends nationhood in a way unlike any other university I know. It is the university of each of the nations of the English-speaking Caribbean; but it is also the transnational university of all these countries. Recently I have been reading the proposal for the University of the West Indies that Sir Eric Williams completed in 1945 and published in 1951. It is an extraordinary document. At a time when all the islands of the Commonwealth Caribbean were still colonies and higher education remained dependent on the mother country, Sir Eric Williams envisioned a great university spread across the Caribbean. He had a lively appreciation of what would be required of a university for the English-speaking Caribbean. And although he discounted the specious prestige to be gained from ceremonial affiliations with universities in the United Kingdom and the United States, he had a keen eye for the genuine benefits to be obtained through collaboration with such institutions.

Best of all, he did not use the opportunity of designing a university as an excuse to discard centuries of proven educational curricula and disciplines in favor of the wide-ranging, not to say bizarre, innovations that educational theorists are prone to. He thus resisted a temptation into which these projectors regularly fall, often with a resounding splash. Rather, Sir Eric designed an institution firmly grounded in educational tradition and political reality. It is not surprising then, that he made his mark as the architect of a university and as the builder of a nation.

Sir Eric was able to proceed on the assumption, now denied college presidents in the United States, that the West Indies would have excellent systems of primary and secondary education that would allow higher education to be higher than something. I trust and hope that the nations and the school systems of the West Indies will continue to cherish and preserve these priceless resources for the development of intellectual capital. My personal experience with graduates of your schools has confirmed my belief in their excellence. The graduates of your secondary schools, no less than those of your universities, far exceed most American college graduates in mastery of the English language.

You should not be misled by the fact that the United States is a rich and powerful country into believing that it is therefore the proper subject for emulation in all areas. In education, the situation is quite the reverse. My country would benefit tremendously by copying your countries in the matter of primary and secondary education. If you use us as an example, review our practice as a cautionary tale: how in the interest of novelty and mindless theorizing by so-called educational experts, we destroyed a highly effective system of public education.

The decline in the primary and secondary schools has inevitably eroded the quality of American colleges and universities. And most have been further diminished by an onslaught of ideologues and educational faddists. This is most evident in the drive towards a goal misnamed "multiculturalism."

This movement correctly observes that culture is a complex creation deriving from contributions of peoples from all over the world. No society can, like a spider spinning its web from its own entrails, generate culture out of itself alone. It must rely in large part on an intellectual tradition. The intellectual tradition of Europe and its cultural offshoots is often miscalled "Western culture," but in fact is a world culture, a human culture. It has as its basis the avoidance of parochialism, the search for universals, the study of the nature of humanity as it is found in any and every human being without regard to the culture from which that person comes, the race or gender of that person. It seeks the truth about virtue and ethics, about beauty, about nature. It seeks universal principles.

It is the nature of general principles that their application to particular cases differ with circumstances. Specific requirements of justice or duty may be dramatically different in different cultures, just as Newton's general statement of the Law of Gravity (still sound for objects in spaces neither too small nor too large) must be applied differently as variables in equations are given specific values. Although the application of fundamental ethical principles differs depending on contingencies, the principles themselves are universal. Except in a descriptive, anthropological sense, there is no such thing as "Western ethics" that can be contrasted with, say, "Mayan ethics" or "African ethics." When the philosophers of Greece struggled to understand the nature of humanity, they were not searching for the nature of Athenians. When Plato asked "What is justice?" he struggled to understand the nature of justice wherever human beings are found. If we accept the idea that there is a Western physics or an Eastern justice, that mathematics is different in China and Uganda, we commit ourselves to a self-refuting relativism that reduces all knowledge to illusion.

Consider chattel slavery. It was a part of the western tradition just as it was a part of the tradition of the vast majority of human societies of which we have any knowledge. The difference is that our culture developed the ethical reflection and mechanisms of education and government which enabled us to understand that chattel slavery is morally wrong, why it is wrong, and then to act on that understanding.

The culture we ought to teach does not – and cannot with integrity – hold that great creative work is the posted preserve of some one race or language group or nation. Our culture finds and recognizes at least as much inspiration and validity in the works of individual Asian, Indian, African, and Caribbean artists as in the artists of Europe or the United States. What is important about the culture we teach is precisely that it is capable of such recognition, or rather that openness to such recognition is one of its defining traits. The university, which is one of the central expressions of our culture, is dedicated to just such openness.

We give the game away if we try to pass off third-rate work by one ethnic group or another, by women or blacks or middle-class white male professors as if such works were of classical importance. We have to call the shots on objective grounds. We are committed to a classification of great art based on its ability to transcend parochial particularities and to speak to fundamental questions of human existence.

"Multiculturalism," as now used in the United States, does not mean one culture with multiple roots, an *unum* that arises from *pluribus*, but rather *pluribus per se*, a society in which many cultures coexist in uneasy competition with each other, each claiming the right to define itself in isolation from anything traditionally understood as American culture. This ideology places great emphasis on the superficial differences in ethnic groups but ignores their common humanity. In so doing, it reduces the search for truth to a thoughtless if sometimes well-intentioned relativism.

In contrast to the bogus multiculturalism that now infests colleges and universities in the United States, stands the genuine multiculturalism that animates the Caribbean, a coherent cultural synthesis of many diverse elements. Here elements from Africa, from Europe, from Asia, and from the Americas are being forged into a vibrant new culture.

At Boston University we have special reason to appreciate this fact because Derek Walcott lives and works among us. No one who has read his masterpiece *Omeros* can come away without a new perception of the complex web that is world culture. Grounded equally in the classical tradition of Homer and the glistening particularities of life in the Caribbean, expressed in a sinewy and elegant English, *Omeros* demonstrates that the tradition of Shakespeare is alive and well. *Omeros* is but one of the brilliant works in which Derek Walcott has demonstrated the power of an intellectual tradition to guide the perennially necessary task of regrounding and renewing culture in the human experience of a particular place.

It should hardly be surprising that the Caribbean, with its diverse traditions and its sense of a center that can and must hold, should have produced so vigorous an embodiment of the classical tradition as Derek Walcott. Like the great archipelago which gave him birth, Walcott has embraced his inheritance, and, as Goethe suggested, truly made it his own. In so doing, he has created a bequest that we can hope generations unborn, not only in the Caribbean but across the world, will themselves embrace and at length make truly their own.

The vigorous culture of the West Indies, a mature multiculture, a melding of diverse cultural influences into a coherent whole, is expressed in the work of your artists and your teacher-scholars in this university. It has nurtured the graduating class here this evening. It is a great inheritance for you to make your own.

Obedience to the Unenforceable

"Authority and civil order depend in significant measure on the consent of the governed. The more civilized and enlightened the country, the greater its dependence on the voluntary respect for standards that cannot be enforced by law."

There are ample signs of deterioration in the civic morality of our nation. We need not speak of crime or moral wrongdoing, but simply of the clear loss of personal responsibility and civility in our political discussions and in day-to-day conversations in the workplace and at leisure. An English jurist defined the characteristics of a civilized society in ways that I found illuminating, and I made his analysis the basis of my remarks in this 1995 commencement address at Boston University.

NEARLY SEVENTY-FIVE YEARS AGO, John Fletcher Moulton, Lord Moulton, a noted English judge, spoke on the subject of "Law and Manners." He divided human action into three domains. The first is the domain of law, "where," he said, "our actions are prescribed by laws binding upon us which must be obeyed." At the other extreme is the domain of free choice, "which," he said, "includes all those actions as to which we claim and enjoy complete freedom." In between, Lord Moulton identified a domain in which our action is not determined by law but in which we are not free to behave in any way we choose. In this domain we act with greater or lesser freedom from constraint, on a continuum that extends at one extreme from a consciousness of duty "nearly as strong as positive law," through a sense of what is required by public spirit, to "good form" appropriate in a given situation, and so on up to the border with the domain of free choice, where there is no constraint whatever on what the individual may choose to do.

Lord Moulton considered the area of action lying between law and pure personal preference to be "the domain of obedience to the unenforceable." In this domain, he said, "Obedience is the obedience of a man to that which he cannot be forced to obey. He is the enforcer of the law upon himself." This domain between law and free choice he called that of Manners. While it may include moral duty, social responsibility, and proper behavior, it extends beyond them to cover "all cases of doing right where there is no one to make you do it but yourself."

Moulton recognized that all three domains are necessary to the life of every individual. The law with its coercive remedies in both civil and criminal jurisdictions is necessary to establish an essential matrix of order and peace. The domain of free choice is rightly treasured by each individual, for it is in this area that "spontaneity, originality and energy arise." Moulton, emphasizing its special importance, said, "It covers a precious land where the actions of men are not only such as they choose, but have a right to claim freedom even from criticism."

Considering the topography of this social order, all of us can recognize at once that the middle land of Manners, as Moulton calls it, is threatened by two tendencies: on the one hand, there are those who wish to extend the realm of law to regulate everything. The Congress and the agencies that have mushroomed from its legislation exhibit this tendency to an alarming degree. On the other hand, there is the tendency to claim that anything not ruled by law is a matter of personal choice. This tendency can be seen in the relativism and unbridled hedonism voiced in our schools, universities, newspapers, movies, and on television by advocates who range from intellectuals and entertainers to the crassest hucksters.

The domains both of law and of free choice threaten to encroach upon the middle domain of manners. Moulton's central point, one of capital importance, is that "The real greatness of a nation, its true civilization, is measured by the extent of this land of obedience to the unenforceable. It measures the extent to which the nation trusts its citizens, and its area testifies to the way they behave in response to that trust."

Obedience to law does not alone measure a nation's greatness. Totalitarian regimes enforce obedience at the price of cruelty and repression. And in the absence of law mere willfulness or license, far different from liberty, is no proof of greatness. The true test of greatness, Moulton said, is "the extent to which individuals composing that nation can be trusted to obey self-imposed law."

In America today the domains of choice and of law have eroded the domain of manners. As the realm of manners and morals has been diminished by those who claim that whatever they think or do is right if it feels good to them, the central domain loses its force. And despite the expansion of the domain of law, the consequent weakening of the central domain has resulted in a diminution of the authority and effectiveness of the law.

It is against the law to deface public property, to steal, to swindle, to drive while intoxicated, to rape, to bomb, and to kill. But our public and private buildings are regularly defaced by graffiti and the territorial markings of juvenile gangs. In our cities many feel imprisoned in their homes, and our persons are at risk on our streets and in our parks. There are twice as many murders each year in New York as in all of England, and twice as many in Boston as in Argentina. Rape is epidemic and deadly assault by drunken drivers is commonplace. Nor is the crime wave confined to the streets: the *Wall Street Journal* estimates that stock swindles and other forms of white-collar crime cost Americans $100 billion every year.

But what of enforcement? Indictments number only a small fraction of the crimes committed; convictions only a fraction of the indictments; punishments, except in the case of first-degree murder, are typically light – a few years, probation, suspended sentence, or community service. Even fines are rarely collected. Of the $4.5 billion dollars owed in fines by stock swindlers, only one dollar in ten has been paid, leaving swindlers with almost all of their ill-gotten gains and their victims uncompensated.

Standards in the profession of law have eroded, as lawyers, judges, and juries have become less obedient to the unenforceable. Judges have accommodated delays and improper importunings of counsel by allowing cases without merit to go to trial. Judges and lawyers frequently exclude from jury duty persons of education and professional and business competence, leaving jury panels composed of the relatively inexperienced and uneducated to try civil cases of great complexity. In criminal cases, worthy jury men and women are rejected by lawyers concerned, not to impanel a jury of twelve good persons and true who represent a cross-section of the community, but a carefully selected jury of persons most likely to respond sympathetically to their client. Impaneling a jury in a murder case, which takes no more than an hour or two in England, takes weeks in the United States. American trials now drag on endlessly, making jury duty a burden beyond the means or endurance of many individuals.

The O. J. Simpson trial, if held at the Old Bailey, would have taken a few weeks. It is now the *reductio ad absurdum* of our system of criminal justice, a bonanza for broadcasters who are provided a year-long soap opera without the expense of producers, writers, actors, or directors. The confidence and respect of the American public for lawyers, judges, and the jury system have imploded as they watch a trial in which the judge has lost control and lawyers flout legal ethics in their reach for irrelevancies to delay the process and create confusion in the minds of the jury.

Even more alarming than the comedy of the courts is the tragedy of the streets: random violence, children killed in drive-by shootings by persons they have never met, and acts of terrorism which demonstrate the inability of a sovereign nation to protect the lives and property of its citizens.

We live in a deeply flawed society moving rapidly toward the state of nature that Thomas Hobbes chillingly described: "No arts; no letters; no society; and which is worst of all, continual fear and danger of violent death; and the life of man, solitary, poor, nasty, brutish and short." Add obscenity and Hobbes's litany sounds just like *Pulp Fiction*.

We cannot end this state of violence and restore the authority of law simply by getting tough on crime, by relying on the police power of the state, or by calling for capital punishment. As both Hobbes and Lord Moulton observed, the sovereign cannot establish authority simply by force or through acts of state terror. Authority and civil order depend in significant measure on the consent of the governed – that is, on obedience to the unenforceable. The more civilized and enlightened the country, the greater its dependence on the voluntary respect and support of its citizens for law and civil order. The rule of law depends upon the morality of the people for its enforcement.

But enforcement requires obedience to the unenforceable. The erosion of manners and morals inevitably undermines the law. Civil society depends not merely on law but on the obedience of the individual citizen who in Moulton's words is "the enforcer of the law upon himself."

The law is not self-sustaining but depends, like science, medicine, higher education, and accounting, on the willingness of scientists, doctors, professors, lawyers, and accountants to obey moral principles that are unenforceable.

There is nothing to guarantee the soundness of scientific experiments and theories beyond the moral integrity of scientists and their faithful adherence to the principles of scientific method. If they falsify data, they are like accountants who cook the books or lawyers who concoct evidence or bring suits devoid of merit. Their professional work is compromised by their lack of obedience to the unenforceable. The integrity and efficacy of all our professions and businesses rest on this moral foundation.

We must not attribute all our social ills to a single cause, for the causes are many. If families had not broken up, if churches had not lost much of their influence, if there had not been an extensive spread of secularism and materialism, if the quality of our schools had not declined despite substantial increases in financial support, if drugs had not become easily available, if some or all of these factors had not been present, we might have withstood the degenerative effects of television and its indiscriminate advocacy of pleasure.

Prior to television and to the breakup of the family, parents typically tried to preserve and extend the ceremonies of innocence in the lives of their children by shielding them from the sordid dimensions of human life, from filthy language, premature exposure to sex, and mindless and indiscriminate violence. But that is now the common experience of children: by age four or five they speak the language of the gutter and teenagers enlarge their experience of violence, obscenity, and sex in all its varieties through television (watched on the average for twenty-five hours a week), through the movies and occasionally even in the schools.

Television is the most important educational institution in the United States today. Since the beginning of human history, mankind has known what Aristotle later set down as the fundamental fact about education:

that we learn by imitation. Common sense alone tells us that violence endlessly enacted on television serves as a model for imitation. In many of our great cities we find teenagers, in imitation of what they have seen scores or even hundreds of times on television, engaged in wanton acts of violence, blowing away parents, friends, or strangers with a totally amoral, psychopathological indifference to the suffering of others. Revulsion and abhorrence, our natural reactions to violence, are suppressed. We become reconciled to violence as though it were a normal part of life, as indeed it has become. Marc Antony made the point when, standing over Caesar's dead body, he prophesied,

> Blood and destruction shall be so in use,
> And dreadful objects so familiar,
> That mothers shall but smile when they behold
> Their infants quartered with the hands of war,
> All pity choked with custom of fell deeds.

And now new opportunities are open for our youth as the Internet makes available to those accessing it simple straightforward directions for the manufacture of bombs. But our government, which has found it necessary to regulate the formula for ice cream and peanut butter, is reluctant to prohibit the distribution on the Internet of handbooks for terrorists. Such communication threatens our lives in a way that shouting "Fire!" in a crowded theater could never do. Can anyone seriously believe that the First Amendment protects instruction in terrorism through the Internet? Its prohibition clearly meets Mr. Justice Holmes's test of a clear and present danger. It may be technically impossible to control terrorism on the Internet, but that difficulty should not be confused with a constitutional protection. The Bill of Rights, as Justice Robert H. Jackson noted, should not be interpreted as a suicide pact.

The power of the media to educate for good and ill can be seen most conspicuously in the way that television advertising and programming floods viewers of all ages with sexual images. This depends upon our first understanding that sex, the most intimate expression between two individuals and a natural sacrament, is debased merely by being enacted before multitudes of third parties. The viewer, who perhaps has no desire to peer into the bedroom, finds the bed dropped into his or her living room. In the global village with millions of Peeping Toms, sex can hardly be intimate and the viewer, like it or not, becomes a voyeur. Children, regardless of age, are bombarded with sexual enticements that they are often too young to understand or, if they do understand, are far too young to cope with.

Only a generation or two ago, society as a whole and parents in particular recognized that there is a period of human development where overt sexuality is totally inappropriate and indeed positively harmful. In years past, persons could be put in jail for contributing to the delinquency of minors by being far less explicit in what they were talking about or what they were showing than what is seen on any television set today. Parents then went out of their way to protect their children from premature exposure to sex. Today, even if they wish to protect them, one must ask: How can they?

What does indecently premature and promiscuous exposure to sex do to youngsters? What harm is it? Can there be any doubt that the preoccupation with instant sex, along with the suggestion that sex is a readily available commodity rather than one of the most consequential aspects of human life, is to an appreciable degree responsible for the growing number of unmarried teenage mothers and fathers in the United States, for the neglect of children born to such immature liaisons and for the more rapid spread of AIDS and other sexually transmitted diseases? What is being taught is nihilism sweetened by hedonism. Television teaches us to seek pleasure wherever we can find it, whatever the consequences. And because pleasure is transient, this commercial philosophy is one of insatiability leading to lives of endlessly frustrated and unsatisfied desires.

The insensitivity and hedonism engendered in many of our youth in the last few years is not due exclusively to television and the entertainment industry. On the other hand, it cannot be explained in the absence of television, for there are no other factors adequate in themselves to account for it. If the influence of television and films were countered, however, by a strong family, a first-rate educational system, or good job opportunities in inner cities, the impact of television would be far less significant and perhaps even negligible.

Television has not had an equal influence on all children by any means. Children from strong homes, children attending vital churches and deeply nurtured in religious traditions, children who have developed sound study habits and who in consequence have little time for television, children who have developed a moral center to guide their choice seem remarkably immune.

As television has ravenously consumed our attention, it has weakened formative institutions and eroded the sense of individual obedience to the unenforceable on which manners and morals and ultimately the law depend. We need to rebuild our families, our schools, and our churches, but we cannot complete these reforms until something is done about television. Both its advertising and its programming have created demands that appeal not to the best in our natures, but to the worst.

Alarmed by the deterioration of standards, and recognizing one clear source of this decline, we may be tempted to enlarge the domain of law by regulating television and the entertainment industry. But this should give us pause.

I do not advocate altering the First Amendment, nor do I advocate congressional limits on what television stations can program. But is it not time for those who own television stations and networks and those who own motion picture companies that supply material for television to demonstrate *their* obedience to the unenforceable?

Let the First Amendment stand as it is. But the moguls of television and movies should recognize that they are contributing directly to the erosion, not only of morals and manners, but of the rule of law itself. Are they going to show obedience to the unenforceable by asserting their moral responsibility for the good of our society, or is the pursuit of profit their only guide?

If the television and the entertainment industries do not control themselves in obedience to the unenforceable, we shall reach the point in the not too distant future where programming on television threatens the life of the Republic. But will the American people recognize that it poses a clear and present danger calling for decisive corrective action?

There is still time for self-correction. But those with positions of responsibility in these industries should understand that we cannot continue indefinitely to tolerate their trashing of our sensibilities and those of our children without endangering our survival.

The barbarians television has nurtured and continues to nurture are not at our gates but in our midst. Recognizing that by its nature, obedience to the unenforceable cannot be enforced, W. Edwards Deming observed, "You don't have to do it – survival is not compulsory."

The members of this graduating class and those of all other classes graduating this spring across our nation are the agents of our future and the repository of our hopes. For good or ill, people of my generation have already made most of our contribution. We have tried to do our best: at times we have succeeded; at others we have failed. But the future for good or ill is increasingly in the hands of the generation of graduates.

If the members of these graduating classes recognize the importance of the domain of manners and morals, and if each is obedient to the unenforceable, we shall see a diminution of license and a renewal of freedom and civilization in this country. If this moral vision strikes fire in the younger generation, our future is secure.

The crisis we face will not be solved by higher or lower taxes, by more or less welfare or Medicaid, by an increase or decrease in the budgets of the military or the police. Our crisis, like that confronting the peoples of the former Soviet Union and Eastern Europe is, as Solzhenitsyn observed, a crisis of moral decay.

We face a crisis of spirit. Its resolution far transcends the power of the state; it is too important, too far-reaching, to be resolved by mere governmental action. Rather, it lies within the grasp of each of us. When we determine to govern ourselves – when each is obedient to the unenforceable – we shall have regained control over ourselves and thus regained as a nation our capacity for self-government.

This will never come to pass without faith in the importance of honor and truth and in the essential role of duty and obligation in our lives.

What we are, what we do, and thereby what we become depends heavily on what we believe about ourselves. Are we Edwin Markham's man with a hoe,

> A thing that grieves not and that never hopes,
> stolid and stunned, a brother to the ox?

Or are we not rather, as Markham puts it, endowed with the power

> To have dominion over sea and land;
> To trace the stars and search the heavens for power;
> To feel the passion of Eternity?

The crisis that will confront graduating classes for years to come lies not in the state or in the stars, but in ourselves. The future of our country, our future happiness and that of our children depends decisively on whether we as individuals and as a people practice obedience to the unenforceable.

The Need for Honesty in Confronting History

"It is important to understand fully what happened in 1945 in Hiroshima and Nagasaki. We must observe that, if the consequences of using the atomic bomb were devastating, the consequences of not using it would have been still worse."

On December 6, 1995, in Hiroshima, Japan, I attended a conference on "The Future of Hope" sponsored by the Japanese newspaper Asahi Shimbun and the Elie Wiesel Foundation for Humanity.

Not surprisingly, some speakers took issue with the United States and its foreign policy, both past and present, while one even compared the bombing of Hiroshima to the Holocaust. But there was no direct discussion of the bombing of Hiroshima and Nagasaki nor any objective moral assessment of those tragic events. As the conference proceeded, I decided it was imperative not to skirt these issues any further but to address them directly by speaking on "The Need for Honesty in Confronting History." The following is a transcript of my address.

FIRST, a prologue. Before I begin my formal remarks, let me create a context for them.

The future of America's relation to Japan depends, as does America's relation to Germany, on all parties – Americans, Japanese, and Germans – being honest with themselves and with each other: all parties must accept the realities of the past. Nothing good, nothing hopeful can come from revisionism, for revisionism is simply a form of denial. We must face our pasts with all our shortcomings as well as our strengths, our virtues along with our vices. If there is to be a future for hope – that is, any hope for the future – there comes a time when all our differences and deficiencies must be put behind us.

Our hope for the future depends on our capacity to forgive. Without forgiveness, without the possibility of redemption, life is without hope. For without forgiveness, we are overwhelmed by our past failings. No individual, no nation, is perfect. We are all guilty of folly and injustice. If we cannot recognize our failings and rise above them through a passionate desire not to repeat them, there will be no basis for hope and, thus, no promise for the future.

Americans and Europeans may find it easier than the Japanese to accept our past failings. The religions of the Bible, the dominant religions in Europe and the United States, also profoundly influence their secular cultures. These religions stress the importance of confessing one's mistakes in the conviction that by repenting our past failures, we may be forgiven and be redeemed. The religions of the Book profess faith in redemption and the possibility of new beginnings – faith in the ability to begin again. Thus they offer hope.

I do not know to what extent the Japanese share this belief in the need for and possibility of forgiveness and redemption. Perhaps the inability of Japan to achieve reconciliation with its Asian neighbors, of which Takako Doi, Speaker of the House of Representatives of Japan, spoke, reflects a profound cultural difference. If it is harder for the Japanese to acknowledge and apologize for their past mistakes, then I suggest it is our obligation and in our interest to try to understand their reticence, asking in exchange that the Japanese try to understand us when we fail to meet their expectations.

Happily, we have succeeded in understanding one another to a remarkable degree: the friendship that now binds together our peoples and nations, fifty years after the bombing of Hiroshima and fifty-four years after the bombing of Pearl Harbor, is truly remarkable.

The total war that raged between the United States and Japan for three years and eight months terminated in fiery destruction. But the victors, the Allies, had learned well the lessons of Versailles, and the war was followed by a generous peace built on enlightened concern for the humanity of the defeated nations. While at war the United States fought, as did Germany and Japan, with all the force and determination we could muster. But once the war was over, we joined the Japanese and the Germans in rebuilding their countries and thus nourished the friendship that binds us today.

THE LEGACY OF THE TWENTIETH CENTURY

It is commonly claimed that the legacy of the twentieth century to its successors will be an unprecedented increase in human suffering. Our introduction of nuclear weapons, the tens of millions of deaths in the Second World War, and the victims of the Holocaust give this claim considerable plausibility.

But consider the fourteenth century: between 1348 and 1351, the Black Death killed a third of the people in Europe. In cities, the death toll regularly exceeded 50 percent: a comparable slaughter in present-day Europe would kill 170,000,000 people. The Black Death was an almost unimaginable disaster, made the more terrifying because of the inevitability of a painful death.

And war no less than pestilence brought great suffering to the fourteenth century. Although the battles were fought by small professional armies, civilians suffered greatly. Armies lived off the land during military campaigns, and during the frequent truces soldiers, demobilized and unpaid, lived for months and years on plunder alone.

The suffering of the twentieth century does not equal in extensiveness that of the fourteenth, but it far exceeds that of the fourteenth in moral horror. For the widespread suffering of the fourteenth century attributable to pestilence bore no trace of wickedness or evil intent; and the suffering attributable to war was largely the consequence of folly.

When famine afflicted the fourteenth century, the cause was poor weather or blight. It remained to the twentieth century to invent the contrived famine, resorted to by Stalin in the 1930s and the Ethiopian government fifty years later, on both occasions the purpose being to subdue unruly provinces.

During the Black Death, urban mobs, panicked by the horrors around them and believing the Jews to have caused the plague, killed many of them. The contrast between the centuries is found in the difference between the cruelty of terrified, maddened crowds and the cold governmental calculation of the Holocaust. The Holocaust and modern war also illustrate the magnification of evil by modern technology. An efficient rail system and Zyklon B were necessary for Auschwitz. Similarly, modern science and technology were necessary for the massive destruction of modern war. Without modern technology, dictators could not have imposed their malevolent intent on hundreds of millions of people.

The suffering of the twentieth century, unlike that of the fourteenth, is overwhelmingly the consequence of moral depravity.

THE LEGACY OF HIROSHIMA AND NAGASAKI

We meet in a city whose name will be forever linked with one event, the nuclear bombing of August 6, 1945. In discussing that bombing, it is not my purpose to arraign anyone. We must not only refrain from moralistic revisionism with regard to the past, we must also understand what actually happened here and what led up to what happened here. It is in this spirit that I now address the question of the bombing of Hiroshima and Nagasaki.

The Pacific War was as much a clash of cultures as of economic and political systems. Prior to December 7, 1941, America was sharply divided over intervention in the European war. But Pearl Harbor ended all division. We Americans believed that Japan, by attacking the United States even as their diplomats were negotiating for peace, had violated the rules so blatantly that it must be punished by decisive military defeat. From the American point of view, Japan's bad faith had foreclosed any possibility of a negotiated end to the war. Although the formula of "unconditional surrender" was not adopted until January 1943, it was implicit from the moment Admiral Nagumo's torpedo-bombers arrived off Oahu.

American resolve was stiffened further by the atrocities inflicted on the American prisoners taken in the Philippines. The Americans followed an international practice in which the war was over for a surrendered prisoner, who became a protected person whose preservation was mandated by the Geneva Convention. The Japanese, by contrast, followed a practice very different from the provisions of the Geneva Convention; they regarded a surrendered prisoner as someone who had failed to fight to the death, a person unworthy of good treatment, an object almost of loathing. Despite its announcement in 1942 that it would respect the Geneva Convention, Japan did not.

On the Bataan Death March, more than 5,000 of the 12,000 American prisoners died from neglect and abuse. Still more were beheaded later. When these facts became known in the United States, the reaction can only be described as one of mass hatred. Americans believed they were facing an enemy with appalling contempt for human life and the rules of warfare.

As the war progressed, the Americans also learned that they were confronting an enemy of extraordinary valor. In the early stages of the war when it still seemed that Japan might win, Japanese forces facing destruction, as at Guadalcanal in 1942, would execute strategic withdrawals in order to fight again elsewhere. But after the war turned heavily against Japan, there were no more withdrawals, and with rare exceptions Japanese soldiers obeyed their orders to die for the Emperor. In the closing days of the war, the Kamikaze pilots gave an extraordinary example of heroic devotion to their Emperor and their country. But there was no more striking illustration of Japanese courage and determination than the resolute defense, island by island, of the outer approaches to the Empire.

On Iwo Jima, with a total surface of only 7.5 square miles, the Japanese defenders inflicted American casualties totaling 6,000 killed and 20,000 wounded. The Japanese figures are even more stark: of the island's 20,000 defenders, only 1,000 were taken alive. General Kuribayashi's order had been, "Die in place; kill as many Marines as you can." His men obeyed.

On Okinawa, the 102,000 Japanese defenders inflicted 85,000 casualties on the Americans. The Japanese who were not killed in action committed suicide by jumping from cliffs.

Such battles set the standard by which President Truman and his military advisers assessed the cost in lives of invading Japan itself.

In preparation for this invasion, Japanese cities were subjected to mass bombing. This tactic was pioneered by the Japanese at Nanking and the Germans at Warsaw and Rotterdam. As the war in Europe progressed, both sides made massive raids on city centers, including the destruction of Coventry by the Germans and the destruction of Hamburg and Dresden by the Allies.

In these raids, civilians were not merely collateral damage but were targeted purposefully. The old notion of civilians as noncombatants no longer held. In the fourteenth century, an invading army was not connected to its home country by a supply line, and the civilians back home had no role in supporting the troops. But in the twentieth century, civilians had become the makers and providers of munitions and supplies to combatants and therefore were considered combatants.

In Hamburg, 300,000 apartments and homes were destroyed and more than 45,000 persons killed. In a single raid on Dresden, 135,000 people were killed and 1,600 acres in the center of the city leveled by a firestorm that burned for four days and could be seen for 200 miles.

Using conventional bombs, the Americans destroyed 64 of the 68 Japanese cities with populations over 100,000. In the March 1945 fire-bombings of Tokyo, at least 80,000 people died – more than at Nagasaki. Nearly a million people – more than the total of Japan's military casualties in the Pacific – were killed in the bombing of Japan. Yet even this level of destruction did not bring Japan close to surrender.

The air war climaxed on August 6 in the nuclear bombing of Hiroshima, killing an estimated 120,000 people.

A comparison of Dresden and Hiroshima is instructive. The casualties were comparable, slightly greater at Dresden. Dresden was destroyed by hundreds of planes dropping thousands of bombs; Hiroshima, by a single plane dropping one bomb.

The main distinction between Hiroshima and Dresden is one of efficiency, and I fail to see a moral distinction between destroying a city with a thousand bombs and destroying a city with one.

But the bombing of Hiroshima did not lead to Japanese capitulation. This fact in itself refutes the revisionist claim that a demonstration explosion over Tokyo Bay would have been sufficient to secure Japanese surrender. There was no reason to believe the Japanese would have been persuaded by it, and there was the risk that it might not work. After all, no atomic bomb had yet been exploded in free fall. With only two bombs in existence, there was none to spare for a possibly failed demonstration.

If the United States had possessed several atomic bombs, if each was certain to explode, and if the explosion could have convinced Japan to surrender, the bombing of Hiroshima would have been unnecessary. But these three conditions were contrary to fact: the United States had only two bombs, there was no certainty that either would work, and on the evidence of Japan's failure to surrender immediately following the bombing of Hiroshima, a failure repeated after the bombing of Nagasaki, it is clear that Japan would not have been convinced by any demonstration.

On August 9, Nagasaki was bombed. Even this did not lead to immediate surrender, but only to an argument between the military and the foreign office, which was referred to the Emperor for decision. On August 13, four days later and seven days after the bombing of Hiroshima, the matter was still under discussion, while more than a thousand American B-29s destroyed two more cities. And two more days passed before surrender finally came.

Hiroshima and Nagasaki cost some 200,000 lives. What did they save? An estimate was that an invasion of the home islands of Japan would cost as many as one million American casualties and possibly many more than one million Japanese casualties. Given the bravery and determination shown by the Japanese in defending remote outposts, this estimate seemed reasonable at the time, as it still does. In consequence, the argument for using the bomb was compelling to a highly moral president whose duty was to end the war as quickly as possible with the minimal loss of American lives. Contrary to the unsupported assertion of the vice president of India, Mr. K. R. Narayanan, the bombing of Hiroshima bore no resemblance to the Holocaust.

If the consequences of using the atomic bomb were devastating, the consequences of not using it would have been still worse. An invasion would have been a slaughterhouse that would have multiplied Iwo Jima and Okinawa many times over. Peace could have come only at the price of annihilation, and relations between the two countries would have been poisoned for decades by memories of savage loss. There could have been no swift reconciliation.

After unconditional surrender, America granted conditions more generous than Japan could have expected to negotiate. Hatred was supplanted by good will and respect, as the Japanese people were, under American protection, encouraged to choose their own destiny as a free people.

HONESTY IN CONFRONTING HISTORY

Many will find unpalatable the conclusion that the atomic bombing of Hiroshima and Nagasaki was not only justified but obligatory. The easy attraction of the revisionist position is that one can assume the mantle of superior morality and use the questionable device of hindsight and unproven and sometimes false assumptions to condemn the conduct of statesmen long dead.

Yet given the circumstances of the time and the experience of those who lived through that time, it is difficult to see how American leaders should or indeed could have acted otherwise. Given the most likely consequences of a failure to use the bomb, it is hard to question their choice.

The twentieth century brought Japan and the United States into a terrible and tragic conflict that destroyed many lives and much treasure. But it also brought them into a deeply committed relationship of economic and strategic interdependence whereby friendship has grown while both peoples have been continually enriched. The need for honesty in confronting the world requires us to face both these facts with equal candor.

Today we are rivals – not on the battlefield but in free world markets. In this arena Americans meet Japanese as equals. The rivalry is friendly, though sometimes Americans must feel envious, and know they must work harder to match Japan's industrial prowess. In such friendship and peaceful competition the future of hope is assured.

Character Education East and West

"East or West, education in character and morals takes place like all basic education – by imitation. What children hear, they say; what children see, they do. It is as simple as that."

I was pleased and interested to address a group of Chinese educators under the aegis of Columbia University in 1995 on the topic of character education - not because I thought current America had a great deal to teach them in this regard, but in order to note that, despite obvious differences, the Chinese and the American traditions have a great deal in common. This commonality, I argued, arose because character education is not fundamentally relativistic as some claim, but is based on objective principles discovered centuries ago in the West and in the East.

I. WHAT IS THE PROBLEM?

I was fascinated when I received the invitation to speak on models of character education at the USA/China Conference on Moral Education. The very fact that we are holding an international conference on this topic is of extraordinary significance.

In every culture for which we have a historical record, men and women have been concerned to educate the young in such a way as to preserve civil order and the possibilities of human fulfillment. Our philosophical and religious literature is replete with moral instruction. Great thinkers East and West (Plato, Aristotle, Epictetus, Confucius, Lao Tze, and Buddha, to name only a few) have spoken or written extensively on this issue.

Until recently no one has thought that the process of character formation, or education in morals and manners, was either complex or obscure. From time immemorial, peoples in countries all over the world have recognized that the character of a nation depends on the character of its people and that the character of its people depends upon the character of its children, which begins to be formed long before they go to school.

Education in character and morals takes place like all basic education: by imitation. In his *Poetics*, Aristotle wrote, "The instinct of imitation is implanted in man from childhood. One difference between him and other animals is that he is the most imitative of creatures, and through imitation learns his earliest lessons" (Ch. 4). That is, education is neither complicated nor mysterious. It is accomplished through the simplest means, and the most complex problem we face is in understanding the power of simplicity.

Ask yourself, "Why do children in Beijing learn to speak Mandarin while American children learn to speak English?" The answer is plain: children do not invent languages from scratch; infants imitate the language of their parents; they have no other language to imitate.

Imitation is the principle behind all education: what children hear, they say; what children see, they do. It is as simple as that.

So why do we need a conference on the subject? The reason can be found in the degeneration of culture in the technologically advanced and prosperous nations of the world. The problem becomes worldwide as films and television programs developed in these nations spread around the globe. They offer examples of degeneracy that too often prove contagious, partly by showing opportunities for economic gain. The development of drug cartels in third-world countries is an apt example.

When societies are well ordered and people are governed under wise and just constitutions, virtue can flourish. As Aristotle pointed out in the *Nicomachean Ethics*:

[M]oral virtue comes about as the result of habit.... [V]irtues we get first by exercising them, as also happens in the case of the arts as well. For the things we have to learn before we can do them, we learn by doing them, e.g. men become builders by building.... [S]o too we become just by doing just acts, temperate by doing temperate acts, brave by doing brave acts.... [L]egislators make the citizens good by forming habits in them and this is the wish of every legislator, and those who do not effect it miss their mark, and it is in this that a good constitution differs from a bad one. (*Nicomachean Ethics*, Book II, Ch. 1)

When the constitution of a nation is sound and its culture is not in disarray, the problem of moral education does not arise, for parents offer their children models for imitation that meet the needs of the oncoming generation. In well-ordered societies, parents take great pains to preserve standards of taste and morals, preserving the ceremonies of innocence in the lives of their young children, offering models for emulation and stories and poems illustrating virtues and virtuous living. Children are exposed to excellent moral examples, and through imitation of teachers and mentors in carefully designed moral exercises, develop habits of courage, temperance, and justice, and begin studies that might eventually lead to wisdom.

When the first English colonists came to America, they shared this understanding of the role of imitation and the importance of examples in character formation and moral education. Although they lived in rigorous conditions that would now be defined as those of poverty, they provided for public education and offered a curriculum that was rich with moral instruction and examples for imitation. Americans continued this concern for character education with the wide distribution throughout the nineteenth century of the McGuffey Readers. Education had a moral core, and until the mid-twentieth century, teachers were selected on the basis of their moral character as well as their intellect.

II. CULTURAL COLLAPSE

But then a disaster befell us that seriously compromised our character education. We became a very rich nation. And as the English philosopher Francis Bacon observed: "Luxury doth best encourage vice while adversity doth best encourage virtue."

Despite our pockets of poverty, the majority of Americans are born into a culture in which affluence is not something to be striven for, but a birthright. In consequence, our national character has suffered. Two young people marry, and because they have no idea that a successful marriage must be striven for, they fail at marriage and, disillusioned, soon divorce. Children learn from television that everyone is rich, that pleasure is instantaneous and without limit, and that sadistic cruelty is a normal part of life. They grow up concerned with little but satiating themselves, and when they fail to become rich or when they find that instantaneous gratification soon palls, they become deeply unhappy and alienated beings who are easy prey to the enticements of drugs and the temptations of easy money through crime.

More laws and regulations are not, and never have been, the solution to the decline of a nation's character. As Tacitus, the great Roman historian, wrote, *Corruptissima re publica, plurimae leges* – the more corrupt the state, the more laws it has. Laws can never guarantee self-regulating behavior; the attraction to what is virtuous preserves the moral fiber of a nation. A nation must trust its citizens, and for this to be possible, the citizens must possess high moral character. The point is made in *The Analects* of Confucius, Book II,

> If the people be led by laws, and uniformity sought to be given them by punishments, they will try to avoid punishment, but have no sense of shame. If they be led by virtue, and uniformity sought to be given them by rules of propriety, they will have the sense of shame and moreover will become good.

In America today, as shame has been replaced by psychiatric and sociological jargon in the assessment of behavior, the domains of choice and of law have eroded the domain of manners. As the realm of manners and morals has been diminished by those who claim that whatever they think or do is right if it feels good to them, this central domain loses its force.

III. EFFORTS TO RESTORE MORALS IN A BROKEN CULTURE

In reaction to these developments, Americans have begun to return to character education. One example of this concern is the Center for the

Advancement of Ethics and Character at Boston University, where we are developing curricula that will instill traditional notions of character in children who would otherwise be defenseless against television, movies, and other degraded elements of our culture.

But the effort to reintroduce moral education into our schools and to encourage parents to offer their children moral education as early as possible has been resisted by relativists who proclaim that whatever one does is right and whatever one wants is good. These advocates of relativism, apparently ignorant of the objective foundation of morals, ask, "Whose morals shall be introduced? Who shall establish which moral standards are to be encouraged?"

IV. OBJECTIVE FOUNDATION OF MORALS

At this point we must not fall into the habit, common in this country, of confusing personal preferences with moral judgments. To speak of moral education is not to speak of subjective preference, but of objective judgment of right and wrong, good and bad. Moral instruction has nothing to do with personal preferences. There are many aspects of life in which we express our personal preference for one thing or another without any claim to agreement on the part of others. If I like X and say that I like X, my statement is true, just because I happen to like it. But it does not follow from my liking X that X is good or right or that anyone else should or does like it.

But if I say that X is good, I assert that the nature and quality of X is such that it should be brought into being or supported in being not only by me but by everyone else. The use of the word "good" carries with it an objective claim not found in mere liking or preference.

In order to teach morals or develop character in the public schools without cultural support, we must rediscover the rational foundations of ethics, the arguments and facts that give objective support to moral principles. We must begin with basics by presenting to children those principles that are necessary for individual self-fulfillment.

First of all, we must acknowledge that no individual is self-sufficient;

this is the first principle of social organization. The evidence is abundant: without society, no individual – even if one could give birth to oneself and survive on one's own following one's birth – would have the power of speech and, hence, the capacity for thought or self-consciousness. Since every individual is dependent on a social organization, it is the obligation of each individual to provide a measure of support for the society on which the individual depends. This is the necessary condition for personal survival, and the factual basis on which morality and ethics rest.

If a ruler has the problem of ensuring the survival of a people (a responsibility faced by Moses, for example, when he led the Israelites out of Egypt), the ruler will of necessity have to establish the principles of conduct necessary to their survival.

Suppose you put yourself in the position of the ruler. What would you propose as the commandments of moral behavior? Would you prohibit murder? Can you imagine the possibility of a society in which there is no agreement that murder is wrong? Can you imagine a society in which there is no agreement that stealing is wrong and that it is wrong to covet the property of others? These are not matters of whim or preference; these are principles on which human existence, both socially and individually, necessarily depends. Why is well-poisoning wrong? It is always wrong, no matter what anyone claims to the contrary, because the community and the individuals who live within it must have water and will be killed if their well is poisoned.

As a matter of fact, powerful arguments based on evidence and logic can be given in support of all genuine moral principles. They are a distillation of wisdom amassed through years of experience by peoples throughout the world. They are principles without which no society can function effectively and without which no individual can hope to live happily.

With regard to basic morality there is not merely an American consensus but an international one. Character educators from China will find most traditional American character education familiar territory, for over the centuries there has been among civilized people across the face of the earth a remarkable consensus as to basic morality. For example, the many formulations of the Golden Rule found in African, Asian,

Middle Eastern, and Western cultures are essentially the same. Confucius was asked, "Is there one word that may serve as a rule of practice for all of one's life?" He replied, "Is not reciprocity such a word? What you do not want done to yourself do not do unto others."

About the same time, the Buddha said, "Hurt not others in ways that you would find hurtful." And a little later, Socrates expressed himself in almost identical terms: "Do not do to others what would anger you if done to you." When Aristotle was asked how we ought to behave to our friends, he said, "As we should wish them to behave to us." The great Jewish sage Hillel stated it this way: "What is hateful to you, do not to your fellow man. That is the entire law; all the rest is commentary." Jesus stated the law affirmatively, "Whatsoever you would that men should do to you, do unto them," and echoing Hillel, he added, "That is the law and the prophets."

This law was given a definitive theoretical formulation by Immanuel Kant, one that is valid in any country or among any ethnic group to which one might belong: "So act that the principle of your act can be a universal law."

Just as elementary ethical principles are common to all civilized people, these principles are also violated in every society and at times in the life of every individual. As long as there is freedom, individuals, even when they have been instructed in their moral responsibilities and nurtured in these principles through moral exercises, may fail to live in accordance with these moral ideas.

There are, moreover, individuals, albeit a very small minority, who seem incapable of accepting moral instruction. Instruction in morals and in character development requires not only a teacher but a pupil receptive to learning. The Taoist Chuang Tze noted, for example, that it is not possible to present, to impart, or to give the Tao to just anyone. "Unless there is a suitable endowment within," he wrote, "the Tao will not abide." In teaching morals, the instructor is like the person who would light a fire. One may blow on a spark, but the spark must be there if the flame is to grow.

It is essential to recognize, however, that the failure to live by moral principles in no way invalidates them. All moral principles are normative. They prescribe what ought to be done; they are not descriptions of what is done. This is as true of morals, which offer rules for virtuous living, as of logic, which offers rules for sound thinking.

V. WHAT IS THE SOLUTION?

Instruction in morals cannot be done through theoretical exercises or mere verbal explanations. Students respond to moral instruction best when that instruction is offered in terms of action and in concrete rather than abstract terms.

In order to build character, we must offer all young children examples of persons and stories that illustrate the moral principles we are trying to teach. Such stories are found in the teachings of our great religious and moral sages.

By the use of aphorisms and stories that illustrate them, children are given models of behavior. These examples must be supported by the actions of their parents and teachers, who must be seen to live by these principles. And in their earliest years, children should be shielded as much as possible from bad examples of speech and action. In America, that means that their exposure to television and movies must be heavily restricted. Only in this way will our children, by imitation, develop good habits that are the very substance of moral character.

For older children we must offer philosophical arguments to explain the validity and soundness of moral principles. We must explain why the moral aphorisms we taught them earlier are true and not mere opinion. In order to succeed in this, the teacher must not only know the arguments and evidence that provide objective proof of moral principles, but must be seen to live by them. The teacher must make these principles clear not merely in words but also in action. Permit me to offer three examples of what I mean from my own experiences as a teacher of ethics.

1. In a philosophy class, I asked students to evaluate Protagoras's statement that, "Man is the measure of all things." One student wrote a remarkable paper in which he defended Protagoras's position, arguing that there was no such thing as an objective assessment of personal conduct, morality, aesthetics, or anything else. He insisted that all such

judgments were a matter of personal preference. I made specific comments on the paper, paragraph by paragraph, but in the end I gave him the lowest grade possible: a resounding F. The student came in to complain, and I said, "Why are you complaining? I was totally convinced by your argument. Since you have shown that there are no objective criteria by which I can evaluate a paper and that all such judgments are matters of whim, I decided to follow my whim and give you an F. What now is your objection?" The student was thunderstruck as he had to face for the first time the practical implications of his argument. Subsequently, he became much more thoughtful.

2. A young student was going through a period of late adolescent turbulence in which she doubted that life had any meaning or purpose. She doubted the value of her own life, and seemed possibly suicidal. I said, "Let's talk about it." We left my office, walked down the street and came to the corner of a busy thoroughfare. Watching as carefully as I could from the corner of my eye while appearing to be lost in the topic under discussion, I walked straight into the oncoming traffic. Just when I was about to be struck by a car, the student grabbed me and pulled me out of the way. I then asked her, "Why did you do that?" She replied, "You were about to get yourself killed." I said, "So what? According to you, life has no meaning, so what difference would it make if I had been killed? And why should you care since you don't even care about your own life?" That was a critical turning point in that student's life. The student knew that I cared enough about her to risk my own life, and in that existential moment she had to admit that she valued my life and hers, even though she could not say what that value was. She had begun to discover meaning in her life.

3. I was invited to visit a college where I was asked to meet with students to discuss philosophy. Our discussion turned to the fundamental distinction between right and power. A young man claimed to be incapable of distinguishing these concepts. All his responses to my arguments were flippant and dismissive. In order to force him to think seriously about the issue, I asked him to join me in a thought experiment. I said, "Let's suppose I suddenly rise from my chair and grab you about the throat." (I was thirty-five years of age at the time, and both larger and stronger than the student.) "Suppose I grabbed you by the throat, threw

you to the floor, and said, 'Now I am going to kill you, but I want to ask you a question before you die. You recognize, do you not, that I have the power to kill you? But I want to ask, do I have the right to kill you?' Can you now discern the difference?" The young man, who had a reputation as the campus intellectual and had been contemptuously arrogant throughout the discussion, blushed deeply, got up, and left the room. I was told later by students that he said that was the first time anyone had exposed his ignorance and arrogance and made him feel like a fool. In consequence, he finally achieved some degree of humility on which the capacity to learn depends.

Moral education cannot be effective with older children unless reasons are offered to support moral principles. But this is not enough. In order to teach character and morals effectively, the teacher must live what he or she professes. The principles he or she teaches must be shown to have practical implications, and the teacher must be seen to act in accordance with the implications of those principles. If teachers are not worthy mentors, they are not likely to be effective teachers of character and morals. Instead, they will induce cynicism. Students will reject their teachers as mere hypocrites.

VI. LEARNING FROM THE AMERICAN EXPERIENCE

We in the United States have no particular wisdom to impart to the rest of the world. But the rest of the world can learn from our mistakes. Our moral culture has been undermined by wealth. Materialism and the pursuit of riches have become the final arbiters of decisions that determine what our children and adults will see many hours of the day and night on television and in movies. We have seen the corrosive effects of the repetitive presentation of degenerate and immoral examples of human behavior. But we have not yet come to terms with the commercial institutions that, by exposing our children to immoral examples, are undermining our capacity effectively to build character and teach morals.

China's economic development has become the wonder of the world. No one can doubt that given its resources – most of all, its resource of an educated and gifted people with millennia of high civilization behind them – China can make the journey from underdevelopment to danger-ous luxury in a period of decades rather than of centuries.

Let us hope that you will be able to profit from our mistakes by careful attention to preserving the character of your people from the assaults of luxury. If you succeed, you will not need to attempt, as we must, to restore it once it has been compromised.

Address to the International Educational Foundation, Columbia University, June 13, 1995

Such Stuff as Dreams Are Made On

"You will never marshal the powers of your own being unless you believe you can attain your highest dreams. It is far better to overestimate the extent of our powers than to sell them short."

In 1996, the student press at Boston University was already anticipating the end of my tenure, though in the event I was to serve another ten years as chancellor. I used this commencement address to reflect on developments at the university in my twenty-six years of service to date, and to reflect once again on the ideals of a university, including its role in fostering that sense of belief in oneself without which the highest striving is impossible.

THIS UNIVERSITY WAS FOUNDED and has lived on dreams of doing the difficult, the unprecedented, and even the impossible. In 1839, a group of New England Methodists met in a building in downtown Boston and planned the first college for the education of Methodist ministers. Thirty years later, William Fairfield Warren, Lee Claflin, Isaac Rich, and Jacob Sleeper set in motion a new dream, the first American university to combine the model of the New England undergraduate college with the professional curricula of the German research university. And they were such dreamers that they also made it the first university in the world to be open to women in all its programs. As President Warren put it, in words that have never been bettered,

> Artificially to restrict the benefits of such an institution to one-half of the community, by a discrimination based solely on a birth distinction, is worse than un-American. It is an injury to society as a whole, a loss to the favored class, a wrong to the unfavored.

At the same time, Charles W. Eliot was beginning his forty-year presidency of Harvard. I am sure you all know I would never criticize our sister institution across the river, nor any president who managed to stay in office for forty years, but candor compels me to note that President Eliot did not share President Warren's views. In his inaugural address, Dr. Eliot announced that Harvard would not admit women. He stated his reason: "The difficulties involved in a common residence of young men and women of immature character and marriageable age are very grave." Dr. Eliot wanted to make it perfectly clear that he was not proceeding out of what he called "crude notions about the innate capacities of women." Indeed, he said, "the world knows next to nothing about the natural mental capacities of the female sex." Given this remarkable ignorance, he concluded, caution was the watchword. At Boston University, we threw caution to the winds.

Our founders, all devout Methodists, also ensured that their university would be open to people of all religious beliefs and of none. Their charter specified that no instructor or student "shall ever be required by the trustees to profess any particular religious opinions."

And from the very first Boston University has admitted students without regard to race.

Fifty years later, President Murlin dreamed of a university that would be centered on the south bank of the Charles River and would recognize its obligation to the city around it. He began to purchase the land on which his dream would be realized. It was brought into being by his successor, Daniel L. Marsh. When land between the University and the Charles River was taken by eminent domain, Marsh had to revise Murlin's original plan. The power of Marsh's belief in the destiny of Boston University sustained him and the University through the harrowing decade of the Great Depression.

Twenty-six years ago, I accepted the presidency of Boston University, in part because I was inspired by the dreams of my predecessors and in part because, like them, I had dreams of my own, dreams of a great university built on their foundations. It should be obvious that in dreaming fantastical dreams of an implausible future I was not an innovator, for that was my inheritance from Warren, Murlin, and Marsh.

I was intrigued with Boston University because I saw it as a school pregnant with unrealized and unsuspected greatness. I soon discovered that there were others here who saw it in the same light.

It seemed obvious to me that Boston University must be moved to greatness, for I believed that a university is either excellent or it is a university in name only.

It is obviously for others, yourselves included, to judge how well I succeeded in bringing my dreams for Boston University to reality. I will only say that to the extent that I have succeeded, it is because many others – staff, faculty, students, and trustees – shared my dreams and worked hard to embody them.

A generation has passed since I first addressed a Boston University Commencement, for among today's graduates are children of graduates at my inaugural Commencement. And now it is time for me to make my valedictory and to graduate with you.

Forty-nine years ago, I left college in times that, although deeply flawed by legal segregation and other forms of racism, were, on the whole, joyous and happy. World War II was only two years past and veterans, supported by the GI Bill, were crowding into colleges and universities, anxious and eager not only to get on with their lives and start families, but to devour books of poetry and philosophy better to understand and express all they had experienced in the years of combat and uncertainty. It was a time full of promise and fulfillment energized by the euphoria of victory and freedom from the bondage of economic depression. We were confident that our future and our country's future would be better and happier than that of previous generations.

It was easier and simpler for us than it is for you members of this graduating class. For us, there was great excitement and joy in finding ourselves alive in a world in which war and economic depression seemed issues of the past. It seemed a world of security and unlimited promise for living intensely and well. Distractions were few, and although TV was on its way, entertainment was still largely a do-it-yourself activity.

As a parent and grandparent, no less than as president of the University, it worries me, as it must worry all who care about the members of this graduating class, that your opportunities in life may be more limited than those of our generation. The world you enter is not known for its domestic tranquility and security. Rather, you move into a world polluted not only environmentally but socially by trash radio and TV, drug dealing, child pornography, and random violence.

Television has greatly accelerated the emergence of a mass culture. This was foreseen as early as 1929 by the great Spanish liberal philosopher and opponent of Franco, José Ortega y Gasset. In that year, he published his *Revolt of the Masses*, in which he described the vertical barbarians – those who besiege civilization not from without the gates but from within. They arise within a culture and pull it down to their level. The rise of trash television would be inconceivable without an audience of vertical barbarians. These programs are not, after all, produced by perverse philanthropists dedicated to debasing public understanding. They are produced by people who know what sells and for whom profits are the only consideration.

How does one live in a civilization under siege? Ortega y Gasset, writing in a Spain staggering towards a bloody civil war, attained great clarity. He divided humanity into two groups: those who make great demands on themselves, piling up difficulties and duties; and those who demand nothing special of themselves. This last group he called "mere buoys that float on the waves."

This is a frankly elitist conception, and in our time, elitism has become a dirty word – except, of course, in sports and in dog-racing where the pursuit and celebration of excellence is the norm. But as a matter of fact, there is nothing wrong with democratic elitism based on talent and virtue rather than wealth, gender, race, or social class. By deciding to pursue your education at Boston University, you have joined the democratic elite. You have expressed your determination to resist the easy way of life by refusing to be satisfied with what you already are. By your decision to accept the demands and duties of a higher education, you have expressed your rejection of a complacent life submerged in mass culture. And you dream of personal fulfillment and of making contributions to society that will require your continuing dedication and your passionate efforts in the years ahead.

You graduate concerned for others and their rights, and with an understanding of the procedures of thought and discovery by which insight and knowledge are attained and the standards by which theories and ideas are tested.

Following the defeat of Germany, the philosopher Karl Jaspers faced a daunting challenge. He proposed a means for the German universities to redeem themselves from the barbarism of the Third Reich. And we should remember that this barbarism was all too often, though with honorable exceptions, heartily embraced by German professors and students. Universities must be free, Jaspers insisted, to pursue the truth wherever the chase takes them. But he denied them any "freedom to engage in propaganda," even when – and indeed, especially when – it was propaganda for what university faculties and administrations believed was the better cause.

Jasper's insight remains a useful guide today, because there are people who truly believe that it is not only acceptable but imperative that universities be committed to political positions and become instruments of political action. This entails a commitment to propaganda and to the suppression of what is seen as politically incorrect. When this happens, universities become dominated by ideologues – by people who derive facts from their opinions rather than their opinions from facts.

Jaspers says,

In the common search for truth there must be no barriers of charitable reserve, no gentle reticence, no comforting deception. There can be no question that might not be raised.

At present there are increasing efforts to introduce taboos with regard to certain forms of research and exploration. Researchers may be sharply criticized, for example, simply for raising the possibility that there are important differences between the sexes. In a university, there can be no taboos against any research that relies on evidence and arguments. No question can be properly excluded from a university if it is asked with honesty and intellectual rigor. Astrologers, alchemists, and those who assert that there was no Holocaust fail to meet this test. They do not accept the discipline by which truth is attainable.

Any question of concern to human beings which can be pursued methodically by means of argument and experimentation is, by contrast, welcome and appropriate in a university. As Jaspers concludes, "We belong together; we must feel our common cause when we talk to each other."

This is the ethos it has been my concern to create and to encourage at Boston University – an ethos in which students can learn, think, and mature in relative independence from the barbaric influences of our time, free from the din and the blinders of mass thought and action to become fully themselves as individuals.

The survival of our civilization depends upon our faith in our ideals, rules, practices, and institutions. Far from illusory, they are more real than tables and chairs, motor cars and computers, which we can do without. What is essential, and therefore real, are our laws, ideals, customs, and institutions that make us civilized and enable us to reach out to one another, to seek and dispense knowledge, beauty and moral insight.

The goals you set for yourselves, the demands you make upon yourselves, will turn on your conception of yourself and your nature as a human being. You will be tempted to accept a debilitating and limiting view of your potentiality prompted by prevailing dogmas that are put forward – falsely – as if they rested on the authority of science.

These limiting views can deny you membership in the company of those who make the highest demands upon themselves. Don't let anyone impose on you a diminished sense of your being and worth. Beware of intellectuals who, disregarding the limits of science, denigrate and diminish the human species, denying the freedom and grandeur of men and women.

I believe that each of us who shares the gift of human life has been given a share in the wonder of mankind, in the greatness of our species. But you can never succeed in realizing your highest dreams and ambitions if you do not strive for them with all the force of your personality; and you will never be able to marshal the powers of your own being unless you believe you can attain your highest dreams. It is far better to overestimate the significance of our lives and the extent of our powers than to sell them short. As William James writes in *The Will to Believe*, "If I refuse to bail out a boat because I am in doubt whether my efforts will keep her afloat, I am really helping to sink her."

To adopt, as if it were true, an unproven materialism which denies all transcendent meaning to human existence, inevitably dwarfs the human spirit. But the possibility of transcendence, of the search for goals beyond our present reach, has been demonstrated in the lives of countless individuals throughout the history of mankind. Your fulfillment is up to each of you, for as Shakespeare said, "We are such stuff as dreams are made on." Without our dreams, without our aspirations, we are nothing.

"Drinking the Sun of Corinth and Reading the Marbles"

"As different as this century will be from fifth-century Greece, it will also be, like that ancient era, a dangerous and challenging time in which to live. The ancient Greeks have much to tell us about how to live and how to die in such a time."

At the University of New Hampshire I spoke on the demanding standards of our Greek heritage and the extent to which it offers us guidance and strength if, as Goethe says, we make that heritage our own. The occasion was the 1998 inauguration of the Rouman Classical Lecture Series established at the university by the Papoutsy family. In evoking our Greek heritage, I also expressed my belief that the humanities are not an idle or useless subject, but in fact a most useful and stringent element of our education, giving structure and meaning to our lives and the courage to live well.

I AM HONORED to have been invited to give the inaugural John C. Rouman Lecture. In establishing the lecture and naming it for Professor Rouman, Christos and Eva Papoutsy have made a magnificent contribution to the preservation and dissemination of our classical heritage. Fifteen hundred years ago, the light of classical learning was nearly extinguished in Western Europe. The Roman authors were preserved by English monks in their monasteries, but the Greek tradition was lost in the West except in Ireland. Geoffrey Chaucer knew Homer only through Latin adaptations, and when Petrarch wanted to learn Greek, he was forced to import a tutor from Byzantium.

The situation is in some ways less perilous now, and in some ways more so. We are in no danger of losing the knowledge of ancient Greek;

but it is now possible to be considered not merely educated but highly educated without any knowledge of either Greek or Latin, a situation that would have been unthinkable a century ago.

Now the preservation of the classical heritage is in the hands of a relatively small group of scholars and teachers at the colleges and universities where the classical languages are still taught. The idea that an institution where the classical languages are not taught is either a college or a university would have been thought bizarre until quite recently.

Professor Rouman, with his thirty distinguished years at the University of New Hampshire, is an exemplar of that band of classical scholars and teachers who defend and preserve our classical heritage as a band of Spartans defended the pass at Thermopylae. Professor Rouman and his colleagues have the additional satisfaction that the Persians have been held at bay.

The ancient Greeks had what amounted to an obsession with education. They rightly understood that the character of their state would depend on the education of their people. Accordingly, the quality of that education was a matter of intense public concern. Understanding that citizens ought to be trained and educated in a variety of ways, they produced a system of education which the German scholar Werner Jaeger was to describe and analyze in his monumental study *Paideia*. "*Paideia*" comprised a broad-based and intensive system of education by which the young of the species *Homo sapiens* were brought to a moral, physical, and intellectual status that made them fit citizens.

This concern with individuals in their full complexity is the great legacy that Greece left Western culture. It is a legacy under attack.

Three hundred years ago that heritage, with its derivative Roman and Christian offshoots, formed the entirety of the university curriculum. Sixty years ago, although higher education had broadened its compass to include contemporary science and a wider range of literatures, the Greco-Roman tradition was still at the core of the humanities, which formed the core of higher education. And even fifty years ago, although there was increased competition from the sciences for space in the curriculum, the Hellenic tradition was still at its center.

How do we stand today? Not well. The Greco-Roman heritage is under siege or is simply dismissed as irrelevant. This is not, I take it, a point of view that would find much favor before an audience of Hellenes. This assembly springs from the civilization that not only devised the notion of *paideia* – of education as a transmission of culture – but that also produced most of the culture to transmit. This was once so obvious a fact as hardly to need saying, although people occasionally found striking ways of saying it: for example, Alfred North Whitehead's remark that "the safest general characterization of the European philosophical tradition is that it consists of a series of footnotes to Plato."

The implication of much of the curricular revisionism of today, with its rejection of the Greeks and their successors in the tradition of humane letters – such as Augustine, Shakespeare, and Hobbes – is that there is no particular reason why an educated person should know these works, or the works of Aeschylus, of Aristotle, of Moliere, of Kant. If we consider the simple facts of educated reading, we can see that this notion is false, if for no other reason than that an educated person must be able to read, with comprehension and without recourse to a reference library, the works of readily accessible poets in his or her own language. Milton's sonnet on his deceased wife is one of the greatest poems by one of the greatest English poets:

> Methought I saw my late espoused saint
> Brought to me, like Alcestis, from the grave,
> Whom Jove's great son to her glad husband gave,
> Rescued from death by force though pale and faint.

Who's Alcestis? If a student has not been exposed to classical learning, he or she must turn to the library to find out, and when this is done, appreciation of the allusion can never be the same as if he or she had immediately recognized it, experiencing one variety of what the critic Edmund Wilson called "the shock of recognition."

This poem and other classics of our culture, high school requirements in the nineteenth century all over the Midwest, the Southwest, the South and other benighted areas of the nation, may now be beyond the educational expectations of graduates of our leading universities.

In such a sterile educational tradition, we will find ourselves in the position described by St.-Exupéry in his book *Flight to Arras*. Anticipating a reconnaissance flight from which he was unlikely to return, he wrote:

> And as I sat there longing for night, I was for a moment like a Christian abandoned by grace. I was about to do my job honorably, that was certain. But to do it as one honors ancient rites when they have no longer any significance, when the god that lived in them has withdrawn from them.

It is typical that St.-Exupéry's climactic simile should be derived from the ancient Greek religion, grounded as it was in the physical presence of the deity. Increasingly, such forceful embodiments of abstractions will be unavailable to a generation that has been educated – if that is the term I want – in isolation from its cultural heritage. For culturally, we are all Hellenes, and a rejection of the classical tradition is a rejection of ourselves.

I believe that many in the university will admit that the god has withdrawn from the ceremonies it celebrates and from the principles for which it allegedly stands, and some will acknowledge that this is a consequence of the weakening of the classical tradition. As educationally dubious as any curriculum must be that does not include the study of the classics as a requirement, what can we say of entire educational institutions where such study is not possible even as an option? Once or twice in my experience as president of Boston University, it was suggested to me, with various levels of stridency, that I should close down the department of Classics and transfer to other departments the money that the University now spends on the teaching of ancient, Byzantine, and modern Greek. My answer on such occasions is this: it is not possible for Boston University to survive without a department of Classics because no institution without one deserves to be called a university. Institutions of higher education that turn their backs on the Hellenic tradition behave as if they wish to have honey without keeping bees. If enough of them adopt this policy, there will be none to keep bees and then no honey. But it is a sad fact that many colleges and universities have lent themselves to this shortsighted rejection of the classics.

What are we losing in the ongoing loss of the Hellenic tradition? Sometimes the loss is of archetypes, for there are now no archetypal moments on which one can depend unless Hollywood has made a movie of them or they are part of a television series.

Sometimes our loss is of pungency and subtlety: when Sir Arthur Conan Doyle had Dr. Watson mourn Sherlock Holmes as "the best and wisest man I have ever known," his readers would have recognized the allusion to Socrates and known that Dr. Watson could find no better words to express his sense of loss than those Phaedo used to eulogize Socrates. The reader deprived of his or her cultural background can still resonate to these moving words, but the force of the tribute can never be what it is to the educated reader.

And sometimes our loss is of pedagogical technique. A hundred years ago, the Platonic dialogue was still a living form in use in our elementary and secondary schools. William Holmes McGuffey prepared readers for our primary and secondary children that included such dialogues as the following, entitled "Let It Rain," in which the Platonic view of the inseparability of fact and value was clearly demonstrated.

ROSE: See how it rains! Oh dear, dear, dear! How dull it is! Must I stay indoors all day?

FATHER: Why, Rose, are you sorry that you had any bread and butter for breakfast, this morning?

ROSE: Why, father, what a question! I should be sorry, indeed, if I could not get any.

FATHER: Are you sorry, my daughter, when you see the flowers and the trees growing in the garden?

ROSE: Sorry? No, indeed. Just now, I wished very much to go out and see them – they look so pretty.

FATHER: Well, are you sorry when you see the horses, cows, or sheep drinking at the brook to quench their thirst?

ROSE: Why, father, you must think I am a cruel girl, to wish that the poor horses that work so hard, the beautiful cows that give so much nice milk, and the pretty lambs should always be thirsty.

FATHER: Do you not think they would die, if they had no water to drink?

ROSE: Yes, sir, I am sure they would. How shocking to think of such a thing!

FATHER: I thought little Rose was sorry it rained. Do you think the trees and flowers would grow, if they never had any water on them?

ROSE: No, indeed, father, they would be dried up by the sun. Then we should not have pretty flowers to look at, and to make wreaths of for mother.

FATHER: I thought you were sorry it rained.

ROSE: I did not think of all these things, father. I am truly very glad to see the rain falling.

Socrates held that one does not know what a thing is unless one knows the good of that thing; what the thing is for. One does not know what a knife is unless one knows what a knife is to be used for. The same goes for water. One does not know the form of anything unless one knows the form of the good in relation to it. Here in McGuffey was a lovely illustration of Plato's point, designed for the moral education of primary school children, that demonstrated the interdependence of fact and value and the factual basis of value judgments. This understanding is the foundation of a wise adulthood.

Here, although sugared over with a sentimentality that would have offended Socrates, McGuffey's method was essentially Socratic, used to bring home some elemental truths to the very young. Two and a half millennia have not given us a better method, and yet we have largely abandoned it and are in danger of forgetting it.

But our greatest loss is the loss of meaning. Providing meaning to human existence amply justifies the humanities. The meaning of the *Iliad* has survived for nearly thirty centuries, for the first five or so by being told around small banquet-fires (on occasions somewhat less grand than this one) to generation after generation of Greeks. These were not men of genius; these were *hoi polloi* who lived in Ionia, on the Aegean Islands, and on the Greek peninsula, and the *Iliad* was a story that entertained them. The *Iliad* and the *Odyssey* are first of all simple stories about fundamental experience, told in a way that anyone can understand, but in a way that will move any person of normal intelligence and sensibility. Any person of ordinary capacity will be elevated and inspired by them.

When, in the *Iliad*, the body of Patroklos is brought back, Achilles goes into great mourning and decides not to bury his friend as long as the man who killed him lives. We are confronted with an elemental understanding of friendship and its obligations. At last Achilles is compelled by events to engage in battle with Hector. When finally they meet each other and after several passes at one another, Hector runs four times around the city of Troy with Achilles in hot pursuit. Then he turns in full dread of his approaching death and fights Achilles face-to-face before the city gates.

Why does he or anyone turn to fight? Why not continue to run? As Patroklos has said earlier, if we had the option of living forever then we would take care not to risk our lives. But since none of us will live long, the important thing is to live well and to bring glory to our lives before we die. Hector is deeply moved by the same thought: he will not die with a spear between his shoulder blades; nor will he forfeit his life to Achilles without trying to prevail over him. Instead he will turn, fight for his life, and lose it with a glory second only to Achilles's own. In opting to die well, he lives well.

Achilles triumphs over Hector's body and drags it home. Then he faces the question of burying Patroklos and what to do with the body of Hector. This leads to a profoundly moving scene. Achilles has already grown in spirit from the time when, angered by Agamemnon's mistreatment, he sulked in his tent, refusing to fight, and thereby inadvertently contributed to the death of Patroklos. Now he has the opportunity of despoiling the body of the man who killed Patroklos and of burying Patroklos with honor.

At this point, however, Hector's father Priam comes to beg for his son's body. The old king kneels before Achilles, who has killed many men who embraced his knees as suppliants. But now through pity Achilles is moved to tears. The powerful young man and the frail old man weep together over the bodies of Patroklos and Hector. They are united in their common grief. Achilles gives the body of Hector to his father for honorable burial.

A person who has read the *Iliad* and attended to it is prepared to live and to die in a way that those who have not read it will not be. Those who have read it know about the obligations and rewards of friendship, about anger and its dangers, about resentment and its demeaning cruelty, about the risks human beings run when they ignore the demands of justice, about the distinction between right and power, the importance of piety, the grandeur and nobility of pity.

The *Odyssey* is no less rich in insights, not merely of adventure and warfare, but of domesticity. When, after twenty years away from home, Odysseus finally returns to Ithaca and meets his son, Telemachos, we are presented with an incomparable picture of a father and son reunited, one that over the passage of thirty centuries still has the power to move us:

[And so Odysseus spoke], and sat down again, but now Telemachos folded his great father in his arms and lamented, shedding tears, and desire for mourning rose in both of them; and they cried shrill in a pulsing voice, even more than the outcry of birds, ospreys or vultures with hooked claws, whose children were stolen away by the men of the fields, before their wings grew strong; such was their pitiful cry and the tears their eyes wept.

Why in one another's arms did the desire for mourning arise in Odysseus and Telemachos? Why not the desire for rejoicing? Because the father and the son had to mourn twenty years of companionship forever lost while Odysseus was away at war and then trying to return home from Troy. Consequently, while they rejoiced they simultaneously mourned. The sensitivity with which Homer recounts this reunion has never been surpassed.

Finally Odysseus is revealed to his wife, Penelope, who has for twenty years resisted the suitors who wanted to take over Odysseus's estate by marrying her. Penelope, wary after those long years of trial, views the person who claims to be Odysseus with suspicion, hardly able, hardly daring to believe that it is truly Odysseus and not an imposter:

So he spoke, and her knees and the heart within her went slack as she recognized the clear proofs that Odysseus had given; but then she burst into tears and ran straight to him, throwing her arms around the neck of Odysseus, and kissed his head, saying: "Do not be angry with me, Odysseus, since, beyond other men, you have been the most understanding. The gods granted us misery, in jealousy over the thought that we two, always together, should enjoy our youth, and then come to the threshold of old age. Then do not now be angry with me nor blame me, because I did not greet you, as I do now, at first when I saw you.... But now, since you have given me accurate proof describing our bed, which no other mortal man beside has ever seen, but only you and I ... [now I know that it is you]."

The way in which Odysseus proves himself the husband of Penelope is significant: he proves it by describing their marriage bed. This would not be evidence had that bed been frequented by others. In our age, in which "intimacy" with strangers is commonplace, not only on television and movies but in real life, an author would have to find some other device for proving the identity of a returning husband.

But perhaps our greatest legacy from the Hellenic tradition is the tragic vision that informs us that all humans are losers. We must remember the poignant saying that Sophocles applies to Oedipus: "Count no man happy until he dies."

This austere, sane, invigorating, and ultimately exalting view of human life is still authoritative. Despite the decadence of our times, the themes and myths that animated Greek culture in antiquity have survived. They are too profound, too tough, too significant to our own lives, to disappear. Among others, modern Greeks have continued to work the rich ore of their cultural heritage. They have read Homer and – more important – they have understood him. In consequence, they have produced works of art that are as powerful and as Greek as the original. Consider, for example, C. P. Cavafy's poem "The Horses of Achilles." It is imbued with Homer's tragic vision of life:

> When they saw Patroklos dead
> – so brave and strong, so young –
> the horses of Achilles began to weep;
> their immortal natures were outraged
> by this work of death that they had to look upon.
> They reared their heads, tossed their long manes,
> beat the ground with their hooves, and mourned
> Patroklos, seeing him lifeless, destroyed,
> now mere flesh only, his spirit gone,

defenseless, without breath,
turned back from life to the great Nothingness.

Zeus saw the tears of those immortal horses and felt sorry.
"I shouldn't have acted so thoughtlessly
at the wedding of Peleus," he said.
"Better if we hadn't given you as a gift,
my unhappy horses. What business do you have down there,
among pathetic human beings, the toys of fate.
You're free of death, you won't get old,
yet ephemeral disasters torment you.
Men have harnessed you to their misery."
But it was for the eternal disaster of death
that those two gallant horses shed their tears.

Nor is this tragic view of life confined to heroic figures, Patroklos, Achilles, Ajax, and Odysseus. It is also applicable to the life of Everyman, to the hoplites at Thermopylae, for example, whose matter-of-fact gallantry has inspired poets from Simonides to T. S. Eliot. Cavafy sings:

Honor to those who in the life they lead
define and guard a Thermopylae.
Never betraying what is right,
consistent and just in all they do
but showing pity also, and compassion;
generous when they are rich, and when they are poor,
still generous in small ways,
still helping as much as they can;
always speaking the truth,
yet without hating those who lie.

And even more honor is due to them
when they foresee (as many do foresee)
that Ephialtis will turn up in the end,
that the Medes will break through after all.

Ephialtis was the treasonous Greek who betrayed the secret pass that let the Medes through to destroy the Greeks. When we recognize that all people, rich and poor alike, face the same end – that everyone dies – we observe that the higher religious and ethical systems have attempted to find ways to transform defeat into ultimate victory. The heroes of Homer could have asked along with St. Paul, "O death where is thy sting? O grave, where is thy victory?" (1 Cor. 15:55) even though they could not have anticipated salvation from their tragic fate. For as St. Paul made clear, faith alone is "the substance of things hoped for, the evidence of things not seen" (Heb. 11:1).

We have in common with the men and women of classical Greece the culture which they developed and which through thirty centuries, as often as not through inadvertence rather than deliberation, has been handed down to us. A substantial part of the humanity of all mankind is Greek. When we study our Greek heritage, we study ourselves.

As different as the next century will be from fifth-century Greece, it will also be, like that ancient era, a dangerous and challenging time in which to live. The ancient Greeks have much to tell us about how to live and how to die in such a time. The world of Homer and the Greek dramatists is not a fair world. Up on Olympus the gods live and laugh, intervening in the affairs of men in ways that are neither predictable nor always admirable or desirable. Unlike the Christian God, they did not make human beings nor do they love them. Rather, their erratic dominion occurs simply because the gods are there – bigger and more powerful than human beings, and immortal.

Living in intimate contact with such gods was a risky business. It taught the Greeks the wisdom of accepting the inevitable and getting on with the business of life. They learned to accept the inevitability and irrationality of the thunderbolt, thinking of it as "just Zeus again." They did not allow themselves to be terrorized into living in caves, and Homer had taught them the stupidity of bitterness. They knew it was not only possible, but essential, to live courageously and well even in the face of an unpredictable and sometimes malevolent universe.

While we have made some progress in taming the forces of nature, the universe is really not much more predictable or less dangerous than it was in Homeric days. If we are to live in a way that justifies the burden of existence, we cannot look for a better guide than the Hellenic tradition, which teaches us to live with the courage that alone brings joy.

That is why I am certain that five hundred years from now we shall still, in the beautiful words of Odysseus Elytes, be

> Drinking the sun of Corinth and
> Reading the marbles.

Procedure or Dogma: The Core of Liberalism

"A position on the left may not be liberal just as one on the right may not be conservative. A true liberal does not adhere to leftist ideology but follows evidence and argument to a reasoned conclusion."

In 1999, the *New Criterion* devoted an issue to the study of liberalism and invited me to contribute. The editor, Roger Kimball, was highly critical of John Stuart Mill and liberalism as he represented it. It was my opinion, however, that Kimball's objection was not to Mill, but to the current confusion of liberalism with left-wing views. I wrote this essay to make clear that one cannot define liberalism as holding left-wing positions – or conservatism as holding to right-wing positions. Liberalism is more accurately defined not as a position but as a procedure by which ideology is avoided through a principled search for truth.

LIBERALISM: has any other word been used in more senses? Is there another word whose definition is so constrained by time and context? I face the issue baffled, and my bafflement is personal as well as conceptual. I have almost always thought of myself as a liberal, yet in the marketplace of ideas I am almost always called a conservative. This seems an ill-fitting description for someone who remembers a time when members of the John Birch Society attended his public lectures and recorded them for transmission to the FBI as evidence that he was a Communist. I am, of course, familiar with conservatives who became such by beginning with Communism and traveling through Trotskyism, socialism, social-democracy, and the whole breadth of the Democratic Party. Along the way they kept changing their minds, but, as far as I can see, I began as a liberal, and with no more adjustments than reality required have remained one.

Enjoying the advantages of hindsight, I see that I have been a liberal since I was a child. One day in San Antonio, I was sitting toward the rear of a bus when a black woman whom I as a ten-year-old perceived to be elderly got on. As she approached my seat in the crowded bus, I got up to offer it to her. This was simply what I had been taught to do by my father. He told my brother and me to offer our seats to the old, especially women, observing, "Your young legs are never as tired as theirs."

The woman thanked me and prepared to sit down. Suddenly there were shouts of "Sit down, Nigger-lover," and "Nigger, get to the back of the bus." The woman moved on and I remained standing. I was furious at the violation of everything I had been taught in Sunday School. That woman needed my seat and those haters were wrong to deny her. What had happened to the Golden Rule? Weren't we supposed to learn something from the story of the Good Samaritan?

This event, still as fresh in my memory as if it had happened yesterday, was the first indication that I was a liberal. A year later, I knew I was a Democrat. The Depression was disastrous for my family. My father's flourishing architectural practice suddenly collapsed: he was forced to dismiss his staff and close his office. Unable to meet the mortgage payments on our house, we moved to a succession of rented houses, each smaller than the one before, until my mother took charge and bought a small house for $25 down and her personal assurance that $25 mortgage payments would follow each month. The size of the down payment proved that the Depression had devastated even property owners. My grandmother and my parents occupied the two bedrooms and my brother and I got the sleeping porch.

As an exercise, my father drew up plans for enlarging our house and making it livable, but there was no money to carry out the plans. One day my father – a staunch Republican, remembering better times under Hoover and deeply disappointed in Roosevelt – announced happily that construction would begin. He had just received approval of a loan from the Home Owner's Loan Corporation, one of Roosevelt's New Deal initiatives. One Sunday, when guests had come to dinner, an unusual occurrence, my father held forth on the virtues of the GOP. I asked him, after the guests had left, "Why are you against Roosevelt? Everything good that has happened to us has happened under Roosevelt." My mother agreed fully, and I knew from that day forward that I was a Democrat.

One New Deal program after another added to the quality of our lives and our community. Schools were built as WPA projects. Mayor Maury Maverick obtained federal funds for the restoration of the Spanish missions, including the Alamo, and for La Villita, the original village of San Antonio. The WPA put men to work building Alamo Stadium, a football field for all the local high schools. Although my father had no political skills or connections, and thus did not win contracts to build any of the federal buildings constructed in the 1930s, the ripple effect of modest recovery brought him some small commissions.

I entered high school pro-Roosevelt, pro-labor, and pro-civil rights. The brilliant musician who directed our band, orchestra, and music ensembles was principal clarinetist of the San Antonio Symphony. With a large family to support, he also played in the evening with dance orchestras. From him I learned what James C. Petrillo and the American Federation of Musicians had meant to musicians. When a group of high school students organized a swing band that began to play major dances, he arranged for them to join the Musicians' Union without paying an initiation fee on the condition that from that time forward they would charge union scale. He explained that when high school kids without families to support charged less than half union scale, they took bread out of the mouths of the families of adult musicians. This seemed right to me: I continued to be a liberal.

After college, I attended Yale Divinity School. As an assignment in Christian ethics I interviewed the relatives, undertakers, and ministers who had taken part in Catholic, Protestant, and Jewish funerals. I called my paper – anticipating Jessica Mitford by fifteen years – "The High Cost of Dying." I was deeply moved by the example of an Italian funeral director who said of infants' funerals, "I persuade the family to buy at my cost the least expensive casket and I urge them to lay the keel for their next child." I was equally impressed with the Episcopal priest of a fashionable New Haven parish who told me he always accompanied the family to the funeral parlor where he insisted that they see the less expensive caskets. He reminded the family that he covered the casket with a black pall before it entered the church and that the parish provided the only flowers. He urged his parishioners not to waste huge sums on the dead but to spend on the living. His ethical standards were in contrast to those of a highly fashionable New Haven undertaker, who argued that a man who drove a Cadillac should be buried in a bronze casket, his principle being – at least in the marketplace – "A man should be buried the way he lives."

In the spring of 1948 the presidential campaign was in full swing. As one might imagine, many of the Yale faculty and their graduate students supported Henry Wallace and his Progressive Party. Many of my fellow students urged me to support Wallace, but I always told them that a vote for Wallace was a vote for Dewey and a vote against every New Deal program they favored. For sticking with Truman and the Democratic Party, I found my liberalism questioned – absurdly, I thought – by many on the left. I would not realize the full implications of these attitudes until many years later.

That summer I returned to San Antonio and worked as an enumerator for the Bureau of the Census on a survey of manufacturers. As part of this survey I assisted the *patrón* of a tortilla factory with his census forms. Leaving his small establishment, I entered a narrow doorway and was suddenly on the inside of the same block of buildings I had been reviewing from without. Behind all of the storefronts, unseen from the streets, was a fetid barrio of hovels occupied by scores of families, a barrio without proper sanitation, and in which all families drew water from a single spigot.

When September came I entered the Law School of the University of Texas. There I had the privilege of studying constitutional law with Professor Jerre Williams, who completed his distinguished career on the Fifth Circuit Court of Appeals. Near the end of my first semester I told him I wanted to bring the rule of law to the families living in the barrios. The owners who rented out those hovels violated sanitation codes, fire codes, and doubtless many others. Professor Williams was sympathetic, but he explained that if I entered the barrios to solicit business, I would be committing barratry and be subject to disbarment. Two decades before they were invented, I was a premature storefront lawyer. A just society, I thought, must provide access to the law courts to all citizens; a society cannot be just if the rule of law is limited to persons of means. Those who cannot afford access to the courts do not live in a society of laws.

The following fall I returned to Yale to complete my PhD in Philosophy. After joining the faculty, I taught a course in the Master of Arts in Teaching program and for the first time came face-to-face with problems of the public schools. I was appalled by the way some teachers treated minority and poor children at an elementary school in which Yale placed students for their practice teaching. I was brought face-to-face with the fact that poor and minority children were being denied equal educational opportunity. This experience added to my experience of the lack of equal opportunity.

In 1955, I was back in Austin as an assistant professor of philosophy. In 1957, a spectacular soprano named Barbara Smith was thrown out of the School of Music's production of Purcell's *Dido and Aeneas* on the orders of the administration. The only objection to Miss Smith was that she was black. This objection had not been made by the faculty or administration, but by members of the legislature and by anonymous callers who threatened violence if Miss Smith appeared on stage with a white Aeneas. The University decided to knuckle under to threats of violence. I challenged that decision by presenting my objections privately and in writing to Chancellor Logan Wilson. He offered no moral or legal justification of the university's violation of Ms. Smith's constitutional rights, now clearly defined by the 1954 decision of the Supreme Court in *Brown v. Board of Education of Topeka*.

I then took my objections to the floor of the faculty council where they fell on largely deaf ears. Despite the fact that Ms. Smith's moral and legal rights were being violated, a committee of senior faculty, including Dean Page Keeton of the law school and other eminent "liberals," found that no reasonable person could disagree with the decision of the Chancellor. I observed then and have never forgotten that persons recognized as liberals sometimes behave as if they were autoimmune diseases designed to attack their own kind. Ms. Smith went on to a successful operatic career and often appeared under her married name of Barbara Smith Conrad.

The phenomenon of liberals attacking liberals was made clear when the *Texas Observer*, under the editorship of the Democrat Ronnie Dugger, endorsed a young Republican, John Tower, for the U.S. Senate and excoriated his elderly Democratic opponent, Coke Stevenson. I pointed out to Dugger that time would soon defeat Coke Stevenson, but that young John Tower would be a senator for decades to come. "Why," I asked, "do you want to be represented for many years by an extremely conservative Republican in order to avoid being represented for a few years by a moderately conservative Democrat?" I found no logical or causal nexus between Dugger's liberal objectives and his editorial policy.

The defection of the liberals elected John Tower and greatly aided the development of a two-party system in Texas. But Dugger had not supported Tower in behalf of a two-party system; he wished to purge a Democrat whose liberal credentials he correctly judged insufficient. The hostility of so-called liberals toward those who failed the liberal litmus test as they defined it led to the wholesale defection of liberal Democrats in the presidential race of 1968. They, not the Republicans, defeated Hubert Humphrey and elected Richard Nixon. There may have been good reasons to vote for Nixon, but there was no reason to believe that he was less committed to war in Vietnam than Humphrey, whose reservations about the war were well-known.

My credentials as a liberal were firmly established by my support of Barbara Smith Conrad and the fuller integration of the University of Texas. My standing was solidified when I helped organize the Texas Society to Abolish Capital Punishment and became its first chairman. In that position I wrote, spoke, and testified in favor of ending the death penalty in Texas. My opposition was not based on the mistaken view that it is wrong in principle to take a human life. The police, in order to save the lives of innocent victims, are frequently forced to kill persons intent on harming others. I also knew that there are serious crimes committed by rational people who deserve the death penalty. A man who bombs an airplane in flight to collect his wife's insurance offers an excellent example. But despite the need to satisfy the understandable public demand for vengeance, the death penalty as an appropriate means for dealing with murder is not so effective a deterrent nor as free from error as the alternative of life imprisonment. It poses unacceptable risks of executing the innocent, of setting the guilty free by juries unwilling to expose the defendant to the possibility of the death penalty, and of its inequitable imposition on the poor and the deranged, who are frequently sentenced to death not so much for their crimes as for their inability to hire a competent lawyer.

Death row in Huntsville, Texas, I observed, was occupied by poor blacks and Hispanics represented by court-appointed attorneys who, in most cases, had presented no evidence on behalf of their clients. These defendants had not received due process of law. Typically, their defense was nothing more than a closing speech to the jury. Quakers in Texas were disappointed that I did not oppose the death penalty in principle, but that did not lead them to expel me from the congregations of the righteous. They supported my work because they knew that on different principles we were working toward the same end.

Continuing my interest in the public schools, I wrote a short paper on the importance of preschool nurture in the home and pre-kindergarten programs in the schools. I sent this piece, which I called "Breaking the Cycle of Poverty," to Senator Ralph Yarborough, the doyen of the liberal wing of the Democratic Party in Texas. As a result, I was invited to Washington to work with Sargent Shriver on the committee that designed the Head Start program. I also evaluated proposals for Otis Singletary, the first director of the Job Corps, and was an occasional sounding board when he wished to review problems in its administration. These liberal initiatives were based on our duty as Americans to provide equality of opportunity and on the fact that equality was denied many children of the ghetto or from dysfunctional homes.

But later I opposed the movement by educators and legislators to confuse equality of opportunity with equality of achievement. That false doctrine destroyed the academic quality of many colleges and universities, including City College of New York, and led to the current classroom fad of treating self-esteem as an inherent right rather than as something to be earned. Television has gone still further, with one children's program having a theme song affirming "the most important person in the whole wide world is you, you, you."

I recount my activities at this length to show how unlikely it would be for anyone to regard me as anything but a liberal. But some persons equated liberals and Communists. I noted that John Birchers had begun attending my classes to record them. These thought police, defining political correctness in their fashion, brought a little innocent merriment to my classes when I would refute their curious notion that the United States could not be a democracy because it was a republic. I pointed out that a republic is a kind of democracy, just as a collie is a kind of dog. There was no question that the Birchers thought that far from being a liberal, I was a Communist. I suspect my FBI file contains transcripts of those lectures, sent thither by the Birchers in aid of their claims that I was a dangerous man. And I have no doubt that many conservative Texans who would never have joined the John Birch Society suspected that I was a fellow traveler.

I began to learn that ideologues, whether left or right, have great trouble in recognizing liberals because they don't know what liberalism means. They confuse the pursuit of goals believed to be liberal with the rigorous procedure of thought and observation by which the genuine liberal discovers his goals.

In 1967, I became dean of the College of Arts and Sciences just as the student protests at Berkeley, Columbia, and Cornell began to erupt. Eventually the movement came to Austin along with the SDS. By 1968, the democratic idealism of the Port Huron Statement had been severely compromised. Forgetting they were students for a democratic society, SDS assaulted the intellectual integrity of the university and academic freedom by using pressure tactics in an effort to determine administrative policy.

I observed the heady effects of "power" on Larry Caroline, a promising young philosopher whom I had personally recruited. He learned that if he addressed a crowd of protesters with outrageous and highly inflammatory statements, he was cheered on the spot and got his name in the papers. For this purpose, lies were as good as truths. Lies were often better, because contrary to conventional wisdom, although truth is sometimes stranger than fiction, this is not the way to bet. Among the lies he told students was that there were five concentration camps in the state of Texas posing a threat to his black brothers who were naturally fearful because of their existence. When I asked for locations of these camps, he had no answer; but he did not retract the claim.

This and other false statements aroused the ire of Frank Erwin, chairman of the Regents, who demanded that Caroline be fired. I responded that his contract had only a year to go, and his appointment had been conditional on his completing his dissertation, on which in the event he had done nothing. This fact alone would have made it extremely unlikely that the contract would be renewed, even had his political behavior been such that Erwin would have considered him a desirable son-in-law. Moreover, I considered his cynical abandonment of the pursuit of truth in favor of notoriety gained by lying to large crowds of students in the presence of the media as a violation of his obligations as a faculty member under AAUP principles. Consequently there was no need to violate his contract by firing him.

As might have been expected, of course, Caroline's claimed status as a political martyr gained him the support of activist junior faculty and even the support of some senior faculty who regarded his political views with amused contempt or downright detestation and thought him an academic layabout. The Department of Philosophy, over the objections of the chairman, voted by a small majority to extend his contract. I, as dean, vetoed the reappointment.

My friend Ronnie Dugger, reflecting the views of many others, argued that Caroline's place at the center of a political brawl in which conservatives were howling for his blood entitled him to a reappointment they would have admitted he did not deserve on academic grounds. Put bluntly, they were saying that the enemy of our enemy is our friend. Outside the academy, the right wing had long engaged in such politicization of the search for truth; now, with seeming enthusiasm, not merely leftists, but those who considered themselves liberals, joined in.

In his recent book *The Politics of Authenticity*, the historian Doug Rossinow writes that I, "the most prominent liberal on campus since the mid-fifties ... started moving toward his later neo-conservatism and worked to get Caroline fired." Aside from the erroneous claim about my having worked to fire Caroline when in fact I had argued before the Regents that he not be fired, this statement encapsulates the now widespread view in the academy that there can be no enemies on the left, and that no careers should suffer for academic deficiencies. It is largely forgotten that the AAUP stressed responsibility in the exercise of academic freedom. Today, few universities and colleges hold a professor when teaching to a higher standard of truth-telling than when he is speaking merely as a citizen. By widely accepted current standards, as long as one holds views accepted as politically correct, there can be no justification for removing a teacher even if that person fails to complete the dissertation, falsifies evidence, or encourages drug use by adolescent students, all of which Caroline did.*

This is a curious inversion of the liberal commitment to academic freedom, which defends the right of individuals to be politically incorrect. That quaint notion is in deep trouble, as is brilliantly and depressingly demonstrated by Alan Kors and Harvey Silverglate in *The Shadow University*.

Shortly after the Caroline case, I found myself fired as dean of my college over reasons unrelated to my political views or indeed any academic issue. But the justifications for my firing never failed to mention my left-wing views, and I came to have the reputation of a card-carrying liberal and, in the views of some, a card-carrying Marxist. This latter reputation, entirely undeserved, eased my way into the presidency of Boston University. My refusal to bow to the irrational demands of the SDS and the black power advocates and my refusal to overlook the incompetence and irresponsibility of Larry Caroline were evidently forgotten.

My name was called to the attention of the trustees of Boston University in the fall of 1970 by Professor Robert Cohen, who in 1948 as a fellow graduate student at Yale had solicited my support for Henry Wallace. He was a leading member of the Boston University faculty, having joined the University in the 1950s along with several other professors of Marxist or socialist persuasion. He wielded considerable influence on the search committee, which included two Marxist undergraduates, two graduate students sympathetic to radical student movements of the time, and faculty representatives including more than one Marxist, in addition to a handful of trustees and administrators.

After having met with the committee on several occasions and with other groups of students, faculty, administrators, and trustees, I was invited in November to a dinner meeting with the search committee and some others. Among these was a strongly anti-Marxist industrialist

---

*It is relevant to note that I was to hear from Caroline again. In 1987 he wrote me that he had returned to Judaism, become a follower of the Lubavitcher Rebbe, father of six children, and, now looking back at his earlier career from his new perspective, he said " ... I truly and literally thank G-d for giving me the opportunity to make amends for the damage I did then. In retrospect, I too would have tried to remove me from the university."

and intellectual named Arthur Metcalf. My support by some of the best-known Marxists on the faculty had alarmed some members of the board. They wanted Metcalf, the most knowledgeable trustee on the subject, to determine my political affiliation.

That evening, a student radical asked me my opinion of the revolutionary movement. I asked him which revolutionary movement he had in mind. He looked deeply confused. Trying to be helpful, I added, "As you know, there is a Marxist revolutionary movement and a Leninist revolutionary movement." He now looked more confused. I added, "Well, as you know, Marx believed that the revolutionary party was coextensive with the working class. And that, of course, is utopian idealism. You can't organize the working class much better than you can organize farmers. Lenin, on the other hand, held that the revolutionary party was an intellectual elite that would lead the working class. And you don't need to ask me my opinion of that revolutionary movement. Its success was demonstrated in October of 1917."

The committee was awash with enthusiasm, impressed with my mastery of the Marxist argot and the Marxists among them anticipated that as president I would establish the People's Republic of Boston University. Metcalf, however, recognized my answers not as advocacy but as the response of a knowledgeable teacher. He reported to the trustees that I was not a communist, and in due course I was offered and accepted the presidency. Members of the search committee and the faculty members to whom they reported disagreed with Metcalf's assessment and were sure of my Marxist credentials. Ideologues, as Marxists are, do not listen carefully; otherwise they would never have been misled about my position. Within months, however, the truth began to out as bit by bit I was exposed as a liberal – or, to use their term of art, a fascist.

I was committed to an open campus on which all invited guests could speak without regard to their point of view, a campus on which any company or institution engaged in a lawful enterprise could recruit, including all branches of the United States Military. My administration would not tolerate the occupation of University buildings or the blocking of their entrances by student mobs.

I was also opposed to allowing minorities a tyranny no one would accept from majorities. The university had for a half century hosted the

ROTC. Faculty radicals had harassed our ROTC units until they withdrew from the campus. I believed the majority of the faculty wanted ROTC, and I ordered a confidential survey by Price Waterhouse sent to the home addresses of the faculty to determine their point of view. Two-thirds of the faculty voted to restore ROTC. They believed, as did I, that civilian control of the military was better ensured when a significant percentage of officers are educated in civilian institutions rather than in military academies. I was also concerned to restore financial aid through scholarships provided by ROTC. In due course, ROTC was restored to the campus. The restoration was proof in the minds of ideologues that I was no liberal.

When Angela Davis was invited to speak on campus advocating revolution, there was no opposition. But when Urie Bronfenbrenner was invited to speak, the situation proved quite different. Professor Bronfenbrenner had published an article in 1967 in which he argued that many black Americans received brutally inadequate prenatal and postnatal care, resulting in grave physical and psychological damage. One would have thought that his attempt to document one of the most vicious consequences of racism would have made Bronfenbrenner something of a hero to the left. But a group of SDS students demonstrated their determined opposition to hearing from that mild, thoughtful scholar. How, I asked, could any true liberal or one respectful of free speech justify disrupting a speaker on the campus of a university?

Robert Cohen, then dean of the College of Liberal Arts, urged me to cancel the invitation on grounds that there might be violence. I told him as years earlier I had told Chancellor Logan Wilson when he canceled the opera performance of Barbara Smith Conrad that civilization does not abdicate in the face of barbarians: it calls the police. I arranged for a dozen or more police officers to be stationed on each side of the lecture hall while Professor Bronfenbrenner spoke. It was a nonviolent but sad affair. In response to hostile questions from the crowd, Bronfenbrenner recanted the views unpalatable to his audience, confessing his errors in the manner of a defendant in a Moscow show trial. His recantation was not enough; a leftist academic present at the lecture announced that Bronfenbrenner's recantation was insincere. Andrei Vyshinsky, Stalin's prosecutor in the purge trials, would have approved.

The student left attempted to suppress another basic human right, that of free association. When recruiters from the Marine Corps came to campus, a small mob blocked access to the building where fellow students wanted to meet with the recruiters. I went down to talk with the protesters. I explained that they were violating First Amendment rights of other students and said that they could continue to protest peacefully as long as they respected the rights of others. When they continued to block the entrance, I said that I would make a civilian arrest for trespass and they could make their case in court. They were outraged by the suggestion and continued the blockade. At that point, I called the police to the campus to remove them and restore the rights of their fellow students. This civilized use of force was a liberal imperative, necessary to assure an open campus on which First Amendment rights are respected.

Our administration kept an open campus to ensure the exercise of First Amendment rights and the rights of free assembly no matter how hard activist faculty and students tried to shut it down. One eminent captain of the Thought Police was Howard Zinn. When our Latin-American Development Center organized an international conference, *Quo Vadis Latin America*, attended by, among others, Presidents Eduardo Frei of Chile and Lleras Restrepo of Colombia, Zinn attempted with the help of his students to disrupt it. The police had to be called to restore order and remove the disrupters. It was once again a civilized use of force to preserve academic freedom and our rights to free speech and assembly. The Zinn principle could be summed up as holding that all academics were entitled to academic freedom, but that some academics were not.

The example of Howard Zinn shows how far we have come from the liberal ideal, practiced by Socrates and developed by Milton and Mill. Socrates taught us to prize those persons of knowledge, candor, and good will who challenge our views, and to be especially grateful when we are shown to be mistaken. For then we exchange a false opinion for a truer one. The Socratic dialectic is not dissimilar to the scientific method, which proceeds by proposing hypotheses to be tested by logical analysis for their conceptual coherence and tested empirically for their confirmation or disproof by relevant facts. Apart from divine revelation, to which I am not privileged, there is no means of attaining absolute truth. Our confidence in the outcome of a Socratic argument or a scientific experiment derives not from our trust in positive proofs, but essentially on our inability to disprove it. We never reach the truth but only the likeliest account, which may require revision or even rejection on the basis of subsequent evidence and argument.

It follows that those who seek the truth as closely as is humanly possible will not begin with conclusions and then look for arguments and facts to support them. Rather, they will examine all relevant facts and arguments in the hope of finally arriving at the truest account of the subject of their inquiry. Those who follow the former procedure have abandoned the search for truth in the defense of an ideology from which they will not deviate no matter what contravening arguments or evidence may be presented. Those who seek the truth, by contrast, will follow the second procedure of inquiry and their conclusions will in consequence be subject to change.

A position on the left may not be liberal just as one on the right may not be conservative. A true liberal does not adhere to leftist ideology but follows evidence and argument to a reasoned conclusion. Liberals will arrive at their position not at the outset but only at the end of their search. For this reason no liberal – unless he or she abandons the search for truth – can be found on the left of every issue.

Liberals who hold fast to any set of doctrines without regard to the existence of contravening arguments and evidence betray liberalism and cease to be liberals. E. B. White provided a useful guide for liberalism: "To pursue truth, one should not be too deeply entrenched in any hole."

This is not to suggest that the liberal will have no fixed opinions, for there are some facts that never change and some arguments that are not refuted. But it is generally true, as the old hymn puts it, that "time makes ancient good uncouth." The world is in flux and if one is an honest seeker of truth one's views must change as experience dictates.

But there are limits on how far one can change one's views and still deserve the name of liberal. One is not a liberal but an ideologue if one joins the thought police to enforce political correctness in society and especially in schools and colleges. One abandons liberalism for ideology. A liberal defends and sometimes exercises the right to be politically incorrect in the Socratic and Millian pursuit of the truest account. Whether evidence or argument leads one to the left or right, one remains a liberal and has every right to object when pejoratively described as a conservative.

Paradoxically, it may be that those of us – whether on the left or the right at any one time – who adhere to the Millian procedure of inquiry in the development of our positions are all conservative in the sense that we conserve a methodology begun by Socrates and essential to all scientific thought. But since this mode of thought was systematically presented by Mill in defining liberalism, those of us who follow that method are justified in calling ourselves liberals and may expect to be recognized as such. (That Mill occasionally violated his liberal principles in no way compromises their nature and importance.) The procedure defines the essence of liberalism, even if well-intentioned liberals occasionally slip into mere ideology.

Many today who wear their liberalism on their sleeves are far from liberal. The rigidity of their adherence to dogmas exposes them as ideologues. And their use of conservative as a pejorative epithet is without justification. Many conservatives adhere to the liberal procedure of inquiry to the best of their ability but while following evidence and argument arrive at conclusions that are right wing. There are also ideologues on the right who use evidence and argument only to support antecedent conclusions. They are more accurately described as dogmatic reactionaries.

If we follow the prevalent but mistaken practice of identifying "liberal" with left-wing objectives and "conservative" with right-wing objectives, we will find persons, such as myself, called conservatives who, on the basis of evidence and argument, support politically correct liberal objectives such as abolition of capital punishment, early childhood education, and affirmative action. But we may be called conservatives because the same procedures of thought lead us to reject as nonsense the views of those who claim privileged access to truth, some unique power of understanding based on gender, race, ethnicity, or some other special dispensation from the hard work required to arrive at the truest account.

Whenever one uses a set of beliefs as a liberal litmus test, one has confused liberalism with dogmatism. One may be a dogmatic adherent to a leftist ideology that defines a revolutionary position, or an adherent to a rightist ideology that defines an equally revolutionary position. Neither is liberal. The anti-abortionist who is prepared to kill those who support abortion is not a conservative, but a revolutionary. Those who, like Herbert Marcuse, are tolerant only of the positions they accept are not liberals but revolutionaries. In "Repressive Tolerance," published in 1969, Marcuse advanced the notion that there was no freedom to be wrong and that right could be determined by the voice of a mass meeting however nonrepresentative or small it might be. Thus Marcuse rejected the liberal concept of a free marketplace of ideas in which all positions are allowed to compete on the basis of evidence and argument. He proposed instead to permit only liberating tolerance, that is only "toleration of movements from the left [extending] the scope of this tolerance ... to the stage of action as well as of discussion and propaganda, of deed as well as word."

The ideologist of the left is no more liberal than the ideologist of the right, for neither believes in humility before the facts and logic, respect for the experience and views of others, and the importance of making a supreme effort to avoid irrationality. Reactionaries and revolutionaries betray conservatism and liberalism alike.

Those who move with some tentativeness and uncertainty as experience and judgment guide them to the best and wisest conclusions of which they are capable, they alone deserve to be called liberals and may claim that name with pride.

Roadblocks to Education Reform

"The reform of education does not turn on money but rather on how it is spent. We should recruit excellent teachers by doubling their salaries."

In 1996, Governor William Weld appointed me Chairman of the Massachusetts Board of Education, with oversight and responsibility for the Department of Education and the primary and secondary schools of the Commonwealth. As is customary on occasions when a governor wishes to make it appear that he is doing something bold and dynamic, Governor Weld's speech appointing me was dramatic and colorful. He referred to me as the "education czar." There was irony in this description. Knowing the history of Russia well, the governor made it appear as if he were thinking of Czar Alexander the Great or at least of Ivan the Terrible. But he really had in mind Czar Nicholas, known for his impotence as he awaited execution by Lenin. Governor Weld offered me a title, but neither he, members of the legislature, nor his successor, Governor Cellucci, removed the restraints that hobbled the position right from the start.

As Chairman of the Board of Education I was asked frequently to report on the quality of our schools. The speech grew with each telling until it became a summary of what I had observed as of May 1999. It became clear that additional funding for education without radical structural reform is largely wasted. In this book I have, with one exception, not offered updates on the numbers cited, but all are substantially larger than they were in 1999.

WE STAND AT the cusp of a new millennium. The year 2000 is only seven months away. When New Year's Day 2000 comes along, we shall still be one year shy of the new millennium. But Americans are impatient people, and we shall introduce the new millennium one year in advance. The numerological allure of the year 2000 is simply irresistible, not only here but also, I suspect, all over the world.

In the field of education, you will recall that the year 2000 should bring in a New Jerusalem. In 1990, President George H. W. Bush and the governors of all our states declared that by the year 2000,

All children in America will start school ready to learn. High school graduation rates will increase to at least 90 percent. All students will leave grades four, eight and twelve having demonstrated competency over challenging subject matter, including English, mathematics, science, foreign language, civics and government, economics, arts, history and geography. Every school in America will ensure that all students learn to use their minds well so they may be prepared for responsible citizenship, further learning and productive employment in our nation's modern economy. American students will be first in the world in mathematics and science achievement. Every adult American will be literate and will possess the knowledge and skills necessary to compete in a global economy and exercise the rights and responsibilities of citizenship. Every school in the United States will be free of drugs, violence and unauthorized presence of firearms and alcohol, and will offer a disciplined environment conducive to learning.

Just think: that educational Promised Land is only a few months away. I can hardly wait. But are we any closer than we were in 1990 when the promise was made? Since 1990, we have increased our budget for primary and secondary education by 38 percent or $79 billion, from $208 billion to $287 billion.* The budget of the Department of Education has grown 74 percent, from $31 billion in 1990 to $54 billion in 1998. Public school teachers' salaries have kept up with inflation and increased slightly, from $34,153 to $34,385 in constant dollars. In Massachusetts, teachers' salaries not only kept up with inflation but also increased by 27 percent in constant dollars from 1990 to 1997. Even with these increases the salaries are inadequate today to recruit women of outstanding skills, while other expenditures of vast sums of money on education have proven ineffective.

---

*These numbers we now know are a pale indication of the huge increases that have followed since 1990. Recent figures put the total at more than $500 billion.

SAT scores appear to have risen from 896 to 1019, which seems a glorious improvement. This improvement in the SAT scores is, however, illusory. The Educational Testing Service recentered all scores in 1995, resulting in a declaration of progress in education reform by discarding one of the few objective, longitudinal standards available for measuring educational achievement. Their justification for recentering was that they wished to keep the mean of the combined verbal and mathematical scores at about 1000 – 500 for each. Since scores were dropping, scoring had to be revised. The recentered score is increased by 103 points, from 896 to 999. Our apparent progress is reduced to an actual increase of only twenty points, from 999 in 1990 to 1019 in 1998.

This, like the "Goals 2000," is merely progress by declaration, progress by words alone. They have all the reality of the declarations of the Queen of Hearts and the Mad Hatter. In truth, there continues to be a crisis in American education.

It is impossible to discuss trends in education reform without generalizing. People often object to this, saying, "Well, that's just a generalization." The fact is, we cannot live or function without making generalizations. Consider, for example, the safety of food. I believe we would all agree with the statement that the food supply in our country is safe. But you cannot claim that all food is safe because sometimes there is an outbreak of food poisoning. But these exceptions are sufficiently infrequent that we can and do assume that food and drink in our homes, stores, and restaurants are wholesome. It is also a generalization that air travel is safe despite infrequent crashes.

A sound generalization applies accurately to a majority of the members of a class. We must distinguish generalizations from stereotypes, which are statements about a class of individuals or institutions that actually apply to only a few. We say, for example, that the English have no sense of humor, yet the English are perhaps the funniest people on earth. Witness Shakespeare, witness On The Fringe, and so many other groups of English comedians. We say that Germans are square-headed and we know from Chancellor Kohl that their heads are pear-shaped. These are stereotypes. They say that Texans are tall, wear cowboy boots and Stetson hats, that they're rich and they're loud. Now, I am a Texan, and I may be loud at times, but I have none of the other characteristics. Those are stereotypes.

In addition, one can make universal statements about classes, institutions, and individuals that are true of all of them. We are all going to die. If you object to that universal statement, your objection should not be delivered to me but rather to God. It is simply true that we are all going to die.

So we need to keep in mind stereotypes, which I shall try to avoid, universal propositions, which I will occasionally use, and generalizations, which are necessary for understanding.

The evidence of our educational crisis was well documented in 1983 in a blue ribbon committee report called *A Nation at Risk*. The committee pointed out that from 1963 to 1980, average SAT scores fell by 50 percent – eventually leading to the recalibration of the test that I mentioned earlier. There has been a precipitous decline in the number of students who score higher than 650 on the SAT. Science achievement scores have steadily declined. In international testing in math and science, the U.S. comes out near the very bottom. There has been a decline in the number of students completing high school with advanced algebra; now most do not even take intermediate algebra. In 1983, only 13 percent of students studied a foreign language.

The decline in the competency of students has been matched by a decline in the intellectual ability of teachers. The committee that wrote *A Nation at Risk* noted that those entering the teaching profession come from the bottom quartile of their high school classes. They are by and large the weakest students in colleges and universities. This, I remind you, is a generalization and not a universal statement. If you are a teacher and were not in the bottom quartile of your high school or college class, I am not talking about you. But the generalization is sound: We are now recruiting teachers from the lowest quartile of our high schools and colleges.

In 1967, college graduates with an IQ of 130 and those with an IQ of 100 were almost equally likely to enter teaching. Those with an IQ of 130 were very bright, while those whose IQ was 100 were only average. By 1980, graduates with an IQ of 100 were four times as likely to become teachers as were those with an IQ of 130. This is a disastrous decline.

We also know that in the United States persons who enter schools of education score on average 50 points below the national average on the SAT. In Massachusetts there is one state college in which the average combined SAT score for students in education is 740. Since one gets 400 by signing one's name, a person with 740 SATs would not even interest an athletic coach who insists that his players be smart enough to know which goal is theirs. That is not the worst of it. There is a private college in Massachusetts whose education students have an average SAT of 598.

The situation at Boston University is different. The combined SAT score for students entering our School of Education is 1238, 240 points above the national average and even higher than that above the Massachusetts average. To achieve these results, we were forced to restrict freshman admissions. We reduced enrollment from 489 students in 1970 to 98 in 1996, costing us about $35 million. We now have about 100 exceptionally well qualified individuals in each undergraduate class where we could have had at least 200 if we lowered our standards. But there are not many universities willing to forego about $35 million in tuition to maintain the integrity of their program.

The standards at Boston College and Harvard are equally outstanding, but the overall evidence clearly supports the generalization that schools of education are inadequate and that a significant number of teachers are lacking in the ability they must have to teach.

We know some of the reasons for the decline in the quality of our teachers. One major contributing factor which we sometimes overlook because so many of its consequences have been highly positive is the movement for equal rights for women. This movement has created choices that were denied to women in previous generations. They now may choose among all the professions – education, the military, medicine, legal, business, financial. Indeed there is no profession or enterprise in the United States today that is denied to women who aspire to achieve in that field.

Enormous talent, intelligence, and energies have been released. There have always been individual women who made great contributions – Joan of Arc on the field of battle, Madame Curie in the laboratory, poets and authors in literature. But now there is a flood-tide of gifted women who enliven and advance all the professions and thrive in thousands of jobs.

No one would now say, as President Charles Eliot of Harvard said as late as 1869, that "the world knows next to nothing about the natural mental capacities of the female sex." No thoughtful person questions the ability of women to succeed in colleges, or wishes to deny them the opportunities now open to them. Certainly not I. With six daughters, I have been pleased to support their entry into careers that enhance their fulfillment.

With all of its positive effects, I think we must also acknowledge that securing equal rights for women is perhaps the most important reason for the decline in the quality of public school teachers. When those rights were denied, women of high IQ, denied other opportunities, chose the teaching profession. Despite inadequate compensation, brilliant women became teachers out of a natural love of children and of teaching and also because the school calendar gave them maximum opportunity to be home with their own children. Teachers were held in high esteem by parents grateful for the inspired teaching by these gifted women. Now highly intelligent and gifted women are less often found in the classroom, and respect for teachers has declined.

The extraordinarily able teachers I had in school in the 1930s and 1940s are now found on the faculties of colleges and universities or in administration. And schools of education have lowered their standards to accommodate the lesser abilities of students planning to be teachers. Many accept students whose IQs are lower than those of the children they will teach. The result has been the certification of teachers of limited ability and limited competence in the English language or in their subject matter.

During the years I served as Chairman of the Board of Education of Massachusetts, I observed many deficiencies during extensive classroom visitations. To select among numerous examples: a geometry class in which neither the teacher nor the students knew the axioms or postulates on which geometric proofs depend; English classes taught in Spanish because the teacher (although certified as bilingual) was not competent in English.

I went to an elementary school in central Massachusetts where they had posted the work of fourth-grade children on bulletin boards. Here are some samples of what I read. "When ice cools, the molecules slow down and melt." Molecules, of course, don't melt. This may show the folly of trying to introduce molecular science at the fourth grade. There are many things a child can learn in the fourth grade, but molecular theory may not be one of them. But if it is to be taught in the fourth grade, why post the work of pupils who fail to understand it? And why post this example of ignorance without any indication that it is wrong?

Now another example: "Hitler wanted more land for Germany and Japan and fought for Japan as if it could not do the work." No one would have been more surprised than Hitler or Hirohito to find out that Germany was fighting the war to win land for Japan. Again, I ask, why was this work posted on the board as if it were exemplary?

I know funny things happen in school; I am not criticizing the child who came up with this bizarre idea. Revisionist history is commonplace these days, and there is no reason why fourth graders should not get into the act. But someone should have corrected the child.

An English teacher asked her students to rewrite the *Gettysburg Address* in their own words. That is an exciting, demanding assignment. No one supposes that in order to get a good grade a child has to improve on Lincoln, but it was interesting to see the ways in which these children decided to rewrite the *Gettysburg Address*. One child wrote, "*Lady's* and Gentleman, we are here at a *berial* ground...." This was the work of a fourth grader, a ten- or eleven-year-old. And it was posted without having been corrected.

I called the superintendent over, showed him this example, and asked, "Isn't this embarrassing? First of all, the handwriting is egregiously bad" (it was partly cursive, partly printed, some slanted to the left, some to the right, some big, some small) "but that aside, what about the spelling? Don't you think correct spelling is a good idea? None of the mistakes in this paper have been marked or corrected. How are children to learn when there are no marks indicating the mistakes?" The superintendent became indignant. He said, "You don't understand, we have to encourage these students. Of course these students make mistakes because they are here to learn." I said, "Of course they are here to learn. But how are they going to learn if you don't correct their mistakes?"

"Well, we don't want to discourage them. We are not trying to put them down, we are trying to boost their confidence."

Nonsense such as this comes straight out of schools of education, where they declare that self-esteem is not something a child earns, but rather is something that ought to be given every child. But does any non-educationist believe a child would have been discouraged if that teacher had called him in and said, "You know, this is a very interesting paper, but you have made some errors in spelling. I would like to put your paper on the board. I would like for all the other children to see your work. Before we do that, though, you need to correct these mistakes. I've put circles around them. I haven't told you what the right answers are, because you know how to find out the right answers. I have indicated the mistakes and when you have corrected them and rewritten this, I am going to post it on the board where everyone will see the fine work you've done." That would not discourage the child. To the contrary, it would build him up, inspire him to work harder and do better.

When I commented about all the terrible writing and printing, the superintendent said, "Thank God we don't teach handwriting. We are not holding children responsible for handwriting in this school. I couldn't pass that test either." Well, it is time for that school district to look for a superintendent who is educated and can write. It is not unreasonable to expect a professional educator to write in a legible hand and to insist on high standards. The idea that computers, spell-check, and calculators are substitutes for handwriting, spelling, and the capacity to do mathematics is nonsense. Are we going to produce a generation of persons who are utterly ignorant if the electricity is turned off? Education has to be something that the individual carries with him. It cannot be dependent on a gadget he carries.

The evidence for the inadequacy of a significant percentage of our teachers and prospective teachers is not merely anecdotal; it was confirmed when Massachusetts was finally able to test the competence of teachers. Perhaps the most important initiative of the Board of Education under my leadership was to implement a law that had been passed in 1985. Eleven years had passed without the Board of Education doing anything to implement a law that required all prospective teachers to pass an examination as a condition of their certification. Our Board was appointed in February of 1996, and by November of that year we had unanimously passed a resolution to require that all persons seeking certification after January 1998 would have to pass two tests: one in literacy and one in the subject matter they were to teach.

The proposal was resisted, of course. The president of a teachers' union declared, "There is no test that will demonstrate my ability to transfer the knowledge in my mind into the minds of my pupils." I replied, "Quite right. But there are several tests that will show us whether there is any knowledge in your mind that might conceivably be transferred into the minds of your pupils."

The purpose of our literacy test was not to determine someone's teaching ability but whether he or she had the knowledge and competence in the English language necessary to be an effective teacher.

The test has now been given several times. The results have been shocking. Sixty percent failed the test the first time around in April of 1998, and 30 percent failed the test at the most recent administration this past January 1999. There is great improvement in reducing the failure rate from 60 to 30 percent. But it is still shocking when you consider the quality of the test. A few examples will enable you to judge whether the test is an accurate measure of the minimal English-language competence or incompetence of teachers.

The handwriting of most of those taking the test was egregiously bad, about the level one would expect of a backward third-grader.

Spelling mistakes by test-takers indicated sheer illiteracy. *Management* was spelled *managmant*. One prospective teacher wrote, "At the present time this policy is in *affect.*" Do we want our children to be educated by a teacher who does not know the difference between *affect* and *effect*?

This person went on to write, "This policy called for fires to be fought *viscourously*" – a vigorously wrong spelling. "This *lead* to large quantities of dead wood on the forest floors," it goes on. Can we not expect a teacher to know the difference between a gray metal that can be melted at a relatively low temperature and the past tense of the word "lead"? Then the prospective teacher writes, "It is also *belived* that the old policy was unnatural and that by fighting fires so *vigerouslly* it killed wildlife and the wilderness." Here is a different misspelling of "vigorously," as well as the grammatical mistake that attributes the fighting of fires to a policy rather than persons. But when the test-taker spells "believed" as "belived," isn't it time to say "enough"?

These misspellings were due not only to ignorance but to deficient intelligence as well, for most of the misspellings were of words that were correctly spelled in the article the teachers were asked to summarize. To fail to spell a word correctly that is printed in the text reflects on the intelligence of the test taker.

To find out whether teachers or potential teachers knew enough English grammar and syntax to be able to write down what they heard, candidates were also tested on their ability to transcribe a passage from *The Federalist Papers*. The passage, read to them slowly, three times, with a minute between each reading, went as follows:

> No man is allowed to be a judge in his own cause, because his interest would certainly bias his judgment, and, not improbably, corrupt his integrity. With equal, nay with greater reason, a body of men are unfit to be both judges and parties at the same time.... It is in vain to say that enlightened statesmen will be able to adjust these clashing interests, and render them all subservient to the public good. Enlightened statesmen will not always be at the helm.

Most persons taking the test could not reconstruct these sentences in a syntactically correct way and did not know how to spell several of the words. For example, "integrity" was misspelled "integerty," "legislation" misspelled "legistration," "citizens" became "citzians," and so on. The next-to-last sentence became, "It is in vain to say that *enlighten* statesmen will be able to adjust these *flashing* interests, and *rendor* them all *subservant* to the public good."

Those objecting to the test claimed that it was a passage with obscure eighteenth-century language and a very convoluted syntax that made it impossible for teachers to know how to handle it. But there were no unusual words or words that had declined in use in the twentieth century. And the construction of the sentences was not complex. The passage was straightforward, but the illiteracy it revealed is widespread and profound. When I was in school, oral dictation was required on a regular basis. Any of us in the eighth grade could have transcribed these sentences with ease.

These mistakes are not isolated examples. They characterize the majority of those taking the exam the first time. These facts support the generalization that those seeking certification were inadequate. This is not to blame or to accuse any individual. Those who were deficient were not fully responsible for being unprepared. How did they graduate from high school? Who admitted such ill-educated persons to college? Who graduated such persons from college? What institutions presented those graduates for certification? Who ever told them that they might be qualified to be teachers? The major responsibility lies with those who educated them and those who hired them.

Unfortunately, I could not muster the support required to deny certification to schools of education that failed to meet reasonable standards. This would have been a much more effective means of raising the quality of prospective teachers than waiting until the last moment to discover their lack of competence and deny them certification.

This is why a genuine reformer must change the standards of the field. It is a tough task, particularly so because any reformer will hear that bogus complaint, "*You're bashing teachers.*" I am not bashing teachers; I have the highest regard for the teaching profession, and that is why I believe the standards of that profession have to be raised. The accusation is a red herring; it is even the case that those teachers in the field who are doing an absolutely first-rate job are criticized by less-demanding colleagues. I am trying to put a stop to the bashing of children by incompetent professors of education and incompetent teachers.

There are many ways in which schools of education fail to prepare even qualified students to become competent teachers. One is the embarrassing habit of concocting absurd ideas and fads to replace established methods of instruction. For example, approximate math is an invention of schools of education. What is the point of approximate math? Would you get into a spaceship and take off to the moon according to approximate math? You would not even want to drive your car and plan gas mileage on the basis of approximate math. You would not go to a grocery store and let them charge you on the basis of approximate addition. At times exactitude is necessary, and if an answer is not right, it's wrong. Mathematics is one of the few areas in which we can expect, indeed demand, a high level of precision and exactitude.

Another folly spawned by educationists is the look-say method of teaching reading – also called the whole-language method – according to which English is taught as if it were Chinese. A principal guru of this method is Professor Kenneth S. Goodman of the University of Arizona. He teaches that "reading [is] a psycholinguistic guessing game," that reading and writing are just as instinctive as speaking, and that children learn to read and write just as they learn to talk. The folly of his claim is shown by the fact that any number of human cultures, some with extraordinary artistic achievement, never developed writing. We have hundreds of American Indian tribes, all with a spoken language, none of whom developed a written language on their own. Professor Goodman might as well claim that the wheel is instinctive.

The whole-language approach goes hand-in-hand with the devaluation of phonics. Devaluing the importance of sounding out a word to find the meaning, whole-language teachers encourage children to guess at the written word without understanding how it sounds phonetically.

The high cost of this fallacious and foolish program has become evident. There is a positive correlation between the decline of literacy in this country and the abandonment of phonics in favor of the look-say or whole language method. At the request of Congress, the National Institute of Child Health and Human Development made a longitudinal study of the decline in the ability of children to read. Congress was concerned about the rapid increase in the number of children diagnosed with special educational needs, excluding the constant percentage of children with learning disabilities or obvious neurological or physiological needs. Although autism and some learning disabilities have increased to some extent, the percentage of children who are deaf, blind, in wheelchairs, who have Down syndrome or some other learning disability has remained relatively constant. But there has been a geometric increase in the number of children with special needs.

The National Institute of Child Health and Human Development found that deficiency in phonemic awareness is a fundamental cause of the increase in the number of children with special needs. Forty percent of our children have a deficiency in phonemic awareness, that is, in the ability to relate symbols on a page to sounds. If you look at the word "cat," can you understand or hear the "kuh" and the short "a," and the "tuh"? Forty percent of our children have difficulty and 20 percent have a serious deficiency in phonemic awareness. Their experience showed that the beginning reader should never guess at a word, never skip a word, and should learn to sound out words. Research showed that with early intervention, phonemic deficiency can be entirely overcome. Rigorous phonetic exercises as early as possible would enhance the recovery of dyslexic children.

In earlier generations the emphasis on phonics – on developing phonemic awareness – was standard practice. In 1930 there were 1.7 children in the first grade for every child in the second grade for the simple reason that if the child had not learned to read adequately – and phonetics was the primary method used at that time – the teachers held the child back for another year. Teachers concentrated on phonemic awareness until the child was ready to advance to the second grade. Now with social promotion we have only 1.1 children in the first grade for every child in the second grade, and many in the second grade are not prepared to learn to read.

Social promotion is another tenet of schools of education, designed to enhance self-esteem. That is one of the reasons given in support of approximate math. We do not want to make a child feel bad because he or she cannot read or calculate that 7 plus 5 is 12. But think about how the child's feelings will be hurt in later years if he or she is illiterate or has to rely on approximate math to find an answer. Being promoted while failing to learn is far more damaging to the child than failure to be promoted until the skills necessary to succeed are acquired. The inability of inadequately educated adults to gain employment and fulfillment is a tragic consequence of the failure to require essential skills in the earliest years of a child's education.

For professors in schools of education, an assault on memory as a component of learning is standard practice. Memory is denigrated as "rote memory." Educators should know that the absence of memory is Alzheimer's. There is nothing more horrible in our experience than the loss of memory; it is the loss of identity.

How can we teach foreign language without requiring memorization? The first framework developed by the Massachusetts Foreign Language Association was an educationist assault on memory in teaching a foreign language. The Board rejected the framework, for it is impossible to teach a foreign language if children do not have to memorize foreign words. If you do not know that *la mesa* is "the table" in Spanish, how will you learn to speak Spanish? It is impossible to learn a language without memorizing its vocabulary.

Why should memory be denigrated as *rote* memory? A history teacher asks a child to remember 1066. Why? Not because it is close to 1166, a cologne made in Germany. Nor is it numerologically important. But 1066 is the date of the Norman Conquest. When England was conquered, the Anglo-Saxon language was transformed by French. Thus began the formation of the English language, the melding of French and Anglo-Saxon that gave rise to Chaucer's Middle English and later to Shakespeare and the full glory of our tongue. The Normans, originally from Scandinavia, had conquered most of Western Europe and had a genius for government and law. The governmental structures in France and in England today are to a very significant degree their heritage from the Normans. The year 1066 is a date around which we can organize an era of history and illuminate our present language and our present forms of government.

Think of the implications of the assault on memory. You are in the operating room about to be operated on by a surgeon. He is going to operate on your heart but cannot remember which organ it is; or cannot remember which nerves control the pulse. Which are veins, which are arteries? Having attended a school of education, he says to his colleagues, "There's no reason for me to remember all this, because as I learned in school, I know how to find out. Please bring me a book on surgery so I can look it up." This is ridiculous, but it is the sort of nonsense generated by schools of education. It is Orwellian in its dimension – that is, it is nonsense so bad only an intellectual could believe it.

Departments of Education contribute their own obstacles to education reform. The Massachusetts Department of Education is composed by and large of dedicated people, but most are educationists dedicated to the ideologies promulgated by schools of education. They stoutly resisted all efforts I and other individuals made to reform the Department of Education. But as the governing body for the requirements imposed on students and teachers, it must be reformed if there is to be reform in education.

The Massachusetts Educational Reform Act of 1993 had charged the Board and the Department of Education with developing Frameworks to guide and test student competency in various areas. During my tenure as Chairman of the Board of Education, the Department submitted unacceptable frameworks in English and language arts, in history and social science, in foreign language and in health. Their standards and their judgment were inadequate. Finding that the quality of their appointments to the drafting committees was inadequate, we proposed to upgrade them.

For example: in drafting frameworks in mathematics and science it is important to have not only some high school teachers on the committee but also some genuine experts in those fields. This is equally true with regard to all academic subjects. But efforts by Dean Edwin Delattre and me to appoint more university faculty to the frameworks committees were met with all too typical bureaucratic inertia. The Board of Education managed to squeeze only one or two faculty onto some of the committees. (We did succeed in putting highly competent musicians, artists, and dancers on the committee to design the framework for the arts.)

Nowhere was the resistance of the Department of Education to reform more apparent than with regard to the test for prospective teachers. The Board of Education determined in November 1996 that no teachers would be certified in Massachusetts after January 1, 1998, unless they had passed a test in the English language and in the subject matter they would be teaching. This decision was reiterated on January 21, 1998, when notice of the teacher test was mailed to all superintendents. It stated that "the law requires candidates for initial teacher certification to meet several requirements including the passing of two tests: a test in communication and literacy skills and a test in the subject matter knowledge for the certificate area chosen by the candidate."

On January 28 the commissioner notified not only superintendents but also education deans and presidents of colleges and universities that public information meetings would be held. He said that consistent with our law, teacher certification candidates were required to pass this test. Then sometime later in that month a question-and-answer booklet on the Massachusetts test was published by the Department of Education. The booklet included the statement that candidates who were to take the test on either April 4 or July 11, 1998, would "satisfy the requirements automatically."

This was treason of the clerks – and I use that term advisedly. The Department of Education, by means of this booklet, attempted to nullify the unanimous vote of the Board of Education. I had to tell the commissioner of the Department of Education to repudiate that mistake and restore our policy. "As Commissioner of Education," I told him, "you should know that if the Department of Education subverts the decisions of the Board of Education, the person responsible will be fired for cause." Unfortunately, I lacked the political backing to make good on this promise.

The Department of Education attempted to and eventually succeeded in subverting another decision of the Board. We know that if children do not read well by the third grade, they are candidates for failure and dropout, and so the Board introduced the Iowa Test to assess according to a national scale how well Massachusetts children could read at the third-grade level. We found that a very high percentage were not reading at grade level, and we recognized the need to introduce the test at the end of second grade to be sure that children did not leave second grade for third until they were reading at grade level. The Board voted to request a supplemental budget of $700,000 from the legislature to support the giving of the Iowa Test at the end of second grade.

Those decisions were forgotten. A member of the Department of Education announced, without the approval of the Board, that the MCAS test for third grade reading would replace the Iowa Test. This was a serious error of judgment. The Iowa Test is useful because it has been given all over the United States and results can be compared with tests given in other states, in England and in most other countries. The MCAS test in reading had never been given anywhere. Its results could not be compared with those in other states, and could not even tell us how this year's third grade class compared with last year's. This decision by the Department of Education undercut the decisions of the Board of Education. Just as disturbing, the plan to test reading at the end of the second grade was dropped.

This kind of subversion must be stopped. It is not the work of wicked people and it is not unique to Massachusetts. It is done by people who are concerned to accommodate the field even at the expense of the education of children. The concern for the field – the teachers, superintendents, school committees, teachers' unions, and the Department of Education itself – is the primary concern of many individuals in the Department of Education. I am sorry to say it is also the primary concern of some members of the Board of Education. They fail to understand that if the field were not the major part of the problem, there would be no crisis in education. If anyone thinks that education can be reformed without reforming the field, they do not understand the problem.

The federal government also poses a serious obstacle to education reform. When it passed the Individuals with Disabilities Education Act (IDEA) in 1990, it expanded the availability of education to individuals with special needs. But the law's provisions were so broad and impractical that the result was an assault on the treasuries of school committees all over the country. In 1967, 80 percent of public school budgets was devoted to regular education. Because of the IDEA, this has declined to 68 percent in 1996. From 1991 to 1996, only 23 percent of the new money to improve education, less than one fourth of it, has gone into regular education. Most has gone to meet the special requirements passed by states or by the federal government. The government passed the new requirements but failed to supply funds to support them.

Of the $274 billion spent every year on primary and secondary education, IDEA spending accounts for almost 22 percent, or $60 billion a year. The Advisory Council on Intergovernmental Affairs reports that IDEA creates the fourth largest amount of litigation of any U.S. statute. I assume that every school district is aware of this. I do not know of a single school district that has not been sued or threatened with a lawsuit over special needs children.

After discussing these issues with many superintendents and teachers, I conclude that only a small percentage of the litigation is on behalf of children who are in wheelchairs, children who have a cleft palate, children who have Down syndrome or suffer from some objectively established learning disability. Few students with such disabilities litigate such claims. More litigation is filed on behalf of normal children whose parents have done nothing to introduce discipline in the home. The parents send an unruly, undisciplined child to school and then invent a disability to require that the child be given special attention and preferably sent to a private school at $30,000 to $40,000 a year. That situation happens repeatedly in school district after school district and is a fraudulent abuse of the serious intent of the IDEA.

I found also that significant problems arise when schools are legally forced into allowing disruptive children to remain in a class, as if only they were special children. Every child is special and has a right to educational development to its fullest capacity. One disruptive child should not have the right to retard the education of an entire class of children who are behaving properly and civilly. But congressional legislation has mandated exactly this.

More recently, new decisions by the Supreme Court have decided that school districts are responsible for providing extensive health care and nursing support to their students. Secretary of Education Bell had determined in 1983 that schools were responsible for every medical service short of attention by a licensed physician, a determination upheld in *Irving Independent School Dist. v. Tatro* (468 U.S. 883, 1984). This year, in its decision in *Cedar Rapids Community School Dist. v. Garret F.* (526 U.S. 66, 1999), the Supreme Court reinforced this definition, noting that "The District may have legitimate financial concerns, but our role in this dispute is to interpret existing law." I doubt that Secretary Bell had any idea of the precedent he was setting. Regardless of the cost of care, or the feasibility of providing that care while also serving every other student, school districts are required to provide all medical support that does not have to be administered by a licensed physician.

The IDEA may become the federal mandate that has caused the greatest amount of litigation in the United States. Unless this law is changed, school systems will go bankrupt or will be forced to cut back on the services they offer.

Teachers' unions create their own obstacles to education reform. Teachers' unions have an extraordinary influence on many pieces of legislation that pass in the Commonwealth of Massachusetts and in most other states. It has been said, and it is not far from true, that the teachers' unions do not rent the state legislatures; they own them in fee simple. Every person who has run for office knows the advantage of selling one's soul to a teachers' union. They will provide an organization overnight.

They will stuff and address your envelopes with your messages; they will assist with all your fund-raising efforts; all summer long, during the primaries, they will stand on the streets with your signs; they will call people and urge them to get to the polls. They will do everything necessary to support the candidate who promises to support the union.

When members of school committees are selected by popular vote, the winners owe their election to the union and lose the independence necessary to represent the interests of parents, students, and taxpayers. Management is not properly represented at the table. Collective bargaining lacks integrity unless parents and taxpayers are represented by an independent individual in negotiations with the unions. When the members of the school committee are elected by the unions, the union sits on both sides of the table.

When it comes to the evaluation of teachers, the teachers' unions in Massachusetts succeeded in putting into the Education Reform Act the provision that teachers must be allowed to invoke evaluation standards set by their unions or professional associations. Thus the Act says that the procedures for conducting teacher evaluations shall be subject to collective bargaining provisions. When the teachers' union designs the criteria of teacher competence, it creates a test that protects incompetent teachers from dismissal. As long as the union contract defines what the standards are, we will not have standards that protect our children.

I am not hostile to unions. I am convinced of their importance. When I was in high school, student musicians started a successful jazz band and were getting very good jobs. Jerome Zoeller, the music instructor in our high school and a superb musician, told them, "Boys, you charge less than half union scale and you're taking jobs away from adult musicians like me who have families to support. This is wrong. Why don't the members of your band join the American Federation of Musicians? I will get you into the union without your having to pay the initiation fee. But you are going to have to agree to pay union dues and charge union scale from then on." The members of that band were thrilled to be treated as adult members of the union and started charging union scale. They did not play as many dances, but they made more money without undermining the livelihood of professional musicians.

I am not attacking the teachers' unions per se but the failure of teachers' unions to restrict themselves to their proper concerns. They should fight for teachers' salaries and benefits; they should not fight, as they have, to protect incompetents from relatively easy dismissal under due process of law, nor should they stand in the way of effective teacher evaluation.

I know also that teachers' unions are necessary because I have seen the way in which politics can interfere with teacher contracts. It is not at all unusual for a superb young teacher to be told at the end of the school year, "I am sorry, but because of budget constraints we are not going to be able to reappoint you next fall." Next August, the superintendent discovers that the money that was not there was there after all. Someone is now appointed who is a relative of a member of the school committee or of the superintendent or of the principal. The teachers' unions are there to put a stop to that and similar scams.

Every organization needs to have someone to check on it. An ombudsman or a watching bird is important in all aspects of life. We cannot depend upon every person trying to live his or her life in a way that is open to surveillance by a very rigorous conscience. We had better have some institutional protection for those who are vulnerable to abuse.

When Boston University took over the management of the Chelsea schools, we told the teachers' union that our negotiator would reserve our right to hire on the basis of quality rather than seniority, and intended to recover all other management rights. When the union learned that we were willing to take a strike – a risk that no elected school committee would willingly take – they became reasonable and gave back management rights in exchange for improved wages. Over a period of only two to three years, we developed a rapport between our negotiator and the negotiator for the union such that we were able to work in harmony for the betterment of the Chelsea schools. During all the years of Boston University's involvement in Chelsea, there were no strikes or job actions. The independence of the two parties at the table is essential if mutual understanding and a sense of common cause on behalf of the schools is to prevail.

It is often the case in education reform that even when solutions to problems are readily apparent, implementation of those solutions is stymied. Among the most important initiatives and the most disappointing failures during my time as Chairman of the Massachusetts Board of Education was our effort to get increased funding for early childhood education. This endeavor met with small success and very little support from the Department of Education or the governor.

We focused on early childhood education because those earliest years of childhood are by far the most important in the development of a child's brain. The brain develops rapidly in the first four or five years and requires stimulation in order to develop fully. Consider the simple example of children who have one strong eye and one so-called lazy eye. Unless someone observes that inequality in the use of the two eyes and puts a patch over the strong eye so that the weak eye has to work, after a few years there will be no neural connections between that weak eye and the occipital lobe of the brain. The person will be effectively blind in an eye that is physiologically sound simply because no neurological connection with the brain has been developed through use.

It is equally important in this period, as brain cells are increasing and synapses are multiplying, that the child hear. Every child should be tested for hearing within the first three to six months. A partially deaf child should be fitted with hearing aids immediately. If the child is totally deaf, other means for encouraging verbal comprehension, such as sign language, must be introduced.

A child must develop language skills in the first three to four years of life or that child's linguistic abilities will be severely impaired. We know this from feral children. Any child who has lacked this verbal stimulation in the earliest years is never capable of acquiring it later. The same thing goes for hand-eye coordination and the ability to learn to focus the ears no less than the eyes. All of us know how to focus our ears – if we go to a restaurant and don't like the conversation at our own table, we start eavesdropping on another table and can shift our attention with no difficulty.

The cognitive development that takes place during these preschool years is critical in preparing a child to learn when he or she reaches school. Without this foundation, children start school unprepared and can quickly fall behind – a situation that too often is never fully remedied. Parental neglect in these years, whether intentional or inadvertent, has the negative effect of limiting the full development of the child's potentialities. Unfortunately the development of the brain is time-sensitive. Unless its potential capabilities are exercised in the earliest years, they will be lost.

In Chelsea, Boston University established an Early Learning Center to ensure educational development for children three and four years of age. The results have been spectacular as children have developed their full potentiality through activities that stimulate their senses and their cognitive faculties. After a year or two in the Early Learning Center, children in Chelsea enter kindergarten or the first grade lively, inquisitive, alert, confident, enjoying themselves and well prepared to learn.

In addition, the Board sought funding for inexpensive and cost-effective child-parent home education programs. Those programs, in operation in eight communities in Massachusetts, cost about $2,000 per child and work miracles. In Pittsfield and Cambridge, for example, they have been going on for over a generation and we have longitudinal results to show just how highly effective they are. A volunteer goes into the home twice each week for a half-hour with books and toys. She shows the mother – or whoever is taking care of the two-to-three-year-old child – how to use these materials to assist the child's educational development. Mothers who have participated with a first child, will, if they have subsequent children, continue to follow the practices they have learned. This natural leveraging increases the cost-effectiveness of the program. Such programs merit our greatest support in the reform of schools. They encourage parents to assume responsibility for homework and for having a place in the home where the child can study.

All of these are important skills and all need to be developed at the earliest possible age. Early childhood education greatly benefits not only children of families with limited child development opportunities, but all children. We need to establish an endowment with the addition of $100 million each year until we reach $1 billion, an endowment adequate to provide education for children ages three and four every working day of the year from 7:00 in the morning until 6:30 in the evening. There is no point in talking about educational reform if nothing is done to provide for children who would have to be abandoned by a parent who leaves welfare to go back to work or to go back to school, or abandoned by parents from middle class or professional families who must be at work. All of us, I presume, favor educating persons on welfare and then restoring them to useful and productive jobs, and all of us recognize that in many families today, both parents must work. Consequently we should be concerned to provide care before and after the school day for children of welfare and middle class parents. Failure to procure adequate funding for early childhood education is a major blow to education in Massachusetts and the United States.

One way to provide funding for early childhood education for all children is obvious: We can transfer the funds for the twelfth grade of high school to support pre-kindergarten education for four-year-olds. In many parts of the country in the 1930s and 1940s, high school graduation occurred at the eleventh grade. Our academic achievement in eleven years was greater then than it is now with a twelfth year of required schooling. If we transferred all resources expended in the twelfth grade to fund a full preschool program, we could easily revise the curriculum to meet current levels of twelfth-grade achievement by the end of the eleventh grade. By offering education to three- and four-year-olds, we could substantially reduce the number of disadvantaged students who in the present system are falling behind.

It is clear from what I have observed regarding schools of education, departments of education and teachers' unions, that creating additional funding for our schools will have no significant positive effect without radical structural change. In the final analysis, nothing will be done substantially to improve the quality of our schools unless highly competent men and women can once again be attracted to teaching.

Salaries available to competent teachers must at minimum be doubled. Salaries are now simply not adequate to attract highly skilled and intelligent persons who can earn much more in other occupations. While there will always be a few who are dedicated to teaching and to the calendar of the schools, general reform will require a radical change in teachers' compensation.

This can be accomplished in large part by terminating no less than 50 percent of redundant administrators. At least that many could disappear without loss. In the late 1990s, the Catholic schools in the Boston dioceses educated approximately the same number of students, and to equally high standards, as did the Boston public schools. But while the Boston public schools employed hundreds of administrators, there were only twelve in the diocesan schools.

We should further supplement the salaries of teachers by passing legislation to provide a federal tax exemption of the first $30,000 of a teacher's salary. That initiative would increase the take-home pay of most teachers by approximately $10,000 to $11,000 per year and would ease the burden of doubling the take-home pay of teachers by local school committees. We also must be able to terminate without endless and costly litigation teachers who do not meet reasonable standards of certification.

If still more funds are needed to double the average salaries of teachers, state legislatures or Congress should respond to what is clearly a national priority. At present they waste billions of dollars in meaningless reforms without improving the quality of teachers. If they wish to effect meaningful educational reform, they must support the most important element in education – the teachers.

Offering higher salaries would make possible improving the quality of teaching by opening the profession to persons who have never attended schools of education. Someone who has majored in English or history or science in a good liberal arts college is far more likely to be qualified to teach than someone who has attended a school of education. There is a pool of highly qualified persons to teach science and mathematics among retired military personnel and scientists and engineers who have been laid off during periods of economic decline. A six-week intensive course in lesson planning and a one-semester apprenticeship would prepare many of them to be effective full-time teachers.

I have two daughters who planned to become teachers. One of them is a certified teacher in a public school. The other, with a master's degree in mathematics and fluency in French, German, and Spanish, tried to get a job in the public schools in New Jersey. But she had taken no education courses and was therefore deemed unqualified. Lawrenceville School, however, was very happy to hire her and she was a sensational teacher from the first day of class. The claims of professional educators that no one can teach effectively unless she has been indoctrinated by educationists are rubbish.

In conclusion, the real question facing the public today is this: Do we care more about the welfare of our children than for the educational establishment, the privileges of teachers' unions and the schools of education? If so, our highest priority will be to provide our children with better teachers. Common sense makes obvious what needs to be done. The question is, do we have the will to do it? By our passivity we, the parents and taxpayers, are in the final analysis the most important obstacle to education reform. We could improve our schools if we tried.

My mother was a teacher from the time she was eighteen years old until she was eighty-two, with the exception of the time she took off to have my brother and me. She retired at eighty-two. I guess she was a quitter. But I learned from her example what a gifted and dedicated teacher is like. My description of the quality of the teaching profession today bears no resemblance to my conception of the profession itself. In my opinion it is not only the most important but also the noblest of the professions. None of us is born to be medicated; none of us is born to be litigated – and that is all that doctors and lawyers do. But we are all born to be educated. Without education we could not become doctors, lawyers, or anything else; education is absolutely essential. It is the teacher, not the doctor or the lawyer, who educates us and under whose tutelage we develop into fulfilled human beings. Are not teachers worthy of our full and generous support?

Reunion College, Boston University, May 21, 1999

Education and Spiritual Formation

"To rid the world of all the conditions that motivate terrorist acts requires more than the condemnation and repudiation of terrorism."

If one wishes to visit the campus of a first-rate school where more than adequate funding has been wisely and gracefully spent, where students are given a superb education on beautiful grounds with splendid buildings including an extraordinarily beautiful chapel, I know of no place better than St. Paul's of Concord, New Hampshire, a school for boys and girls from the ninth though the twelfth grade. Invited to offer remarks at a service of evening prayer in 2002, I was assured that my audience would be primarily seniors, faculty, and alumni. I was referred to remarks by the theologian Paul Tillich on the occasion of the centenary of the founding of St. Paul's and asked to contrast the role of the church in our time with that examined by Tillich almost fifty years earlier.

I worked hard on this address and hoped it would be worthy of my audience and of Tillich. What I did not know is that the audience would in fact be composed largely of students in the ninth grade. I felt almost like a war criminal in subjecting these boys and girls to a rather stiff dose of intellectual inquiry. Indeed, so heavily did those young faces weigh upon my mind that I had difficulty completing this address.

FOR ALMOST A CENTURY and a half, St. Paul's has stood for values of infinite worth that are acquired only through education and induction. Its educational program, as its motto proclaims, centers on learning "on earth those things of which knowledge continues in heaven;" that is, St. Paul's is concerned to educate the young on matters both finite and infinite, quotidian and transcendent. It claims that "none shall go away unimproved." No one can fault these ideals and objectives; but constant effort is required to reach these lofty goals.

229

In 1956, on the centenary of the founding of St. Paul's, the school invited the celebrated theologian Paul Tillich to address a symposium on the topic of "The Church in Our Time." Culturally speaking, our time is many centuries distant from the time when Tillich spoke. Profound changes in our culture over the past forty-six years – scientific, technological, political, economic, social, educational, linguistic, and religious – have been more extensive and transformative than changes over the previous centuries. Developments in communication and travel – radio, television, the jet, and the Internet – have provided the engines of this acceleration.

Back in 1956, Tillich spoke from the perspective of one of the happiest, most self-confident and religiously observant periods in American history. Dwight Eisenhower was president and, as a song in the musical *Call Me Madam* put it, we liked Ike. A generation flourished, having survived the Great Depression with its acute suffering and deprivation scarcely known to the students and faculty of St. Paul's. It was a generation that had also survived World War II and the Korean War in which graduates of St. Paul's were conspicuously and honorably represented. The blessings of peace and prosperity had never before been known on so broad a scale. The modest houses of Levittown, costing about $7,500 (or $60,000 in today's dollars), were within the reach of almost any family and were mansions to those who moved out of rented tenements to buy them. Education was suddenly available to many millions of veterans whose tuition and living expenses were covered by the GI Bill, a piece of legislation that democratized higher education and the professions. Family and children were the focus of a generation tempered by hardship whose members were content to move step by gradual step toward personal fulfillment – to education, a job, a car, a spouse, a house, and children – as each could be afforded.

Ample entertainment was available for a dime or a quarter in movies or free of charge on radio and television. Wholesome entertainment was imposed on movies by the edicts of the Hays Office and on radio and television by regulations of the FCC.

I knew by heart the FCC regulations outlawing profanity and obscenity on the air because as a disc jockey at station KONO in San Antonio I was required to pass the FCC examination as a condition of employment.

One day while on the air, I forgot to change the gear of my turntable from 78 to 33 rpm. So when I changed from a dance record to a long-playing recorded commercial, the advertisement sounded like the chattering of Disney's chipmunks. Forgetting that my mic was open, I said "son-of-a-[…]!" and those words were on the air as commentary on the chipmunks. For days I waited for the Feds to descend on me. Actually, I had nothing to fear, for apparently my show was so popular that no one was listening.

In the '50s, television was only a minor though emerging force. It began its march towards dominance by aiming first at a discriminating audience with programs such as *Omnibus* and *Playhouse 90*, shown not on PBS, but on commercial networks. Public health was improving dramatically: tuberculosis and polio were being wiped out, and there was no AIDS. Drug usage was so rare that Tom Lehrer could joke about "The Old Dope Peddler" in one of his songs. Unmarried pregnancy was still discouraged. Rape was still a crime involving strangers, and murder typically a crime involving friends and relatives.

Church attendance was high, and millions listened on radio to the sermons of Fosdick, Sheen, Peale, and Sockman; theologians Niebuhr, Barth, Murray, and Tillich had national and international followings in addition to their influence in universities and seminaries.

In the middle '50s, the Cold War was bracing but not yet the threat it was to become in the next decade. Under Eisenhower, the country, though alert, was content under a popular president who was denigrated only by intellectuals, too many of whom never learned that common sense and the common touch are necessary qualities of wise democratic leaders.

But the world and the times of 1956 are no more, having disappeared in a series of revolutionary changes. The standards of taste once imposed by Hollywood and the FCC have for the most part been ignored or abandoned. Two filmed versions of *Hamlet*, Laurence Olivier's 1948 film and Kenneth Branagh's of 1996, illustrate the decline into degeneracy: in Olivier's film, as in Shakespeare's play, Ophelia is chaste and virginal. In Branagh's, she is Hamlet's whore. Young women today are caught in a crossfire between feminists who decry the use of women as sex objects and urge career over marriage and motherhood, and those who urge them to get all the mileage they can from their sex, to become "Pretty Women" modeled after Julia Roberts or her successor Britney Spears. It is difficult for young men and women today, in an age that denigrates enduring commitment, to know the fulfillment of marriage or even the ultimate fulfillment of love as an intimate private union unobserved by others.

The present generation reared in luxury need not temper its moves toward personal fulfillment by prudential steps. Its members are encouraged to believe one can have it all at once. The harvest is AIDS, herpes, drug addiction, theft, a new crime of date rape between close friends, and drive-by murder not of friends or relatives but of total strangers. The end result is satiation, giving poignant, sobering meaning to Peggy Lee's song "Is That All There Is?"

Most of these phenomena are the consequence of complex forces released by three decades of unprecedented luxury with its attendant disappointments and boredom. Now we confront an added contingency, more disconcerting than that aroused at the height of the Cold War: terrorism. Terrorism is no longer characterized by relatively isolated acts; rather, it has become a global and domestic epidemic. It can be carried out anywhere by an individual, an organization, or a country; its motivation can be personal, ideological, or religious.

The terrorist threat reverses the condition laid down by the Athenian ambassadors at the Melian Conference when they explained that the strong do what they can while the weak suffer what they must. The relation is now reversed: the weak do what they can, while the strong suffer what they must. In this age of advanced weaponry, massive destructive power can be placed in the hands of a weak individual. An individual properly equipped can not only destroy an airplane or a school but armed with a virus can destroy millions in a widespread epidemic.

We had good reason to believe that the Cold War would end peacefully, for common sense would compel restraint in the face of mutually assured destruction. But we have no reason to believe that the threat of terrorism and the high level of contingency and uncertainty that follows from it can be contained, much less eliminated. We have no idea how to settle all old scores and grievances peacefully, reconcile all those who are resentful or alienated, satisfy all those who are bitter because their dreams have been shattered. In the absence of a universal system of belief that condemns the slaughter of the innocent and repudiates terrorism in all its forms, we have no means – cannot even conceive of means – by which to rid the world of all the conditions that can motivate terrorist acts.

The cultural milieu of today is so fundamentally different from the milieu in which Tillich spoke, though only forty-six years ago, that we must ask, "What is the relevance of what Tillich said regarding the education and the spiritual formation of young people?"

Despite the differences in the times, Tillich's tripartite analysis of education appears as sound today as in centuries past; it includes technical education, humanistic education, and induction, that aspect of education so often overlooked but which Tillich called to our attention. As he observed, these aspects of education vie with one another for dominance. Today, technical education is generally accepted as the educational ideal. Technical competence in reading, writing, mathematics, computer skills, science, and engineering is what we emphasize most and do best in our finest schools and colleges. But this technical education makes little contribution to the spiritual formation of the young or to the development of sound character. Nor does it necessarily contribute to the development of stable, vigorous, humane communities.

No one can doubt the technical competence of Nazi and Soviet scientists and engineers. But everyone is appalled by the uses to which they put their technical know-how. The educational program in Nazi Germany and in the USSR was not merely technical. Elements of humanistic education are present in all forms of technical education which, Tillich notes, include "discipline; subjection to the object in knowing and handling it; participation in the community of work; subordination to and criticism of the demands of the expert and the community." While these are part of the aim of humanistic education, they fall short of the humanistic ideal which, according to Tillich, concerns "the development of all human potentialities, individually and socially." Humanistic education is incomplete apart from its relation to what Tillich calls "elements of inductive education." Inductive education aims to develop the potentialities of the individual not in any direct way, but rather indirectly by anchoring the individual through participation in the "life and spirit of community, family, tribe, town, nation, [and] church."

We can readily understand the role of inductive education in Nazi Germany and in the Soviet Union. Without it, morale could scarcely have been sustained through the horrendous losses and crimes suffered by and committed by these regimes and their citizens. Inductive education also has its humanistic component in the intellectual interpretation of the symbols and institutions of the communities into which individuals are inducted. But as Tillich observes, "induction precedes interpretation." Then, as he says, "interpretation makes induction complete."

The ideology of the master race and the ideology of communism offered interpretations of the Swastika and the Hammer and Sickle that inspired and motivated the Wehrmacht and the Red Army to fight and die for *Vaterland* and Mother Russia. The successful induction of individuals into these communities by means of symbols and their interpretation – as shocking as it appears to those who were not inducted – offered inductees plausible justification for the atrocities of the SS, the solution to the Jewish question, the concentration camps in Germany, and for the atrocities of the KGB, the show trials, the massacre of the kulaks, and the Gulag in the Soviet Union.

But still small voices of individuals formed by humanistic and inductive education into the community of the church were still heard. Dietrich Bonhoeffer's induction into the Christian church was deepened and strengthened through his humanistic education in Germany and the United States. Finally the symbol of the cross was sufficiently powerful to compel his return from the U.S. to imprisonment in Germany and to sustain him even unto death. Similarly, induction into the community of Junkers with their ideals of honor and duty sustained Claus von Stauffenberg, Helmuth von Moltke, and other German dissidents who plotted against Hitler at the cost of their lives. Russian orthodoxy and humanism sustained Solzhenitsyn throughout his long imprisonment in the Gulag.

Inductive education of all kinds is practiced by wide varieties of groups and communities. One is inducted into the Boy Scouts and Girl Scouts through a variety of symbols and practices, just as one is inducted into a church by different but similar means. Basic training in the armed forces, though in part technical, is primarily inductive. In Boston there is the perennial effort to induct all of us into the community of Red

Sox nation, binding us with undying loyalty to the symbol of the Green Monster at Fenway Park. The *Globe* and the *Herald* participate in this inductive education in support of community spirit. Induction into stable, two-parent families, unfortunately, is now far less pervasive, having been weakened by social legislation and by radical changes in sexual mores.

Programs of inductive education also include those of gay advocacy groups and groups of feminists who compete for the hearts and minds of the young. But the most pervasive program in inductive education, on which more money is spent than on any other form of education, is advertising. All advertising, while it may introduce technical elements, is essentially an exercise in inductive education whose aim is the creation of insatiable desires for products of dubious value.

With this array of competing educational programs, what should be the focus of St. Paul's School? It cannot be all things to all groups and communities. One would assume that some guidelines can be found in the community of the Episcopal Church, if there remains a sufficient core of doctrine and supporting theology to offer guidance. Tillich warned in his address to St. Paul's that "when the religious substance of humanism disappeared, the mere form was left, abundant but empty." He noted not only the emptiness of humanism but also the "indifference, cynicism, despair, mental disturbances, early crimes and disgust of life" that follow. All these factors are more abundantly in evidence today than they were forty-six years ago.

Secularism, which Tillich deplored, led him to observe that the contemporaneous church school "is dependent on a small section of the religious life, a special denomination or a special confessional group [but not] the spirit of our society as a whole."

I cannot be sure that St. Paul's School is still committed to an essentially religious orientation, for in the material I was sent I find the ambiguous declaration, "We seek to be faithful to our Christian heritage while being inclusive (and inoffensive to) people of other faiths or no faith." Jesus on hearing this might say, "If the salt has lost its savor, it is good for nothing" (Matthew 5:13). Or, "He who is not with me is against me" (Matthew 12:30). Or, as an old-fashioned Episcopalian like St. Paul's founder George C. Shattuck might say, "Neither fish nor flesh, nor good red herring." I doubt that you can achieve the objective of being all things to all people while adhering to your motto.

I now wish directly to address those responsible for the future of St. Paul's. The times have changed radically, and St. Paul's, while attempting to retain what it can of its founding purpose, must likewise change. It is not only understandable, it is inevitable that those directing St. Paul's and other Episcopal schools are confused and uncertain about the means by which to contribute to the development of community and character, and to the spiritual formation of young people. It is perhaps their honest doubt and confusion that best prepares them for this task.

All of us, I suspect, feel oppressed today by forces of fate or destiny that are beyond the control or responsibility of any individual, institution, or nation – forces that seriously limit our choices. We cannot create new symbols by which to inculcate the younger generation in a system of beliefs that meld and unite harmoniously all the diversities of our time. Rather we must await a new cultural synthesis with a persuasive power comparable to that of medieval Christianity or eighth-century Islam. We can only wait for a *Kairos* – a fullness of time in which a compelling revelation is apprehended and accepted, a compelling revelation in which all the wounding divergencies of our times are reconciled. This opening of hearts and minds to the acceptance of a healing synthesis of belief is beyond our power; it requires, as Christians have recognized, a breaking into the temporal of the eternal – perhaps tomorrow, five hundred years from now, or perhaps never – and we can do nothing to hasten it. But neither can we wait like first century montanists for the Second Coming. Creatures of the present, we must act now. Thus the question reasserts itself: what should we do?

I am embarrassed by the modesty of what I can offer. My answer, the limits of which I am acutely aware, is this: look for and teach what is common to us all, those eternal verities of birth, friendship, love, disappointment, loss, and death that are the gifts of the humanities.

Tillich said that, cut off from religion, the humanities are empty. But it is hard to say where the humanities end and religion begins. It is especially difficult for Tillich, who defined religion as "the ultimate concern for the ultimate." Socrates held precisely that view of philosophy. Both require, as Tillich said, "initiation into the mystery of existence and the symbols in which it is expressed." Humanism, Tillich observes, "starts with … the question of being – of being generally and of my own being particularly."

Students who enter St. Paul's having been inducted as young children in the symbols of the Christian faith or some other religious faith should be assisted, as Tillich recommended, with conceptual interpretation that transforms a primitive literalism without destroying the power of the symbols. This will prepare them for a curriculum suitable to all students, including those without a religious induction, whom St. Paul's now welcomes.

Can we do better in the education of all students than to induct them into the humanistic community by immersing them in the wisdom of the world's great teachers and by grafting to their souls the emotional power, the archetypes and symbols, of our Greek heritage which knows no cultural, racial, or ethnic boundaries? Can we improve on the Hellenic tradition that once was central to education both in the schools and the universities? Sir Henry Sumner Maine observed that "except for the blind forces of nature, nothing moves on this earth that is not Greek in its origin."

In the *Republic*, Plato laid down the first principles of social organization. No individual is self-sufficient. Without society, that is, without community, no individual would have the power of speech and hence the capacity for thought or self-consciousness. Since every individual is dependent on a social community, it is the obligation of each individual to provide a measure of support for the community on which he or she depends. This principle of non-parasitism is the necessary condition for personal survival and the factual basis of morality and ethics.

There is also the question of moral motivation, and here let us make use of the motivating force of the *Iliad* and the *Odyssey*, of the Hellenic archetypes and of poetry. In a school like St. Paul's, to the extent that it is open both to those with faith and those without it, initiation into the mystery of human existence may be best achieved through poetry. If St. Paul's students would know the meaning of life, let them read and commit to memory Cavafy's poem "Ithaca":

When you start on your journey to Ithaca,
then pray that the road is long,
full of adventure, full of knowledge.
Do not fear the Lestrygonians
and the Cyclopes and the angry Poseidon.
You will never meet such as these on your path,
if your thoughts remain lofty, if a fine
emotion touches your body and your spirit.
You will never meet the Lestrygonians,
the Cyclopes and the fierce Poseidon,
if you do not carry them within your soul,
if your soul does not raise them up before you.

Then pray that the road is long.
That the summer mornings are many,
that you will enter ports seen for the first time
with such pleasure, with such joy!
Stop at Phoenician markets,
and purchase fine merchandise,
mother-of-pearl and corals, amber and ebony,
and pleasurable perfumes of all kinds,
buy as many pleasurable perfumes as you can;
visit hosts of Egyptian cities,
to learn and learn from those who have knowledge.

Always keep Ithaca fixed in your mind.
To arrive there is your ultimate goal.
But do not hurry the voyage at all.
It is better to let it last for long years;
and even to anchor at the isle when you are old,
rich with all that you have gained on the way,
not expecting that Ithaca will offer you riches.

Ithaca has given you the beautiful voyage.
Without her you would never have taken the road.
But she has nothing more to give you.

And if you find her poor, Ithaca has not defrauded you.
With the great wisdom you have gained, with so much experience,
you must surely have understood by then what Ithacas mean.

If those who graduate from St. Paul's commit poems like this to memory, they will not leave without having been improved. And those of religious faith leave better prepared, as Milton says, "to serve therewith [their] Maker ... lest He returning chide." Those who have been offered induction into the symbols of a religion may live in faith which includes the hope of heaven in which tragedies of life are overcome. Those without faith but inducted into the symbols of Hellenism may live with courage and joy befitting anyone who knows that the journey of life is worth the struggle, the pain and the loss and who, like Yeats's Homer, can go open-eyed and laughing to the tomb.

Ethics and Corporate Responsibility

"The U.S. is in danger of becoming a service economy – that is, a third-world economy, belonging to a country that lives at the sufferance of more productive countries."

In the decade since this speech was given, the trends I outlined in it have continued and indeed accelerated. Management has become increasingly separated from ownership. When this happens, managers are tempted to betray the long-term interests of their institutions in favor of short-term gains, on which their personal compensation is based. This misuse of power threatens to undermine the long-term interests of corporations and even the life of the nation.

I first gave this speech as a keynote address to corporate executives of UBS in Zurich in 2003. The members of that audience were for the most part college graduates who had studied Immanuel Kant's ethics in the process of completing their education.

FIRST, I want to thank UBS for inviting me to give the keynote address at this conference on the critically important issue of corporate responsibility. There are few subjects of greater complexity or import for the future than responsibility as it applies to the administration of corporations.

My host wondered whether chief financial officers would be interested in hearing about issues that are actually the responsibility of chief executive officers. But if CFOs are guided by the recent experience in the United States, they should be interested. For in most cases where there have been improprieties and wrong-doings in corporations, it is the CFOs, not the CEOs, who go to jail.

A brief discussion of responsibility per se offers a useful preparation. The term *responsibility* concerns the way in which individuals or corporations act with regard to their technical and moral obligations. We, as individuals and corporations, are responsible both for what we do and what we should have done but have failed to do. Responsibility defines one's performance or activity in relation to one's obligations. This places us squarely in the realm of ethics and has given rise to a demand for ethical behavior by corporations.

Schools of business or management have responded by introducing courses in business ethics; many books and articles have been written and are being written on the subject, and symposia and conferences, much like this one, have been organized to address this issue in an effort to encourage greater corporate responsibility. When responsibility is used in this sense, it refers to the normative dimension of corporate activity. Many corporations have prepared codes of ethics and documented the standards of responsibility by which they will operate.

This is not to overlook the other meaning of responsibility, where we use the term to note, for example, that the CEO of X corporation was responsible for its going bankrupt. This usage is neutral – neither good nor bad in itself – but merely an assertion of the agency of the individual or corporation. The corporate responsibility movement is concerned to promote responsibility in its normative sense, that is, to encourage strict observance of moral and ethical duties by those who exercise corporate power. In this way, it encourages corporations to contribute to the common weal by behaving according to legal and ethical norms. Courses and conferences on business or corporate ethics are designed to determine for us what those legal and ethical norms actually are.

Although ethical issues arise in all human activities, thus in all professions and businesses, in individual life and in institutions and corporations, it is a mistake to believe, I suppose, that differing individuals, institutions, or professions have their own special ethic by which to assess their responsibilities, the direction of their own lives or in the direction of the institutions and corporations they direct. The first and most important thing I can say about business ethics or any of the so-called professional ethics is that there is no such thing. Business, legal, medical, or military ethics are nothing but the application of universal ethical principles to a particular field of human activity. Neither ethics nor logic comes in varieties. There is no business, legal, medical, or military logic, for logic lays out the principles and procedures of sound thinking according to which one may move in thought from true premises to true conclusions, no matter what the subject of one's thinking may be. Like ethics, logic is normative: it tells us how we ought to think. It does not describe the way we actually think, for we often think irrationally. Just as logic sets forth universal principles that apply in any and every context in which thinking is involved, ethics sets forth universal principles to guide one in matters of right and wrong as they arise in any context.

Philosophers and sages have for thousands of years tried to formulate the basic principles of ethics. No one has formulated the principles of ethics or morality more rigorously than Immanuel Kant. By this I do not mean that Kant invented ethics or morality any more than Newton invented gravity. Rather, Kant described ethical principles in formulations that meet strict philosophical standards. He recognized that Confucius's statement "Do not do unto others as you would not have them do unto you" and Jesus's statement, "Do unto others as you would have them do unto you," were useful steps toward the formulation of the fundamental principle of morality. But while they partially expressed a sound ethical point of view, they were inadequate formulations of the ethical principle. The formulation of the Golden Rule "Do unto others as you would have them do unto you" can be observed by two heroin addicts who reciprocate in giving each other injections. As each addict gives and receives a shot, each does to the other as each would be done by. This is a gross misapplication of the intent of the Golden Rule, but it is in full accord with its formulation.

Kant reformulated the Golden Rule as the Categorical Imperative: "So act that the maxim [that is, the applied principle of your act] can be a universal law." Or, "So act that the maxim of your act can through your will become a universal law of nature"; or, "So act that you treat others never as a means merely but always as ends in themselves"; or, "So act that you are a lawgiver in a kingdom of ends of which you are also a subject." (By "a kingdom of ends," Kant meant a community of rational beings who by virtue of their capacity to establish rules and objectives and make free decisions are ends in themselves, centers of moral worth whether good or bad, depending on how they exercise their freedom.)

These formulations are only various ways to restate the one Categorical Imperative in order to make its meaning and its application more obvious. Kant further clarified its meaning by saying "Think for yourself," "Put yourself in thought in the place and point of view of others," and "Having done so, think consistently." One who follows these procedures will most likely do the right thing, while one who fails to carry out these procedures in determining what one should do is almost certain to violate his duty. This is true both of individuals and corporations. The purpose, for example, for the enactment of labor laws specifying the conditions of employment is to ensure that corporate managers put themselves in thought in the place and point of view of employees and consider the consequences of corporate decisions as they affect them.

As we will see, there are often situations in which the right thing to do is also the most advantageous action. This would not have bothered Kant. A man might act entirely in his own interest, Kant agreed, and yet do the right thing. He would act according to the moral law though not for a moral motive. Kant noted that this outcome is far preferable to a man not doing the right thing at all. We can make a case, in other words, for "enlightened self-interest" and not violate the requirements of the Categorical Imperative.

This brief discussion of ethics is relevant, I believe, because the kind of prosperity that the West enjoys depends on its moral order as much as on its technology, economic wisdom, and law. That moral order is not universally obeyed or perfectly envisioned. But it is recognized as a relevant norm.

II

But what is the relevance of morality's universal demands when corporations are so large that no one individual directs them? What do the universal demands of morality mean in an age when corporations can abandon the democracies that can gave them birth and deal instead with dictatorships?

If one asks what is the responsibility of the milkman, the answer is straightforward: deliver the milk on time to the right customers without contaminating it. The house painter: to prepare the surface first so that the new paint will adhere and to apply the final coat or coats according to specifications. Personal responsibility of individuals and their responsibility as professionals practicing outside the corporate structure are all relatively simple and straightforward.

But when we ask what is the responsibility of a corporation, the question is anything but simple. First of all, we confront the complexity of corporations. Within the limits of time I shall focus on the responsibility of large industrial, agricultural, service, and financial corporations with brief glances at governments and international agencies, themselves corporations, as they pass laws and regulations affecting the exercise of responsibility in other corporations.

Let us begin by considering the elements of a corporation. There are owners, managers, boards of directors, a variety of employees fulfilling widely different functions, buildings and materials, and products and waste produced by corporations. A corporation consists of all these elements. When a corporation through its CEO and other officers thinks for itself, it must include consideration of all these aspects of its corporate existence, for all are internal to the corporation. No administrative team or owner can make any major decision responsibly without taking into account how it will affect the owners (whether individuals or stockholders), how it will affect the employees, what will be required in the way of facilities or materials, how its products will affect the communities in which businesses are located or in which their products or services are sold, and how it will dispose of waste materials. If there is a board of directors, each director in order to fulfill his or her responsibility must ask to what extent is management taking these factors adequately into account.

One reason corporations have become less accountable to their communities and employees is that it is harder to identify whom one might hold responsible. If we go back one or two hundred years, we find that most industrial corporations were managed by the individuals who owned them. In such cases, extremely rare today, no conflict of interest can arise between management and the owner, for they are one in the same. Today, however, corporations are run by men and women but owned by millions of shareholders. Adolf A. Berle Jr. and Gardiner C. Means of Columbia University in 1933 addressed the implications of the separation of ownership from management in a seminal book, *Modern Corporation and Private Property*.* They pointed out that when the managerial class is separate and distinct from the owners, as is the case in publicly traded corporations, where there are many thousands of stockholders, the stockholders by their dispersion and physical distance from and lack of knowledge of the activities of management have no adequate means of ensuring that management acts in a way that is in their interests. "[T]he shareholder in the modern corporate situation," they write, "has surrendered a set of definite rights for a set of indefinite expectations. The whole effect of the growth of the powers of directors and 'control' has been steadily to diminish the number of things on which a shareholder can count, the number of demands he can make with any assurance that they must be satisfied.... The stockholder," they continue, "is therefore left as a matter of law with little more than the loose expectation that a group of men, under a nominal duty to run the enterprise for his benefit and that of others like him, will actually observe this obligation.... As a result, we have reached a condition in which the individual interest of the shareholder is definitely made subservient to the will of a controlling group of managers even though the capital of the enterprise is made up out of the aggregated contributions of perhaps many thousands of individuals."†

For a corporation to be governed responsibly, it is essential that management, including the board of directors and the officers of the corporation, share the long-term interests of the shareholders and act accordingly. This problem did not arise when the owner of the corporation directly hired managers. The unity of ownership and management was maintained, for the owner could remove the manager anytime he wished.

*New York, The Macmillan Company, 1933.
†*Ibid.*, p. 277.

Henry Ford Sr. offers an excellent example of the owner-manager. He did not worry about quarterly reports, and he was not interested in hiring a chief financial officer or an accountant who could assist him in padding one quarter's earnings so he could influence the value of his stock. His interest was long-term sustainability – not in years, but in decades, for he envisioned the company being owned and operated by his children, grandchildren, and great-grandchildren. Likewise, he was concerned for his employees. During the Depression of the 1930s, he recognized that unless the wages of workers all across the United States were increased, they would not be able to purchase automobiles to sustain the Ford Motor Company and its competitors or business in the non-automotive sectors. Following a meeting with President Hoover on November 21, 1929, Ford announced that he would pay his workers seven dollars per day, a munificent salary in the 1930s, so that his workers could afford to buy Fords and other products. He urged major business leaders not to cut wages but to follow his lead and to increase them. He argued soundly that this policy would help restore the purchasing power to the working classes that was essential for economic recovery. His words went unheeded by the government and by corporate leaders, and the Depression continued with only moderate amelioration until 1939, when an impending war began to fuel the economy.

Ford eschewed the notion that he was an idealist, but we cannot dismiss his actions as merely opportunistic. His self-interest coincided with the broader public interest and the sustainability of his and other corporations.

But the dynamics of corporate responsibility are fundamentally altered when ownership shifts to thousands of stockholders in publicly traded corporations. Once this shift occurs, there is no guarantee that either the directors or the managers will share the interests of the stockholders, or be committed to the long-term sustainability of the corporation, or consider the effects of management decisions on all those sectors affected by them. Under the happiest circumstances, which usually only occur in smaller companies, the CEO may be the largest stockholder, and he can ensure that the interests of the stockholders are foremost in his mind by serving with a modest salary and by relying on dividends for most of his compensation. That situation, unfortunately, is not possible in the case of very large corporations in which no individual owns more than a very small percentage of the equity.

Now that management is separate and distinct from ownership, we have become increasingly aware of the way in which directors and managers have betrayed their corporate trust to act responsibly. Compare the owner-manager Henry Ford Sr. with Kenneth Lay, CEO of Enron. Lay sold over $100 million of personally owned stock while urging all employees to purchase Enron stock and while he invested the retirement funds of his employees exclusively in Enron stock. All the while he must have known the company was in financial difficulty, which was obscured from view by creative bookkeeping and the connivance of bankers, lawyers, and auditors. Both Enron and its auditors, Arthur Andersen, crashed as a result of this chicanery. It is hard to believe that this would have happened had Enron been owned by its managers or had the personal fortune of the directors been aligned with the long-term success of the company.

Neither the directors nor the top managers of Enron met the test of the Categorical Imperative. When Lay sold his stock while recommending its purchase by employees, he failed to act as a lawgiver in a community in which he subjected himself to the laws he enacted. The most superficial effort on the part of Lay, other managers, and directors to follow the procedures required by the Categorical Imperative would have revealed that moral, legal, and possibly criminal culpability. But management and the directors never put themselves in the place and point of view of others – their employees whose jobs and retirement benefits were forfeited by their policies, the stockholders and their families who lost their entire investment or the communities devastated by the collapse of Enron.

Subsequent events have shown that their shortsighted policies were not only a disaster for employees and stockholders but also harmed the policy makers themselves and in the end may send Lay and other managers and directors to prison.

Part of the responsibility for economically disastrous developments in corporate management has been the elevation of financial gurus to the position of CEO. Harold Geneen, a superb accountant and financial officer, provides the finest example. He assembled the ITT conglomerate not by combining corporations that enhanced one another and functioned symbiotically to create more and better products at lower costs while capturing market share in complementary areas. Rather, he added to his conglomerate any company whose acquisition increased earnings over the short run. When time ran out, as it must in any such scheme, it was the obligation of Geneen's successor, Rand Araskog, to dismantle that dysfunctional conglomerate and rebuild a smaller company on sound footing. Geneen is important in any discussion of corporate responsibility because he showed the way, I believe, for others like Kenneth Lay and Dennis Kozlowski to rely on financial tricks to create the appearance of enhanced value rather than to develop sound products or services to create genuine, sustainable value.

Once the separation of management and ownership takes place, directors have greatly enhanced responsibility, for they alone are in a position to ensure that the interests of the stockholders are protected. Unfortunately, the failure of directors to protect the interests of stockholders and employees has become increasingly apparent both in the United States and in Europe. While shareholder returns declined 18 percent for Disney, the directors increased Michael Eisner's compensation by 498 percent. When the stockholder returns in Delta Airlines declined 58 percent, President and CEO Leo F. Mullen's compensation more than doubled by action of the directors. Similar practices were followed by Abbott Laboratories, Cardinal Health, Honeywell International, and Tyco International.*

Part of the problem is that members of boards of directors, even when apparently independent, are actually dependent on accommodating the CEO, who can remove them from the board that pays lucrative fees for very little work. It is also true that many directors have little if any knowledge of the business of the corporation they putatively direct or even knowledge of accounting. These pliant directors too quickly fall prey to what The Economist calls the "Lake Wobegon Effect," named after a fictional Minnesota town where "all the children are above average." In today's corporate climate, directors behave as if all CEOs are above average and deserve outrageous compensation whether or not they perform

---

*"Executive Pay: A Special Report," by Patrick McGeehan. The New York Times, April 6, 2003, Section 3, p. 1.

exceptionally. But would directors be so eager to cater to their CEO *Wunderkindern* if they imagined themselves as shareholders who had lost their investments, or employees who had lost their pensions?

Worst of all, many directors serve reciprocally on one another's boards. Two or three CEOs may serve on each other's boards and on one another's compensation committees. In this latter capacity, they follow the maxim: I will raise your salary if you will raise mine. In this they observe the literal demands of the Golden Rule but fail to meet the requirements of the Categorical Imperative, according to which the interests of stockholders, workers, and all concerned must be taken into account.

This phenomenon is not limited to the United States. Stockholders in Europe are becoming increasingly outraged by the compensation and pensions offered to CEOs, and some countries are taking steps to ensure restraint and to rein in pay. In the United Kingdom, pay packages must now be approved annually by shareholders. In France, disclosure of top executives' salaries is mandatory for public companies. In Germany, shareholder complaints have prompted a growing number of executives to begin disclosing their pay packages.* And in Italy, listed companies must disclose purchases and sales of shares by their executives. None of these regulations will ensure corporate responsibility, but they can certainly help.† The situation cannot be handled adequately by law, for "it's a case of total moral bankruptcy," said Muriel Siebert, the president and chairwoman of Muriel Siebert and Company. She continued. "The Enron mess could not have happened without the banks, the lawyers, and the accountants."‡

Corporations do not necessarily act responsibly even if directors and managers transcend their own interests to think of what is best for their employees and their communities. Corporate responsibility requires management to think also of all those outside the corporation who are affected by it. Environmental laws have been enacted to compel

*For a prime example, see "After Huge Merger, German CEO Faces Trial Over Payout," by Marcus Walker. *The Wall Street Journal*, November 6, 2003, p. A1.

†"Mad About Money," by Dan Bilefsky. *The Wall Street Journal*, April 14, 2003.

‡"Private Sector; An Insider Judges Wall St.: Profits 'Too Fast and Too Vast'," by C. J. Satterwhite. *The New York Times*, April 6, 2003. See also McGeehan, *The New York Times*, April 6, 2003, Section 3, p. 2.

corporations to ask what are the effects and consequences of corporate decisions as they affect those outside the corporation. Paper companies in the United States, for example, have been notorious for dumping into rivers and streams the chemicals and dyes used in paper manufacture. For years, they simply ignored the damage done not merely to the environment as a conceptual abstraction but to the lives of persons living along those rivers and to communities relying on those waters for the municipal water supply, as well as to the fish and other living creatures that depend for their lives on clean water. In Europe, industrialists have used the Rhine as a great sewer for generations. An entire morning could be used in cataloging in briefest format the damage to the environment and to human, animal, and vegetable life that has followed from corporate irresponsibility.

The inefficiency of the corporate responsibility movement follows from the obdurate fact that most businessmen and corporate leaders, though aware of what they ought to do, are, unfortunately, also and even more keenly aware of what is in their personal interest. Lincoln Steffens, America's finest investigative reporter who flourished from the 1890s through the 1920s, became famous for his series on "The Shame of the Cities," in which he outlined the collusion of political officials – mayors, aldermen, governors, functionaries, and corporate managers – in the violation of the public interest by improper and often illegal alliances. The directors and managers of public utilities were particularly tempted by the riches to be gained through bribery and graft. And politicians were easily seduced by the proffered rewards.

Being something of a philosopher, Lincoln Steffens speculated about the cause. Was the character of the individuals or corporations at fault? He answered in the negative by retelling the story of the Fall of Man. After Adam and Eve had angered God by eating of the fruit of the tree of knowledge, God questioned them. Adam explained that the woman was to blame; Eve explained that it was the serpent. But Steffens observed that they were both wrong. It was the apple. The corruption of government and business is caused, he observed, because there are substantial rewards for dishonesty. Greed lies at the heart of the problem, and all the courses in ethics and conferences on corporate responsibility will do little to dampen the seductive power of financial riches.

Only a system with legal checks and balances will effectively encourage and enforce corporate responsibility, but nothing will ensure the probity of directors and managers short of a moral ethos in which there is general acceptance of the duty to obey the unenforceable. Enron and Tyco reveal the limits of law in controlling corporate behavior. Or consider the board of directors of the New York Stock Exchange: they approved a compensation package for the CEO of $140 million and retirement packages totaling $133 million for other top managers. The management of the New York Stock Exchange incurred no financial risks that could have explained this exalted compensation. Though outrageous, this compensation is apparently legal. They merely took advantage of their situation.

Unfortunately, the moral failings of CEOs in the West have corollaries in the global marketplace as well. If reform is a pressing concern at home, it is an urgent necessity worldwide.

III

Since the collapse of Communism in 1989, international development agencies such as the IMF, the World Bank, and the World Trade Organization have argued relentlessly in favor of free trade and private enterprise around the globe. This consensus, along with unprecedented investment abroad and accelerated technological developments in transportation and communication, has been described as "globalization."

We know, of course, that the world's peoples have been trading across long distances for thousands of years and that colonialism and mercantilism accelerated this trade. A global economy has existed for several centuries, but, in the past, only the developed world had the capital, ships, technology, and coercive military power to enter the global economy on its own terms. The underdeveloped world – the so-called third world – was once totally ignorant of the possibilities of a better life in the second or first worlds. The developed world, by contrast, was for centuries aware of the second and third worlds and capitalized on the economic advantages they have offered, either through colonization, imperialism, mercantilism, or a combination of these relationships.

The "globalization" we now see is quite different from past trading patterns. The global village – no longer a prescient catchphrase coined by Marshall McLuhan – is the world we live in. The migration of peoples – legal and illegal – demonstrates that people in the most isolated and benighted areas of the world are now aware, largely through television, radio, and jet travel, of the possibilities of a better life in other parts of the world.

Today the concept of a global economy invokes openness between all nations and free trade on a level playing field in which, presumably, all nations and peoples may prosper together. In the past, exploitation to the advantage of developed countries was the accepted standard. No more. World opinion is officially opposed to exploitation and endorses the ideal of fairness and an even playing field as globalism officially espouses. We can now picture a world in which international economics are conducted to mutual benefit – a world in which the rules of the game, like the laws of Kant's imagined kingdom of ends, are written to suit both the powerful and the weak.

Like all ideals, that of globalism remains to be fully realized. Many of the realities of the global economy are deplorable. Russia, China, and other nations have sold weapons that fuel wars in the Balkans and in the Middle East and civil war in Africa. The IMF has been the financier of emerging African nations whose leaders have too often used IMF grants not to build infrastructure and industry within their countries but instead to buy arms and build armies to retain political power and engage in wars of ethnic cleansing or wars to relocate boundaries along ethnic lines that were ignored by colonial powers when they divided the continent.

The global economy has also opened the way to American cultural and political preeminence, to the frustration of many. It was perhaps inevitable that the United States, with the largest and strongest economy and by far the strongest military, would become the global hegemon. But it was partly by default: many European nations gladly reduced military appropriations while relying on the United States as their military shield. Cultural hegemony has been driven by the global reach of American corporations, which have used the opening of markets to export music (I use the term loosely to include rap and other dubious categories), movies and television programs, clothing (blue jeans, baseball caps, T-shirts), Pepsi-Cola, Coca Cola, and the ubiquitous double arches of McDonald's. Cultural globalism has led to a remarkable degree of homogenization, even while the doctrine of diversity is preached by every activist and politician. I can sympathize with the French, who must be appalled to find that their exportation of *pomme frites* has returned to France as American French fries.

These problems, however, are not the result of serious malfeasance among the CEOs of Western firms. The managers and directors of McDonald's have served well the interests of their stockholders, franchisees, and employees by expanding globally. All have prospered. They have given jobs to citizens of the countries in which they do business. Their products are wholesome, if fattening, but it is the customer who is responsible for moderation in the consumption of high-caloric foods. Is McDonald's to blame because teenagers the world over love the Big Mac?

The global economy has also introduced new business opportunities in less-developed countries where the rule of law and international conventions regarding copyrights and patents are ignored. Businesses that pirate music, movies and television properties and books, and manufacture generic versions of drugs protected by international patents are thriving. India and China are leading supporters and defenders of such illegal enterprises. The owners and managers of these businesses and the governments that condone them could not justify their actions if they considered their reaction if their products were pirated. But this moral lesson will not evoke any corrective action. Although it is flagrant corporate irresponsibility on the part of the businesses and governments involved, theft of these properties will continue until economic countermeasures force a reconsideration.

But, incredibly, the countermeasures are decried by some as inconsistent with the commitment to openness and free trade. In the meantime, if not for all time, businesses engaged in piracy will happily enjoy the profits of an illegal trade. Morally speaking, however, they are no worse than the thousands, if not millions of Americans who illegally copy films and CDs from the Internet. Once again we must remember the apple. When substantial economic rewards are there for the taking, those who are driven more by greed than by principle will eat of the forbidden fruit.

Fortunately, these examples of corporate malfeasance, while significant, do not threaten to derail the global economy. But as anti-globalism demonstrations in Davos, Seattle, and Cancun made clear, there is an emerging conflict between the rich and poor countries that must be resolved if the ideal of a global economy is to be attained. It is neither fruitful nor enlightening, I believe, to describe the economic relationship of rich to poor nations in terms of traditional imperialism or colonialism – terms that protestors often use. But we can discern, I believe, a new variety of old-fashioned mercantilism.

Mercantilism was a common practice among developing industrial countries from the sixteenth through part of the nineteenth centuries. Governments passed laws or issued charters to encourage favored industries to export manufactured products to colonies or other countries and also licensed the same or other corporations to import raw materials and commodities from the countries to which the manufactured goods were sold. Often the transactions were bartered. This exemplifies globalization as it has existed for centuries. It is distinct from the current ideology of globalism, which presumes that all parties to international trade will benefit fairly from it.

As Enlightenment social theorist Adam Smith recognized, mercantilism favors a few well-connected businesses over others who might have traded in a free market. It also flouts any pretence that international trade is for the mutual benefit of importer and exporter alike. To the mercantilist, trade is not a matter of mutual benefit; it is the brutal business of "beggar-thy-neighbor." Although globalism's advocates today speak of mutual benefit and respect among trading nations, rich and poor, in reality no one could fashion a Categorical Imperative from the way many corporations treat poor countries.

In the current exchange of goods and services, developed countries are practicing a reverse type of mercantilism: they outsource the manufacture of products and services to take advantage of cheap but adequately skilled labor in underdeveloped or developing countries while exporting their own raw materials and commodities – particularly subsidized agricultural products that undermine local producers.

This new mercantilism, supported by government and international agencies, has been far from salutary. Arundhati Roy, writing in *The Nation*,* describes globalism in India as "a process of barbaric dispossession." Rather than leading to the eradication of poverty worldwide, it is, she claims, "a mutant variety of colonialism" or, more accurately, I think, a mutant variety of mercantilism. Whether it is good or bad depends, she admits, on whom one asks, for it affects those in rural villages where 700 million Indians live and work on small farms and those in urban slums quite differently from the way it affects the much smaller middle class or the relatively few leaders of big business. It has greatly benefited, for example, those employed in providing computer services, an area in which India is internationally competitive and gaining increasing market share. But it is a different story in agriculture.

In March 2000, the Indian government was pressured by the World Trade Organization in the name of free trade to lift "import restrictions on 1,400 commodities, including milk, grain, sugar, cotton, tea, coffee, and palm oil." But these commodities were produced in abundance by Indian farmers and farm laborers. In the name of "fair and free trade," heavily subsidized corporate farms were allowed to destroy the livelihood of many of India's 700 million subsistence farmers. In desperation, these farmers and farm laborers have been forced in ever-increasing numbers to abandon the countryside to seek a marginal livelihood in the desperate poverty and squalor of urban centers.

Roy notes the mocking arrogance and hypocrisy of the WTO's motto "Trade Not Aid." "'Creating a good investment climate,' " she writes, "is the new euphemism for third world repression." It is mercantilism under a new name and imposed by the international agency, another corporation, responding to the dominant member nations that determine its policies. This, I submit, is a glaring failure in corporate responsibility. Germany, France, Japan, and Sweden, along with the United States, participate in this practice of destroying domestic agriculture in India, Africa, Mexico, the Philippines, and elsewhere. No moral justification can be offered for this practice of rewarding heavily subsidized

* "Shall We Leave It to the Experts?" February 18, 2002.

prosperous agricultural corporations and individual farmers at the expense of the world's poorest people.*

Not surprisingly, perhaps, Enron provides one of the best examples of rapacious mercantilism. Following the openings made possible by pressures from the WTO, Enron secured a contract to build private power plants in Maharashtra. "Privatization" is another mantra of the advocates of globalism. Enron was to receive $430 million for a 740-megawatt plant in Phase I of the project. Phase II called for the construction of a 1,624-megawatt plant. The Maharashtra State Electricity Board had to pay $30 billion for both phases. The contract offered Enron $12 billion to $14 billion in profits and a return on equity of over 30 percent. This contract held no benefits for Maharashtra, for the power generated by Enron was twice as expensive as power available from its nearest competitor, and seven times more expensive than the cheapest power produced in Maharashtra. When the government informed Enron that it was unable to pay these prices, Enron did not consider renegotiating the contract but demanded that the government auction off for Enron's benefit the public property that had been offered as collateral.

This example of corporate irresponsibility in the global economy is an outrage. One cannot fail to observe how such corporate exploitation globalizes hatred for the United States and the WTO. Nothing feeds the cause of anti-globalism more than the practice of developed countries to export agricultural products and technologies at subsidized and artificially low or coercive prices to third-world nations, destroying the livelihood of those engaged in domestic agriculture and in other businesses.

This is the message of Cancun, where representatives of the poorer nations demanded an end to the exportation of subsidized farm products and the removal of restrictions on the importation of goods produced by the poorer countries. The outcome of this test of will must go one way or another: either the developed countries will end their exportation of subsidized farm products and open their markets to the poorer

*Subsidies to the American cotton industry are especially destructive to developing economies, since cotton is common in the underdeveloped world and is harvested on labor-intensive farms that keep millions employed. See "The Case Against King Cotton," an editorial of *The New York Times* published on December 7, 2003.

nations, or they will refuse. If the former, the global economy should continue to flourish and more closely approximate its ideal. If the latter, the opposition to globalism will intensify and the goal of free and fair trade worldwide will remain an illusion.

But again, let us not forget the apple. Although fewer than 2 percent of the American people are engaged in farming, their political influence is enormous. A similar situation exists in France, Germany, Sweden, and Japan, where only a small percentage of the population are the beneficiaries of the enormous farm subsidies. What shall motivate these privileged parties to relinquish their unfair advantage? And consider the consequences if they do. The standard of living of those from whom the subsidies are taken will be reduced. I am not aware of any volunteers to share in this radical realignment.

Rather than reforming our subsidies and practices, we might well conclude that moral concerns have no place in the savage world of international trade. We might decide that this new mercantilism in fact suits us. But what if ambitious and ruthless leaders of some of the countries we exploit decide to turn the tables and use our crude mercantilism against us? If the moral case for dismantling modern mercantilism does not persuade, perhaps we ought to consider whether financing the industries of emergent global rivals is in our enlightened self-interest.

China receives investments from the United States of more than $60 billion per year. This year China enjoys a trade surplus with the United States that is approaching $130 billion.* This dramatic trade imbalance seems to be in part a result of Beijing's manipulation of its currency. China seems, for example, to hold the value of the yuan artificially low, making Chinese goods especially cheap for those buying with dollars or euros. Given the great advantage China already enjoys in labor costs, this monetary advantage shatters any illusion that China competes on the kind of level playing field that is essential to openness and free trade.

But as it makes its bold entry into the global economy, China has enjoyed an additional advantage – the complicity of Western corporations. American and European firms have helped to accelerate China's economic development by competing with one another to build

* "US warns China patience wearing thin as trade deficit soars," AFP, October 28, 2003.

factories that take advantage of skilled and inexpensive Chinese labor and by importing vast amounts of goods that these factories produce. This has accelerated the economic development of China beyond all historic precedents. China has not been forced to save the way England, Germany, France, and the United States were forced to save in order to finance their industrialization. Nor has it had to bother with such quaint notions as the rule of law, the sanctity of contract, and freedom of speech and assembly.

China beckons corporate leaders with the alluring prospect of access to its vast market of potential customers and offers skilled and willing workers whose wages are but a small fraction of those in the first world. In consequence, the management of major automotive corporations compete with one another to gain access to the Chinese market. After General Motors and Ford invested heavily in China along with other automobile companies, the Chinese have announced that they will now build their own automobile and restrict the sales of foreign-made cars to no more than a 50 percent share of their market. The Chinese car will be very inexpensive, their Volkswagen, more in line with the economic means of Chinese workers. The Chinese are also interested in moving globally. They have announced the building of an automobile manufacturing plant in the United States and are arranging for dealerships through which to sell their car to Americans.* Who will be the winner in these ventures?

Airbus and Boeing have been competing to see which will be allowed to build wide body jets in China. There is no doubt that with guidance from either corporation, the Chinese can learn to build excellent jets. And the price of their planes will be the lowest in the global economy, for their workers earn less than 5 percent of the wages of aircraft workers in the U.S. and Europe. For the first ten to fifteen years of this venture, if it is consummated, the corporation that wins this contract will have a virtual monopoly in the sale of wide body jets. But what happens when the Chinese, having acquired all the requisite knowledge and skill, take over the enterprise? What excuses will be offered by the directors and managers

* "China's Factories Aim to Fill the World's Garages," by Keith Bradsher. *The New York Times*, November 2, 2003, Section 1, p. 1.

when they attempt to explain how they have been put out of business? There will be no problem for those who made the original decision, for they will have retired years before the finale.

What is happening in automobile manufacture and what is possible regarding aircraft construction is already underway in the manufacture of computers and electronic devices and is far advanced in the manufacture of household goods and furniture. It is the avowed intent of China to become the manufacturer to the world, and the Chinese are moving rapidly in that direction as corporation after corporation outsources its production to China. India, Malaysia, and Latin America are also in the hunt, but China clearly has the lead. The older industries of Western Europe and the United States have already suffered the effects of China's determined effort. Italy's textile business is endangered.* America's tool-makers, one step up the industrial food-chain, are also under enormous pressure.† The erosion of jobs in developed countries, moreover, is not limited to manufacturing. The United States and Europe are also losing jobs in the high-technology sectors in which the most advanced research and development takes place. Documents leaked from IBM in December of this year have revealed that the company planned to replace 4,700 employees in the United States, exporting their high-paid programming jobs to India and China.‡

If the United States and other developed countries lose to India and China not only their "rust belt" manufacturing jobs, but also jobs in the most advanced fields of research and technology, what will be left of their economies? No nation that depends on other countries for its manufacturing in both low-tech and high-tech fields will remain in the first world. A service economy is a third-world economy, the economy of a country that lives at the sufferance of more powerful countries. Will India and China sell us their most sophisticated products if our desiccated

---

* See "Threat from China Starts to Unravel Italy's Cloth Trade," by Christopher Rhoads. *The Wall Street Journal*, December 17, 2003, p. A1.

† See "With Foreign Rivals Making the Cut, Toolmakers Dwindle," by Timothy Aeppel. *The Wall Street Journal*, November 21, 2003, p. A1.

‡ The plan, named "Global Sourcing," was exposed by *The Wall Street Journal*. See "IBM to Export Highly Paid Jobs to India, China," by William M. Bulkeley. *The Wall Street Journal,* December 15, 2003, p. B1.

economies can offer them nothing of value in return? Will they, with employment problems for their vast populations, use our services?

It is possible that Switzerland, given its size, complexity and central location, may be able to sustain both its manufacturing and research economies despite these trends. But if the shift of employment to the underdeveloped world continues at the present pace, we can predict the steady decline in the economic strength and standard of living in the developed countries of the West.

Sometimes international corporations seem determined to subvert not only the security of the America's economy but even the country's ability to protect itself. During the Clinton era, businesses such as Hughes Electronics and Loral Space and Communications lobbied the White House to reduce restrictions on technology that could be sold to China and eventually won permission to export missile guidance systems. These technologies were ostensibly for use in China's burgeoning commercial satellite business, but their military applications were obvious to anyone who wanted to see. Those who held stock in these companies benefited, along with their employees. But what of the long run? Is the world safer as China catches up with the West in the manufacture of sophisticated weapons? If China becomes the world's manufacturer, will we buy our fighter aircraft, our aircraft carriers, and our missiles from China? Will China sell them to us? Will our "service economies" be able to withstand economic and military pressure from a China that enjoys flourishing manufacturing, innovative technology, and sophisticated research?

One might like to argue that free trade with China – including products of strategic and military importance – is good for American business and contributes to the liberalization of China's economy and, eventually, its politics. But free-trade absolutists made similar arguments in the 1930s. In 1934, British Premier Neville Chamberlain was so determined to promote his nation's exports that, overlooking Winston Churchill's objections, he permitted the sale of 118 Rolls-Royce Merlin airplane engines, suitable for use in fighter aircraft, to Hitler's Germany.*

* "Profiles in Self-Absorption," by Hugh Hewitt. *The Daily Standard*, November 26, 2003. www.weeklystandard.com.

The management of major corporations in the United States and Europe and the directors of their governments and international agencies (who are also corporations playing in the global economy) have been blinded by the glitter of promised rewards from the China trade. The apple again. All fail in their responsibility because they never consider the sustainability of their policies and practices, while the Chinese always do.

When guided by our better angels, we all know that there should be some rough equality among the peoples of the earth. Can anyone believe that the wages in the first world should be one thousand times greater than those of the third world?

We must also ask if the long-range dream of the global economy is even possible. It is an obdurate fact that the industrial world can already produce many more goods than it can sell. But according to the credo of the global economy, new markets are supposed to be created as people the world over prosper and become customers for our manufactured goods. But as production doubles, triples, or quadruples as China, India, Brazil, and other countries achieve their goals of industrialization, where shall we find customers for all the goods that they can produce? A Malthusian day of reckoning may approach.*

And now one final observation. When, as I suspect will be the case, China by 2050 (or, if not, by 2080) has become the world hegemon and the most powerful militarily and economically, when China has captured the lion's share of the world's manufacturing and deploys military forces second to none, how many in Europe and elsewhere will breathe easier knowing that the United States has been eclipsed? Will China be as restrained and as benign as the United States in imposing its will on the rest of the world?

And if current managers and directors could live to see that day, how will they assess the policies that accelerated China's ascension to that

---

* "New Global Trade Lineup: Haves, Have-Nots, Have-Somes," by Larry Rohter. *The New York Times*, November 2, 2003, Section 4, p. 3; also, "U.S. Overcapacity Stalls New Jobs," by Louis Uchitelle. *The New York Times*, October 19, 2003, Section 1, p. 1; and "Factory Employment Is Falling World-Wide," by Jon E. Hilsenrath and Rebecca Buckman. *The Wall Street Journal*, October 20, 2003, p. A2.

position of world dominance – a position that would have been impossible without the financial support of the most prosperous corporations?

Corporations are responsible in a global economy for much of what happens now and years hence not only as they direct their own affairs but also as they influence the positions taken by the elected and appointed corporations of government and international agencies. To act wisely, they must not think only of the apple, but rather of the well-being of all affected by their decisions. In order to have the freedom to act in accordance with this enlightened perspective, they must first create systems of checks and balances that make difficult, though unfortunately never prevent, the misuse of their offices. But ethical principles can help us determine which corporate practices require regulation and intensive oversight. Our ethical principles should guide us in the development of legal and regulatory structures to ensure that the global economy develops in ways consistent with the well-being of all peoples.

NOTE: *I twice had occasion to give this speech in American venues, where I was each time denounced (the word is not too strong) by a listener who said that American ingenuity would triumph and that I did not know what I was talking about.*

Life Is a Series of Surprises

"One of the great surprises in life is the discovery of one's true self – the fulfilled person he or she can one day become."

With the rising cost of higher education, community colleges and junior colleges serve the invaluable purpose of providing relatively inexpensive opportunities at times of the day convenient for those who have to work while they pursue their education. I felt honored to address at their commencement a group of dedicated and hardworking 2004 graduates of Lackawanna College, individuals who had earned their degrees despite disadvantages that would have deterred many others. It occurred to me to share with them some stories of the role of education in the surprises and difficulties of my own life and that of my parents.

BY THIS TIME, all of you must know that life is full of surprises. It is the surprises in life that I want to talk about this morning. And since I am about fifty to fifty-five years older than you members of the graduating class, both you and I may be surprised if I have anything to say that might be of interest or help to you.

Although I am no longer as vigorous as you and have far less time ahead of me, I can remember what it is like to be your age and to share your joys and anxieties, your hopes and fears.

When I was your age what concerned me most was that I did not know who I really was or what I might become. I suspect that many, if not most of you, are similarly in the dark. One of the great surprises in life is the discovery of one's true self – the fulfilled person he or she can one day become.

I was pleased to be asked to address you today because Lackawanna College stands for and practices America's commitment to the surprises that come with equality of opportunity. By offering open admissions, the college gives all students the chance to discover themselves. By offering a demanding educational program, it proves John Adams right in his observation that education makes a greater difference between one person and another than nature has made between humans and beasts.

We often fail to recognize the importance of education and its surprises because we learn so much before we are consciously aware of it and long before we go to school. Without the nurture of your parents, you would have no language; you would be mute in a world of incomprehensible noises. As a baby only a few months old you began to understand what was being said to you and by two years of age you were talking, already in possession of that greatest educational gift – the gift of language. This wonderful surprise was yours before you knew it.

In school you earned that second greatest educational gift – the ability to read with comprehension. That skill, once acquired, reveals all the surprises that come with knowledge. Those who can read well can, like Abraham Lincoln, become autodidacts – persons who can teach themselves. Lincoln, with no more than five years of schooling, was able by his own efforts in reading to master geometry and the logic on which that science depends. With the Bible and Shakespeare as his sources and guides, he became the American Shakespeare. His poetic speeches, unequalled by any other president, expressed what this country stands for – the meaning of the Civil War and the course of action by which the wounds inflicted in that war might be healed. Education, mostly acquired by his own efforts, transformed an ignorant country boy reared in desperate poverty by parents of limited education into the wisest and greatest of our presidents. Education was the foundation of Lincoln's success and just as plainly it is your ticket to a fulfilled life. But neither Lincoln's nor your education comes passively. Rather it requires supreme effort and dedication by each of you, for no one else can learn for you.

Education is so important for your fulfillment that I hope all of you will continue your education. Most of you are now qualified to seek a bachelor's degree in a four-year program and thereafter perhaps a graduate or professional degree. For those who must work full-time, education is still available, either by attending evening and weekend classes, or on your own in the manner of Lincoln.

At this point in your lives, you are all looking forward to what will be a series of discoveries and unexpected events. When I think back on my life, I find a series of surprises. From 1912 to 1930 my father was a highly successful architect. But the Depression put an end to most private construction, and he lacked the political skills to land federal, state, or municipal work. So for the decade of the '30s he earned only $400 to $800 a year from small remodeling jobs. My family was sustained by my mother, who in 1932 went back to work as a schoolteacher. Desperate for work, she had to accept an annual salary of only $810, which, along with my father's income, kept us alive. But my mother could not have kept her job without more education. So for the next eight years, while working full time, she went to night school and summer school to complete her BA and MA degrees. It was not easy for her to teach all day and then attend several hours of classes at night. But her ambition, diligence, and self-discipline paid off. As her qualifications increased, she advanced to more responsible and better-paying positions. In 1937, she was appointed supervisor of teachers in the Bexar County schools, and her success in developing the skills of the teachers she supervised led to an unanticipated appointment to the faculty of Trinity University in San Antonio.

The point of this story is that if you have the ambition and desire to make more of yourself, and the discipline that is required, you can open new doors through continuing your education.

But there is another point to remember. When, in 1932, with only a certificate based on her high school education, my mother returned to teaching, she did not know what her full potential might be or what she might become. That was a surprise in store for her.

To illustrate further the important element of surprise, let me tell you something about myself. When I was your age I had no idea what I would do when I grew up. I was a fine trumpet player in high school, so as a college freshman I registered as a music major. But the following summer I entered the excellent music program at Northwestern University. There I found myself among superbly talented musicians in comparison to whom I was clearly an amateur. That summer I learned one of the most valuable lessons education can offer – the discovery of what one is not good at. I had to look further to discover what I could do best or at least better. I sampled widely, majoring in fine art, philosophy, and religion and minoring in speech and debate. After graduation I spent a year in the Yale Divinity School studying theology. The next year I studied law at the University of Texas. When I dropped out of law school, my exasperated father asked me, "What are you going to do when you grow up – be a soap box orator?" I made the mistake of replying, "What's wrong with that?" Disgusted, my father threw up his hands and turned on his heel, muttering, "What's wrong with that!"

I was not trying to be a smart alec. I just did not know what to do, what I was best qualified to do, or how I might make a success of my life. I thought my father had given up on me.

But the next summer, while I was working for a few weeks as a draftsman in my father's office, I learned that, on reflection, he had been pleased with my answer. One day he introduced me to one of his friends, saying, "I want you to meet Johnny. He is the boy I was telling you about. When I asked him, 'What are you going to do when you grow up – be a soap box orator?' he answered, 'What's wrong with that?'" My father had come to recognize that, although I was still in the dark and searching, I was not complaining. I had not declared myself a victim. Rather, I had merely asserted my independence as a grown man with the right to decide for myself. My father relaxed, realizing that he could stop worrying about me, and I suspect he felt pleased in having guided and goaded me to adulthood.

When that summer was over I returned to the Yale graduate school of philosophy and earned my PhD. I had finally found the field – philosophy and teaching – in which I could be more fully myself.

That is my story. And consider my surprise when on becoming a college president, I found that my wandering studies had equipped me well for my new responsibilities. Such are the surprises in life, for I had never planned to be a college president. By taking all those extra courses in painting, sculpture, music, speech, philosophy, theology, and law, I had a range of knowledge quite useful in assessing the qualifications of programs and faculty in many areas. My study of law was useful in the review of contracts and in preparing briefs in cases where the university was plaintiff or defendant. The construction or remodeling of buildings is a major concern of college presidents, and my ability to read plans and specifications and spot mistakes in architectural or engineering design was useful and saved the university both time and money. My experience in speaking and debate was useful every day in engaging the faculty, students, and alumni. Every aspect of my education contributed to my success in my new assignment.

Now where does it stand with each of you? The discovery of your true self can come early or late. Mozart's musical genius was evident by the time he was five, but few of us have one such dominating talent. Most of us can do many things reasonably well, and it is difficult to know where our greatest abilities and opportunities lie.

That is why, if we want to become our best, we must set goals for ourselves that force us to perform beyond what we already know we can do. Setting higher and higher goals is the agenda of Lackawanna College and every college worthy of the name.

Admittedly, there are risks in all such adventures. You may try and fail. But you are then tested on how well you respond to failure. The right answer is found in the lyrics of an old song: "Pick yourself up / Dust yourself off / And start all over again." But in starting all over, sometimes one must start in a different direction. Having clearly failed to reach professional standards as a trumpeter, I would have been foolish to continue to try. I had reached the limits of that endeavor, and it was time to resign myself to amateur status. I would not have known this, of course, without initially striving for excellence.

We run far greater risks if we fail to heed the maxim, "We all learn from experience, but smart people learn from the experience of others." You do not have to try Russian roulette in order to find out that it is dangerous. There are risks you need not take, for they have already been tested and the results are well-known. It will come as no surprise to those of you who are ambitious that seeking pleasure as your goal in life will not carry you far. Observe the celebrity icons – some of enormous talent, like Elvis Presley, Marilyn Monroe, and Dennis Rodman – who in search of pleasurable highs wasted themselves on drugs, alcohol, and indiscriminate sex.

There is still much to be said for the virtues extolled by Benjamin Franklin: industry, honesty, thrift, loyalty – virtues that are urged from every pulpit. These virtues are still relevant if you want to reach the best that is in you.

Why not take a shot at the best that is in you? None of us can be greater than what we believe ourselves to be. With the gift of life, we have been given a share in the greatness of our species. No matter how modest our abilities may be, each of us can add to the richness of life and to the joy and fulfillment of the lives of others by partaking in the surprises that inevitably attend us when we strive.

Science vs. Scientism

"The assertion by scientists of dogmas unsupported by objective scientific procedures has been an unrelenting assault on the dignity of the human spirit."

I was invited by Cardinal Sean O'Malley of Boston to speak after the Archdiocese's annual Red Mass – an occasion having nothing to do with Russia or Marxism but rather with the profession of law, red being in this context the Church's traditional color for the tongues of spiritual fire to be invoked for attorneys, judges, and other officials. Addressing an audience that was intellectual in its orientation, I took the occasion to consider ways in which scientism, a reductionistic perversion of science, assumes in intellectual discourse an authority unsupported by either its methodology or its evidence. The following essay was adapted from that address for the *New Criterion* in 2005.

ON GRADUATION FROM COLLEGE I entered Yale Divinity School, not because I had decided to become a minister, but because of increasing doubts about the religious faith in which I had been reared. I supposed God had a purpose for my life, but I had no idea what that purpose might be. I entered the seminary to find out, but was required at once to accept field work as pastor to a small Baptist church. I found that having to deliver pastoral prayers and sermons in my state of confusion increased my growing doubt. As a Protestant, I had direct access to God, but while I could call on God, I never could hear God's reply. Finally my tie to Christianity became so tenuous that it was perhaps best expressed by Augustine's prayer: "Thou hath made us for thyself and we are restless till we find our rest in Thee."

In that frame of mind, while still in the divinity school, I was invited by a good friend to attend his high nuptial Mass, rich in ceremony, music, and liturgy. I am embarrassed to recall how deeply that Mass

offended my Protestant sensibilities. In the midst of incense and the reci-
tation of an almost endless Latin liturgy, I heard only mumbo-jumbo
incantations that seemed to me barbaric and in violation of the clarity
of Protestant Christianity. I had a hard time believing Calvinist doctrine, but, I asked myself, how could anyone buy into this dumb show
and noise?

Subsequent events set me straight. Reared in a Protestant sect whose
members were expected to demonstrate that exalted piety and virtue
appropriate to the elect, I had not yet discovered the importance of a
church that welcomed everyone – sinners as well as saints. Despite the
differences between Catholics and Protestants, all Christians profess
a faith in a loving God whose love was made tangible by the incarna-
tion. Unlike the laughter-loving gods of the Greeks who from Mount
Olympus made sport of finite human beings, the Christian God, Creator
of human beings, cared deeply for them. Distressed by their behavior
and concerned to save them, God decided to become human in order to
share fully the human experience.

But what, I asked, did it mean that Christ was wholly God and wholly
human? If God were wholly human, I wondered, would God while fully
human still be fully God? If God became wholly human, God would
have to accept and suffer all the ills that flesh is heir to, the abuse of other
human beings, and even a totally undeserved death. In the throes of
death God would know what we human beings know: beyond physical suffering and death, God-as-human would also know the horror of
being totally alone, defenseless, abandoned by God. Even God, once
fully human, would be alienated from God and cry out from the cross,
"Why hast thou forsaken me?"

That conception of God is profound. If one could believe it, one could
know that God fully understands each human heart, sinners no less than
saints. Because God has shared their experiences, God would have compassion for them like the father of the prodigal son.

Another striking feature of Christianity is the parity of perfection
and forgiveness. Each Christian is called upon to be perfect as his or her
Father in Heaven is perfect. But the call to perfection is merely a call to
striving and in every case a call to failure. The guilt that follows would
be utterly corrosive and prompt one to villainy (as Richard III, knowing

his deformed and wicked nature, says, "I am determined to prove a villain"). But this temptation is overcome by the availability of full forgiveness through repentance and confession, thereby restoring a spiritual equilibrium.

This parity of perfection and forgiveness makes it possible for Christianity to require that each of us strive to do our very best without being destroyed by guilt in our failure to achieve that goal.

As the years passed, I observed that not only these theological doctrines but also the rich traditions of humanistic secularism were losing their influence. An anti-humanistic, deracinated secularism was spreading in concert with the decline of attendance in mainline churches. The public square was increasingly emptied of religious symbols and practices. Religious instruction, prayer, and even Christmas carols were banned from the public schools, and manger scenes were prohibited on public grounds. At the same time, a variety of sects was flourishing: the Moonies who captured young people, brainwashed them, and separated them from their families; the Krishnas who panhandled in every airport; and the Jonestown sect that terminated itself in mass suicide.

Although I remained a searcher, I began to be aware of the importance of a church that, while open to all, would set minimum standards of religious orthodoxy to which anyone could turn. I began to appreciate the particular strengths of Catholicism. The demands of the Catholic Church were not so stringent as those of Protestant sects. The Catholic Church offered a spiritual home to all and instructed each communicant on the minimal elements of Christian orthodoxy. I came to see that the Catholic Church served a purpose in religion and theology like that of the meter bar in Paris that set the standard of spatial measurement throughout the world. I recognized the Church in its doctrines, its practices, and in its parochial schools as a great teaching institution alongside other schools and colleges, businesses, the law, and the courts.

One of the most important teachings of the Church – an insight applicable to all institutions – was pronounced at the Council of Trent, when it held that the validity of the Mass does not depend upon the moral quality of the priest. The individual priest may fail in his obligations, but the Mass he performs is still valid. This insight is relevant to many aspects of personal and intellectual life.

Just as the Church is not destroyed by the failures of individual clergy, neither are schools and universities discredited by the failures of faculty, nor businesses by the venality and cupidity of some CEOs and boards of directors. The legal profession is not discredited by the presence of shysters nor the courts by errant decisions from the bench or the improper conduct of judges in private life. All these institutions retain their appropriate authority and relevance despite the inevitable shortcomings of individuals who serve in them.

This doctrine of the Council of Trent applied to all institutions offers a powerful reassurance that our institutions can survive the failures that inevitably tarnish them.

We are all too painfully aware of the ordeal through which the Catholic Church has gone in consequence of the sexual predation of some priests. And none of us if honest can fail to observe the way the legal profession has abandoned traditional professional standards in the pursuit of business opportunities. Ambulance chasers advertise their wares and encourage those possessed of any injuries, illnesses, or losses – imaginary or genuine – to join in the hunt for deep pockets.

We are equally aware of the failures of business leaders and boards of directors who in pursuit of personal riches have violated their fiduciary obligation to protect the long-term interests of stockholders, employees, and the communities affected by their presence.

I would be remiss if I failed to enlarge on the failures of our universities. No institution has contributed so extensively to the deracination and diminishment of our humanity as university faculties. A remarkable prophet of this devolution was Friedrich Nietzsche, who in 1882 announced the death of God in *Die Fröhliche Wissenschaft* (*The Joyful Science*). Nietzsche was completely misunderstood by the graffiti author who inscribed on a wall, "Nietzsche Is Dead, (signed) God," for Nietzsche was not making a theological statement or a declaration of atheism. Rather he was announcing the world-shaking fact that God no longer had any significant influence in the lives of educated Europeans. Copernicus taught them that our world is not the center of the universe, and Darwin that humankind is not a special creation descended from Adam but merely the end result of millions of years of evolution. Educated Europeans were the inheritors of scientific rationalism.

Enthusiasm for Darwin was not dampened by the humorist who reported the father–son conversation of a pair of monkeys. Handing his son Darwin's *Origin of Species*, the father monkey said, "Read this, son, it will make a man of you."

The emerging dominance of an anti-humanist secularism, absent God, gained strength with every passing decade and now, with the exception of those places where Muslim, Christian, or Jewish fundamentalism holds sway, dominates the intellectual climate of the educated in the United States and most parts of the world.

Nietzsche also prophesied the consequences of God's absence, summarized in the epigram of Dostoevsky's Ivan Karamazov: "If God is dead, everything is permitted." Nietzsche foretold a bloody twentieth century of unprecedented, catastrophic wars, to be followed by a twenty-first century in which human beings, retaining an atavistic sense of guilt but absent a God offering forgiveness and absolution of sins, begin to loathe one another and themselves. Faith in God, he predicted, would be replaced by allegiance to barbaric brotherhoods at war with non-brothers. Although Socrates, Kant, and many others denied the necessary dependence of morality on a divine foundation, Nietzsche foretold the total eclipse of all values in the absence of divinely sanctioned moral codes and denied the possibility of belief in moral obligations without the authority of a God who supports them with a divine imperative.

Although the gloom of pessimism as the millennial year of 1900 approached was apparent among many Victorian writers, including Alfred Lord Tennyson, none was so specific as Nietzsche. His prophetic powers have been accurately assessed by Tom Wolfe. In *Hooking Up*, Wolfe writes, "[I]n the peaceful decade of the 1880s, it must have seemed far-fetched to predict the world wars of the twentieth century and the barbaric brotherhoods of Nazism and communism.... Behold the prophet!" Who can now question the accuracy of Nietzsche's and Karamazov's dire predictions?

The scientific assault on the place and dignity of humankind has continued and accelerated. While Copernicus and Darwin announced their findings with reluctance and trepidation, their followers announced further denigrations of the human species with the enthusiasm of tub-thumping evangelists. Freud, in claiming to have discovered the unconscious, proclaimed that individuals were no longer masters in their own houses; thoughts and behavior were determined instead by irrational and largely unconscious motivations. Edward O. Wilson in his *Sociobiology* and Richard Dawkins in *The Selfish Gene* further extended Darwinism by reducing humans to the levels of animals whose behavior, like that of ants, is genetically determined. B. F. Skinner easily matched their extreme reductionism with his denial of the relevance of conscious thought in human action. (Sidney Morganbesser spotted his error: Skinner thinks, he said, with dripping irony, "We shouldn't anthropomorphize people.") What are we to make of our own experience if the mind – thoughts, ideas, and consciousness for which there is no scientific understanding – is held to play no role in the behavior of individuals? According to these reductionists, all mental phenomena are at most epiphenomena, associated in totally inscrutable ways with brain functions responding to genetic mandates. In the final analysis, what an individual human being thinks or does cannot be an expression of will or consciousness but, to use the current metaphor, of the way that person is wired. Criminal behavior, for example, is simply an expression of the genes. The self, understood "scientifically," disappears as a causal responsible being. Praise and blame, guilt, pride, and shame are all equally misplaced and illusory ideas. Scientism, this reductionistic unscientific extension of science, has furthered the climate of anti-humanist secularism and practical atheism in universities and intellectual circles.

Carl Sagan, Steven Weinberg, Stephen Hawking, and legions of cosmologists and physicists have proclaimed that science, not religion, explains the origin of the universe. We all know their view: our universe originated in the Big Bang. But when they are asked what banged, they have no answer, unless it is the matter left over from a prior universe, now collapsed into a black hole. But when pushed to explain where the earlier universe came from, these cosmologists are faced with an infinite regress which leaves unanswered the philosophical and theological question: Why is there something and not nothing?

Theologians have offered the view that God created the universe *ex nihilo*, from nothing. This is no explanation, but, except for Biblical literalists, it leaves the issue as the mystery it is. Is it not better to admit that no one knows the answer than to propose a "scientific" answer so patently inadequate?

And what shall thoughtful individuals say about Darwinism in its fulsome development and extension? First, we ought to acknowledge that it is impossible to confront facts objectively and deny that species have evolved. The evidence showing developments in physical structure that relate the human species to hominids is compelling, and the similarities in the DNA of humans and chimpanzees provide undeniable scientific evidence of their kinship. Thus far, evolution is not merely one theory opposed to another but a scientific truth amply confirmed by facts. And there is convincing plausibility to the idea that physical or intellectual advantages have survival value. We can recognize the soundness of the view that those species have survived which possessed qualities lending them a clear advantage over species that have become extinct. An animal that can see, for example, is clearly advantaged over those that are blind. Survival of the fittest based on specific advantages provides factual support for the process of evolution.

The critical question posed for evolutionists is not about the survival of the fittest but about their arrival. Biologists arguing for evolution have been challenged by critics for more than a hundred years for their failure to offer any scientific explanation for the arrival of the fittest. Supporters of evolution have no explanation beyond their dogmatic assertion that all advances are explained by random mutations and environmental influences over millions of years.

This view was challenged a century ago by Henri Bergson when he asked for an explanation of the extraordinary eye of the giant squid. Once the eye is fully developed, one need not question its survival value. But its development required hundreds of thousands if not millions of years. Why were random mutations so marvelously contributory to the development of this complex structure? No scientific explanation has been offered; the view is only a working but unproven hypothesis. The empirical scientist becomes a fanatical dogmatist by insisting that random mutation devoid of any formative principle explains it all. (One need not appeal to an intelligent designer in order to ask if there is an organizing force in the universe offsetting entropy.) A magician who shows you his empty top hat at time t_1 and then at time t_2 produces a rabbit from the hat has never had the gall to offer the mere presence of the rabbit as an explanation of how it got there. He claims it is magic. The evolutionists can do no better.

More recently, even some scientists and mathematicians have begun to question the adequacy of theories based on an emergent aspect of evolution, largely for their failure to explain what Michael Behe, professor of biochemistry at Lehigh University and author of *Darwin's Black Box*, calls the "irreducible complexity" of organisms. Random mutation cannot explain scientifically this complexity and the addition of so many complex elements before any survival value is established; hence, the black box or the rabbit in the hat. In *Abyss: The Deep Sea and the Creatures That Live in It*, C. P. Idyll considers once again Bergson's preoccupation with the eye of the squid. Idyll notes, "What the scientist finds hardest to understand in considering the squid and the human eye is that two entirely independent lines of evolution should have converged at the same point." Why should evolution have produced eyes in two vastly different species through totally independent lines of evolution such that each has the eyeball with its lens, its cornea, its iris, its retina, its vitreous humor, and its optic nerve? How did random mutation produce such extraordinarily similar structures in the absence of any teleological or formative principles? And how many hundreds of thousands of years passed before each additional element significantly contributed to the final capacity of sight that would enhance survival?

Random mutation might be the answer, but there is no evidence to prove it. Scientists should acknowledge the difference between what is proven and what is merely a hypothesis. One is not attacking or denigrating science to point out its hubristic extensions unsupported by any evidence or methodology that could be described as scientific.

Creationists cannot responsibly deny the fact of evolution – the development over extended periods of time of new forms of life and the survival of those forms that are the fittest. These aspects of the theory of evolution are adequately confirmed by facts and must be accepted as facts by rational observers. Those who insist that human beings were originally created in their present form are as irrational as those who believe the world is flat.

But those who believe that an intelligence or some formative principle has guided the development of new forms of life have a right so to believe. At the same time scientists have the right to believe that random mutation alone accounts for the arrival of new forms of life. Each has the right to that credo or faith that best supports their view of the nature of things. At the same time, however, each should recognize that faith, not facts, supports their positions, for there is no scientific evidence or proof for either intelligent design or random mutation as a fact-based explanation of the arrival of the fittest. On my view, scientists and laymen should prefer to leave the issue as the mystery it is rather than commit to an answer for which scientific evidence is lacking.

If scientists do not claim to know anything as factual unless it is supported by empirical evidence, they will, as Kant observed in his *Critique of Pure Reason*, leave room for faith.

I recall as a child the sermons I heard in which ministers railed against evolution. I asked then, as I ask today, what are the theologians complaining about? Presumably God can use evolution as a method of Creation if God so desires. I could not understand the conflict between science and religion then, and I cannot understand it now, except when literal fundamentalists interpret the Bible as a scientific book and treat the account of creation in Genesis as a factual scientific account – or when scientists dogmatically assert as scientific fact their hypotheses to explain the arrival of the fittest.

The public places mistaken emphasis on the bane of political correctness in universities. Most examples of political correctness, however stupid and irritating, are relatively harmless. But the constant drumbeat and march of scientism – that assertion by scientists of dogmas unsupported by objective scientific procedures – has been an unrelenting assault on the dignity of the human spirit. In the intellectual climate of the present we are left with diminished human beings whose complex experience is denied by reductionistic scientism.

Those who challenge the reductionistic doctrines of scientism have been subjected by scientists to verbal abuse and contempt that equal in intensity the denunciation from pulpits of those who question the literal interpretation of Scripture. Those scientists approach in hubris and ignorance pastors who rely on the literal interpretation of the Bible without knowing that the canon was not handed down in English at Sinai but was determined by the fathers of the Catholic Church.

With regard to the literalists and the reductionists, I would say, a plague on both houses.

The literalists have no standing in universities. But what standing, we must ask, should the reductionists have who claim the authority of science in areas of inquiry beyond scientific evidence or proof? I do not question their right to develop their ideas and their research as they deem best. Freedom of inquiry should not be challenged. But neither should any scientist or researcher claim an immunity from criticism. The right to err is fundamental for, as Goethe remarked, "Man must err so long as he strives." We have, moreover, the assurance of the Council of Trent that all our institutions, including the university, retain their validity despite the failures and mistakes of our members.

We have, therefore, every right to demand of the reductionists: What is the relevance of your pronouncements that trivialize or deny outright the full range of human potentiality in the face of the demonstrable wonders of mankind? Do your claims account for or diminish the beauty of the Parthenon, the music of Bach or Mozart, the frescoes and sculptures of Michelangelo, the plays of Shakespeare, or the genius of Lincoln's prose?

The miracle of human existence is reflected in an incident recalled by the late choral conductor Robert Shaw. At the conclusion of a concert in southern France, he met an elderly parish priest who said, "When the angels want to give particular pleasure to God, they sing only Bach. But," he continued, "when they wish to give greatest pleasure to themselves, they perform only Mozart." As Shaw observed, there are "a billion billion ways to organize the words in the English language – but there was a Shakespeare." And there are "a trillion trillion ways to organize simultaneous and sequential pitches – but there was a Mozart." Individual persons make the difference and expose the shallowness of the exponents of the view that we humans are merely responses to the dictates of mindless genes.

Why should anyone as an act of faith – one dominant among the proponents of scientism – accept a view according to which our experience as conscious, purposeful, and morally responsible individuals is dismissed as illusory? Edward O. Wilson's assertion that an "organism is only DNA's way of making more DNA" is refuted by organisms like Mozart, Shakespeare, and Michelangelo, whose DNA made few off-spring but many enduring works of art.

While one may be in doubt about the existence of God or a design, no one should deny the rich fabric of human experience on the unproven claims of a faith that empties our lives of all meaning and purpose. Preferable is the recognition that there is undeniable greatness in the human spirit and nothing can be truthfully said, much less proved, to deny so obvious and obdurate a fact. We fail to achieve our full humanity unless we affirm in belief and in action the wonder of our natural endowments and, in harmony with others, putting aside self-doubt, knowledge of our finitude, and the reality of death, strive to achieve the greatness that lies within us.

The Choices Are Ours

"Greed has now infected all parts of our government; a growing relativism erodes our moral sense, which has gradually been replaced by unreflective partisanship and ideological rigidity. But we are not at the end of our greatness."

In concluding this book, I briefly considered recent developments that have seriously altered American life and our political system. I suggested that the solution to our problems lies almost entirely in our own hands and depends on the choices we make. I thought it appropriate to develop this piece as another speech and was pleased to be invited to deliver it to the Algonquin Club and the Boston Consular Corps. *[Note: In the event, ill health prevented John Silber from delivering this piece as a speech.]*

As I noted in the Preface, I have selected for this book speeches on issues that I believe have the greatest import for how we live and our influence on succeeding generations. The speeches I have included seem to me as important and pressing as ever, and the suggestions regarding ways we might resolve or at least ameliorate our problems seem to me still worth pursuing. These essays and insights are a large part of any legacy I might leave my children and grandchildren.

Although I might update some of my observations and numbers to give some sense of how financial and other problems have increased over time, this would add little to what I have to say. Rather, since most of these speeches were given more than twenty years ago and, except for the last, some seven years ago, I have asked myself, "What would I choose to speak on were I invited to speak today?" This speech addresses developments that were not so apparent in 1971 or even when I spoke in 2005.

Two issues of particular import have emerged. The first, just beginning to be apparent forty years ago, has now transformed and begun to dominate our lives. An unprecedented luxury has flooded our country, profoundly altering our perceptions and ourselves. The second issue is a growing relativism and the substitution of ideological conviction for the search for truth.

In the late 1940s and '50s, we were just emerging from the brutal austerity of the Depression. While life was still difficult for many of our citizens, they were determined to improve their condition by hard work. Jobs were suddenly available; unemployment was low; there was a general feeling of optimism and well-being, a general contentment among our people. Most of us believed that for the foreseeable future things would be better and better still.

I noted in the Preface to this book the joy I felt in 1960, when my family and I returned to the United States after spending a year in Europe. Everywhere there were hopeful signs. Although prejudice and bigotry continued to victimize minorities, substantial progress was being made in civil rights and in equality for women. Progress was accelerating in medical research and clinical practice, resulting in extended life expectancy and in the reduction of suffering. The GI Bill opened higher education to intelligent, knowledge-hungry GIs, who by their seriousness stimulated great scholars and teachers to outstanding levels of instruction. The average standard of living was at an all-time high and still rising. There was a remarkable balance between materialism and spiritual aspiration.

But this balance was precarious and already beginning to disintegrate as prosperity evolved into luxury. When luxury flourishes, removing economic limits on choice, materialism and consumerism begin to dominate. Desires multiply and pleasure or whim replaces principle as the basis of choice. The guidance of morality becomes less certain and seems arbitrary. The limits imposed by reality, what I have called the Tremble Factor, grow weak. Unlike the Roman engineer who was the first to stand under the arch he had built, we no longer feel in jeopardy from the consequences of our choices.

As I have noted previously, when the moral North Star is obscured, relativism and dogmatism – mere adherence to ideology – are on the rise.

The search for truth and the ability to approach it most closely through evidence and argument are increasingly abandoned. Obedience to the unenforceable, the cornerstone of any highly developed civilization, is drastically weakened, while increasing numbers of people, confused by the ambiguity of all choices, find strength in the specious certainty of an ideology.

Juvenal's observation that luxury is more ruthless than war is now evident. Items and activities that were once rightly considered luxuries came to be looked on as necessities. To paraphrase Shakespeare, our appetite has increased by what it fed on. We have collectively given businessmen, bankers, industrialists, celebrities of film, radio and television an exaggerated sense of their personal and professional importance. They have rewarded themselves with, or we have given them, ever-increasing compensation in salaries, bonuses, and benefits. Even many public service employees demand and receive salaries, pensions, and benefits that are neither justifiable nor sustainable. Luxury has encouraged greed, and greed has begun to erode the character of those with public responsibilities.

Leaders of institutions once noted for their integrity, forbearance, and probity began to enlarge their gains through means once illegal or inappropriate. A top executive at Goldman Sachs noted in his resignation from this distinguished firm that its principals were pursuing their own interests rather than those of their clients. Accounting firms such as Arthur Andersen falsified the evaluation of assets for the benefit of clients. Investment bankers spent many millions of dollars lobbying Congress to repeal the Glass–Steagall Act and other regulations that were enacted in the 1930s to guarantee the integrity of banks. With the removal of restrictions, banks chartered in one state began to acquire others outside that state. In Boston, for example, the Bank of Boston, Shawmut, the Bank of New England, and FleetBoston Financial all disappeared into the maw of Bank of America, a bank now too big to fail. When its greed resulted in disaster, not only was the institution bailed out, but the architects of disaster were rewarded at taxpayer expense.

Without restrictive regulations, investment banks could legally acquire depository banks and proceed to use the funds of depositors, whose primary concern was for safety, for risky derivatives. Bad mortgages were bundled with sound ones to win AAA status by rating agencies although the bundles more often deserved rating as junk bonds. Greed driven by luxury was the ever-present motive and engine of these changes.

The erosion of financial and political probity was matched by a weakening of the social fabric. At the close of World War II, most of us were firmly anchored in the institutions of family, church, and country. Slowly these verities, their hold weakened by the relativism brought about by luxury and greed, became no more than assertions, no longer objective truths but only ideologies grounded on unproven assumptions. And in the conflict of ideologies, truth was a casualty. Loss of moral, social, and spiritual anchors was replaced by ideological conviction in all levels of education, in the thinking of many citizens, and in the behavior of our politicians.

Business leaders and special interests of many sorts discovered that greed can transform and corrupt even high-minded public servants. Government, including the Congress and the administration, fell under their influence as greedy special interests dominated congressional legislation and administrative regulation. I do not suppose anyone would claim that a member of Congress can be bought, but the decisions they make lead me to wonder, for many members of the Congress walk away from their responsibilities when the pressure becomes intense.

Greed has now infected all parts of our government; a growing relativism has eroded our moral sense, gradually replacing it with unreflective partisanship and ideological rigidity. How else can we explain the failure of the Congress and the administration to address our appalling deficit?

Our departure from the search for truth is of profound importance. It is a huge obstacle to any corrective course we might propose. To an alarming degree, we have ceased to live in a civil order in which persons can disagree in a spirit of toleration and work together for the common good. This is due in large part to the triumph of ideology over common sense and the search for truth. Arbitrary conclusions based on selective evidence, with contravening evidence ignored, are presented as certain. A partisan dogmatism replaces dialogue. As a result, the concept of compromise has been vilified and denounced as if it were evil by ideologues who profess by their intolerance an infallibility for which there is no justification. Ideological rigidity leads inevitably to legislative deadlock and makes it extremely difficult if not impossible for any president of the United States to be effective. The situation today is in striking and alarming contrast to the situation in the Eisenhower, Kennedy, and Reagan administrations when the members of the Congress, whether Republican or Democrat, worked amiably with the administration to forge legislation in the national interest. No democracy can survive this level of rigidity and dogmatic conflict.

Justice Holmes once remembered that the happiest day of his life was the day he discovered that he was not God. Let us hope that this discovery will be made by all members of the Congress and the administration and that it will free them from the folly of infallibility, opening their eyes to the virtues of evidence, common sense, and compromise.

In the meantime, our government continues billion-dollar subsidies for tobacco, ethanol, and other products, and permits the investment of billions in start-up companies that pursue dubious programs of green energy. These billions of dollars are provided on the recommendation of ignorant bureaucrats who fund start-up enterprises whose worth and promise have not been tested in a sophisticated market by an IPO. Grants and bailouts provided by Congress boost the fortunes of banks and private individuals without requiring the recovery of public funds supplied by the taxpayer and without restricting the amount of bonuses the beneficiaries of these grants may claim for themselves.

Unlike traditional Congresses of the 1960s, few members of today's Congress have served in the military. More than a few are multimillionaires, and close to half are millionaires. Greed has prompted them to exempt themselves from the laws and regulations they impose on the people of the United States. Thus they have been free to ignore affirmative action in the staffing of their offices and for years exempted themselves from the prohibition on insider trading. The Congress has thereby separated itself and its interest from the interest of the people it governs.

These developments are changing our form of government from a democracy to an oligarchy – that is, from government that is of, by, and for the people to government of, by, and for the rich. The enormous expense of running for office – whether for the House, the Senate, or the presidency – has also contributed to this transformation to oligarchy.

And the Supreme Court in its 2011 decision in *Citizens United v.*

Federal Election Commission has given constitutional authority to oligarchy. It has interpreted the Constitution to say there can be no limit to the amount of money that corporations or individuals can anonymously devote to the political process. The Supreme Court's endorsement of Super PACs as a constitutional right of free speech has altered the fundamental nature of our government. Elections can be and are now bought and sold by hugely wealthy individuals or groups of individuals who need not even identify themselves. They must only pretend along with the candidates that there is a Chinese wall that separates the Super PAC from the candidate – a glaring legal fiction.

Justice Holmes in *Schenck v. The United States* held that falsely shouting "Fire!" in a crowded theater was not privileged free speech. One wonders how the provision of untold millions through Super PACs accountable to no one, with contributors who are not even identified, can be privileged free speech. When one falsely shouts "Fire!" in a crowded theater, a small percentage of the audience is exposed to injury or death in the resulting confusion. But when a government is transformed from a democracy to a system based on greed and controlled by moneyed interests, the loss is profound for everyone. Every citizen who is not an oligarch is effectively disenfranchised.

Today we need a war on greed more than we need a war on drugs or poverty. We do not need a new ideology; we need a return to common sense, responsible politics, and the search for truth.

In order to avoid excesses of compensation for the administrators of banks and other corporations bailed out by the federal government, we need to reintroduce over the opposition of investment bankers and industrial leaders many of the regulations contained in Glass–Steagall and other measures that were set in place in the 1930s to protect the banking industry from the possibility of failure.

I do not claim that the Supreme Court erred in its interpretation of the Constitution by permitting the Super PACs. Whether right or wrong, however, their decision should be overturned by the only means left to us. We should amend the Constitution to place severe limits on the role and influence of money in our elections so that individuals with minimal obligations to those who have financed their campaigns can win seats in the Congress while remaining free to represent the people.

In addition to placing limits on Super PACs, we should also reduce the cost of running for office. Television and radio stations licensed by the FCC can and should, in exchange for the privilege of their license, provide without cost a reasonable amount of time to all credible candidates for public office. Candidates who avail themselves of this provision should assume a liability for the value of air time until they establish themselves as serious candidates by receiving a reasonable percentage of the vote. This or some other measure must be found to deter frivolous candidacies while making it possible for honorable persons to run for office without the expenditure of gigantic sums of money, thereby lessening their dependence on special interests.

Candidates campaigning on the Internet compete on a relatively level playing field. They can use the medium not only to present their programs but also to meet the cost of their presentations by soliciting contributions from Internet viewers. This proved to be an excellent source of financing in the last presidential campaign.

The Constitution should also be amended to require members of Congress and the administration to obey all of the laws and regulations they impose on the people of the United States. This would restore the public's sense that the members of Congress and the citizens for whom they legislate share common interests. We may be encouraged by the current initiative to limit insider trading by members of Congress. However, a constitutional amendment is still necessary to ensure that all members of Congress and all those who draft regulations be subject to all laws and regulations.

Two things might persuade the chattering class, the celebrities and the owners of television and radio, to recognize that humility and self-restraint are in order. One is if we stop listening to them. The other possibility is that they will hearken to obedience to the unenforceable and recognize that they have been elected by no one, that they have no authority to push their views on the American people. They are loyal Americans; they care deeply about our country and wish it well. But it is time that they, along with the unnamed bureaucrats and regulators acting without public oversight or sanction, recognize the way in which they themselves undermine the ability of our country to survive and prosper.

When I consider the future of America, I am still optimistic because I believe Americans are, despite some appearances to the contrary, realists at heart. I am confident we will learn from the example of Greece and other Euro countries that have followed with even more reckless profligacy the course we are following. If we monetize our debt, we will unleash an inflationary spiral that will consume all of our wealth, leaving us destitute. The example of the Weimar Republic should not be ignored. These examples show how severe and dangerous is the disaster that lies ahead unless we alter course.

I am confident we will confront and begin to deal with the financial abyss that threatens us. Understanding the realities of our situation will free us from the shackles of ideology and restore our common sense and dedication to evidence and argument. When that awareness takes hold, I am convinced Americans will take the corrective actions that are necessary not only for our own sake but for our children and grandchildren.

I have frequently observed that realism calls for us to confront death and human finitude even as we strive for the best that is in us. I have argued that confronting death is the most important and transforming realization provided by education. Death faces us all, and the shallowness of greed is revealed in the fact that nothing is permanently ours.

This insight was brought home to me when my father died. He kept his personal belongings in a top drawer of his dresser, and my brother and I would not have dared to open those drawers when my father was alive. But after his death, we did. And what did we find: collar buttons, tie clasps, cufflinks, a watch, and other small personal items.

I was overwhelmed by the realization that my father owned none of these things. He only had a lease on them for the duration of his life. Although we may possess things for a time, none of us own anything.

Greed offers nothing permanent but only relatively brief possession. For some, the thought of death leads only to thoughts of material possessions and hedonism. But those capable of deeper insight will, I believe, see the ultimate futility of greed. They will be encouraged to accept the sacrifice that is required by a corrective response to our financial crisis. They will recognize that failure to restrain their greed and make the sacrifices that corrective action requires will leave little or nothing for their descendants.

Faced with national bankruptcy, greed itself becomes an incentive for change. Concern for future generations can prompt individuals to go to extreme lengths to pass their wealth on to their descendants. But unless we alter course, the financial collapse facing us today threatens to wipe out wealth for all of us, the rich no less than the poor. Greed itself will stimulate those concerned for the well-being of their descendants to resolve the present crisis by putting an end to our excessive spending.

We are not at the end of our greatness; we are not at what Saul Bellow referred to as "the dwarf end of time." Our financial crisis is actually a legislative crisis, a crisis of political paralysis. As serious as it is, it does not compare to the crisis that confronted our nation in the Civil War and can be overcome by far less radical means than those Abraham Lincoln was called upon to use. If each American citizen thinks through these issues, nearly all will unite to demand an end to dogmatic ideologies and a submission of opinion to the tests of evidence and argument as we seek through compromise the likeliest solution to our problems. We will demand a democratic process that sends free, unencumbered men and women to the House and Senate and to the office of the president. We will repudiate oligarchy and demand reforms that put limitations on special interests such that they can no longer control Congress, allow-ing rational and thoughtful individuals a chance through compromise to lead this country in better ways. The principle of community, by which we owe support to those institutions that sustain us, will once again pre-vail and will encourage obedience to the unenforceable.

We have the time, we have the intelligence, we have the energy, and I believe we have the honesty to face the reality of our situation. We all possess the prudence to make reforms that are necessary for our long-term survival and for the provision of opportunity for our children and grandchildren.

The problems we face are serious, but the solutions suggested here and in other chapters of this book are not wishful thinking. Given the American character, they are possible and even probable. Many highly motivated, intelligent, and educated young people who only a few years ago would have headed straight for Wall Street are starting or joining companies that seek not only to turn a profit but also to improve life for the elderly or those faced with poverty. Others are coming up with new avenues of research and invention that will boost the economy. While there are serious problems with microfinancing, these may well be overcome, and the spread of the idea is a hopeful sign. Teach For America continues to attract some of the best of our beginning teachers. Massachusetts has seen the dramatic reform of the Chelsea schools through the provision of an Early Learning Center for three- and four-year-olds. No one who visits that Center can fail to be impressed by the joy and intensity of the children's participation in the various activities. Whether rich or poor, their minds and senses are stimulated to the fullest, and they enter kindergarten or first grade ready and eager to learn.

Our young people aspire to a better life for all; they are motivated by idealism and full of energy. They want to know that the American dream is not dead and will dedicate themselves to its renewal. The postwar and baby-boomer generations will assist because most of us feel a deep sense of failure and guilt at having betrayed our children and grandchildren by profligate living on borrowed funds.

This perennial idealism of our youth, who are never blind to the possibility of a better world, is a powerful source of hope. The growing distress of those who confront with realism the problems we face is another source of hope – for where there is major discontent, there is growing demand for reform. Discontent combined with youthful idealism and energy for action ensures a brighter future. If we were ever to lose discontent with the present and the idealistic demand for a better future, we would lose hope and forfeit all chance for a better life. Our existence and our fulfillment depend upon the knowledge of our history, on what has made us great, on the knowledge which nourishes our capacity not only to hope for a better world but also to believe it possible and to make the sacrifices necessary for its realization.

Acknowledgments

This book would not have been possible without the assistance of my colleague Brian Jorgensen. I am grateful for his help. Samuel McCracken and Jon Westling, colleagues of many years, have been an ongoing source of advice and criticism. I am grateful as well to my assistant Kelly O'Connor and to my assistant Jennifer Horgan. I also want to thank Paul Montrone for his close reading of the text and his penetrating criticisms. Tom McCann has provided invaluable insight and advice. My thanks to Gerald Gross for his help in finding a publisher and to Joseph Mercurio, trusted friend and colleague. My deepest debt of gratitude is to my late wife, Kathryn, who was throughout our marriage a source of wisdom, support, and laughter.

Index

A Man For All Seasons, 42, 43
A Nation at Risk, 207
Abyss: The Deep Sea and the Creatures That Live in It, 276
Academic freedom, 104, 120
Achilles, 88, 181–182, 184
Adams, John, 50, 73, 75, 82, 264
Adams, John Quincy, 52–53, 82
Adams, Samuel, 83
Advertising, 8, 79, 145–146, 235
Advisory Council on Intergovernmental Affairs, 220
Affluence, 33, 86, 124, 160
Agnew, Spiro, 41, 44, 45, 49
Airbus, 258
Alienation, 5, 17, 29, 32
Alter, Robert, 121
Ambition, 80, 265
Amos, 23, 25, 26
Analects, The, 160
Ancient Greek, 176–187
Anti-globalism, 254, 256
Antigone, 59
Anti-hero, 23
Antony, Marc, 145
Aphorisms, 165
Apocalypse, 124
Approximate math, 214, 216
Araskog, Rand, 248
Aries, Philippe, 56–57
Aristophanes, 32, 104
Aristotle, 18, 117, 122, 144–145, 159, 160, 164

Arnold, Matthew, 98
Arrowsmith, William, 54, 130
Arthur Andersen, 247, 282
Atkins, Susan, 78–79
Atomic bombs, 155–157
Aurelius, Marcus, 54–56, 58
Autonomy, 103–104, 112–113

Bacon, Francis, 160
Bailouts, 284
Banks, 249, 282, 284, 285
Barzun, Jacques, xxxii, 29, 31
Bataan Death March, 154
Behe, Michael, 276
Belafonte, Harry, 135
Bellow, Saul, 62, 288
Bergson, Henri, 275–276
Berle, Adolf A. Jr., 245
Bernstein, Leonard, 13
Bible, 25, 36, 43, 60, 87, 88, 124, 151, 186, 264, 277, 278
Bicentennial speech, 72–83
Birchers, John, 194–195
Black Death, 152
Bloom, Harold, 29
Board of Education, Massachusetts, Chairmanship, xli–xlii, 204, 209–220
Boeing, 258
Bolt, Robert, 42
Bonhoeffer, Dietrich, 234
Borges, Jorge Luis, 121
Boru, Brian, 96

Boston, 99, 131–132
Boston University, xv, xxii–xxiii, 66,
    108, 127, 130, 131, 132, 161–162,
    169–171, 179, 197–200, 208
    faculty, xvi, xviii, xxii, xxiii, xxxvii,
        xl, 108, 127–130, 171, 199, 200,
        218, xxxviii–xxix, xl–xli
Branagh, Kenneth, 231
Brandeis, Louis, 43–44, 46
"Breaking the Cycle of Poverty," 194
Brecht, Bertolt, 89–90
British soldiers' grave, 20
Bronfenbrenner, Urie, 199
Brookshire, 39
Brown v Board of Education of Topeka,
    192
Buddha, 89, 164
Bunker, Archie, 79–80
Bush, George H.W., 205

Cancun, 256
Caroline, Larry, 195–197
Categorical Imperative, xxiii, 242–243,
    247, 249, 254
Catholic Church, 271–272
Catholicism, 100, 269, 271–272
Cavafy, C. P., 184–185, 237–239
Cedar Rapids Community School Dist.
    v. Garret F., 221
Center for the Advancement of Ethics
    and Character, 161–162
Centuries of Childhood, 56
CEOs, 246–249, 253
Chamberlain, Neville, 260
Character education, 158–168
Chaucer, Geoffrey, 31, 176, 217
Chelsea Public Schools Project,
    xxxviii–xli, 223–225
Child-parent home education
    programs, 225
Children, xxiv, xxvii–xxviii, xxxv,
    xxxvii, 10–19, 25, 36, 54, 56–57, 63,
    64, 91, 124, 132–133, 144, 146, 147,
    158–168, 204–228, 237, 246, 289

China, 167–168, 257–261
Christian Church, 35
Christianity, 60, 62, 90–91, 186, 234–
    236, 269, 270
Christians, 90–91, 235–236
Chuang Tze, 164
Church-related universities, 123–125
Citizens United v. Federal Election
    Commission, 284–285
City College of New York, 194
Civil disobedience, 24–25, 46
Civil War, American, 20, 82, 264, 288
Civilians, in wartime, 152, 154–155
Civilization and Its Discontents, 35
Classicists, 29
Classics department, 179
Cohen, Robert, 197, 199
Colleges. See also Education;
    Universities
    church-related, 123–125
    multiculturalism in, 138
    parents and, 126–134
    reality avoidance and, 36
    "tremble factor" and, 36–37
Commencement speeches, 5–21,
    66–71, 114–118, 135–139, 140–149,
    169–175, 263–268
Commonwealth Caribbean, 135–136
Communism, 234
Confucian scriptures, 59
Confucius, 161, 164, 242
Congressional bailouts, 284
Conrad, Barbara Smith, xiv, 192–193,
    199
Continuity, in family, 54, 56, 61
Contrived adversity, 116, 117
Cooper, David, 56
Copernicus, 272–273
Corporate responsibility, 240–262
Corporation(s)
    accountability of, 244
    board of directors, 248–249
    CEOs, 246–249, 253
    cultural hegemony of, 252–253

elements of, 244
environmental considerations,
    249–250
in Europe, 249
in Germany, 249
global economy and, 251–254,
    256–257, 261
greed in, 250
management of, 244–245, 247–248,
    261
ownership of, 245–246, 248
responsible governance of, 245
in United Kingdom, 249
Council of Trent, 271–272, 278
Counterfeits
of democracy, 72–83
of education, 76, 104–109
Courage, xxxi, xxxii, xl, xliii, 3, 16, 23,
    30, 39, 68–69, 76, 82, 83, 160, 186,
    187, 239
Creationists, 276
Crime, 44, 49, 62, 82, 142, 193, 231, 232,
    234
Critical theory, 122–123
Critique of Pure Reason, 277
Cultural globalism, 253
Cultural hegemony, 252–253
Curtis, Staton, 108

Darwin, Charles, 273
Darwinism, 275
Darwin's Black Box, 276
Davis, Angela, 199
Davis, Mac, 67
Dawkins, Richard, 274
Death of the Family, The, 56
Death, xliii, 8, 10, 11, 31, 69, 91, 92, 152,
    182, 184–186, 193–194, 234, 236,
    270, 272, 287
Death row, 194
Deconstructionism, 120–122
Delattre, Dean Edwin, 218
Deming, W. Edwards, 148
Democracy

description of, 72–83
external threats to, 80–81
free enterprise and, 102–103
Democratic elitism, 74–75, 172
Dependency principle, 64, 162–163,
    237
Derrida, Jacques, 123
Developed countries
erosion of jobs in, 259
mercantilism by, 254–257
Dido and Aeneas, xiv, 192
Diogenes, 11
Disraeli, Benjamin, 54
Dogmatism, 202, 281, 283
Domains of human action, 140
Dooley, Martin, 94–95
Dostoevsky, Fyodor, 61, 273
Doyle, Arthur Conan, 180
Dreams, 23, 169–170, 174–175
Dresden, 155
Drug culture, 8, 29, 34, 63, 86, 144, 161,
    267
Dubos, René, 29
Dugger, Ronnie, 192–193, 196

Early childhood education, xxxix,
    224–226
Early Learning Center, 289
Easy Rider, 6
Education. See also Colleges; Teachers
in ancient Greece, 177
for autonomy, 112
budgetary increases for, 205
continuing of, 264
counterfeits of, 76, 104–109
in democratic versus
    nondemocratic societies, 103
early childhood, 224–226
equal rights for women movement
    and, 208–209
ethical distinctions in, 88
Horace Mann and, 76
humanities, 28–31
ideology and, 106–109

imitation and, 159
inductive, 233–235
liberal, 76
Massachusetts Department of,
    217–220
multiculturalism and, 137–138
in Nazi Germany, 233
in 1960s and 1970s, 119
overqualification myth and, 66–71
parents and, 126, 132–133
pollution of time in, 12–14
purpose of, 14, 37–38, 69, 91–92,
    96, 103, 105, 109, 115–116, 119,
    125, 128–130, 172, 174
and the "real world," 69
relativism and, 104–105

SAT scores, 206–208
Schools of, 214–217
teacher salaries, 205, 226–227
Tillich's analysis of, 233
as transmission of culture, 178
tremble factor in, 32–39
Education reform
child-parent home education
    programs, 225
Frameworks, 218
generalizations about, 206
Individuals with Disabilities
    Education Act effects on,
    220–221
teachers' unions effect on, 221–223
Eisenhower, Dwight, 2, 230, 231, 284
Eisner, Michael, 248
Eliot, Charles W., 169–170, 209
Eliot, T. S., 70, 185
Elitism, 74–75, 172
Elytes, Odysseus, 187
Encounter groups, 35
Enlightenment, 61
Enron, 247, 251, 256
Epictetus, xi, xviii, xxx, 158
Ephialtis, 186
Equal achievement, 77–78, 130

Equal opportunity, 77, 130
Equal rights for women, 208–209
Erwin, Frank, xiv–xv, xxiii, 195–196
Ethical principles, 164
Ethics, 14–15, 137, 162–163, 237, 241–
    243, 262
Ethnic groups, 77
Evolution/evolutionists, 275–277
Excellence, 115–116

Failure, 115–116, 267
Family
affection from, 57–58
Aries's writings about, 56–57
biblical references to, 60–61
Confucian scriptures about, 59
continuity in, 54, 56, 61
Hindu scriptures about, 60
historical references to, 57–60
interdependency of, 64
personal nurture in, 64
purpose of, 56
Federalist Papers, 15, 213
Fili, 96
Financial crises, 288
First Amendment, 120, 145, 147, 200
Fish, Stanley, 122
Flight to Arras, 179
Fonda, Henry, 6
Fonda, Peter, 6–7
Ford, 258
Ford, Gerald, 40–51
Ford, Henry Sr., 246–247
Foreign language instruction, 207,
    216–217
Forgiveness, 47, 150–151, 270–271, 273
Four Noble Truths, 89
Fourteenth vs. Twentieth Century, 152
Franklin, Benjamin, 50, 74, 267
Free association, 200
Free choice, domain of, 140
Free enterprise, 102–103
Free speech, 285
Freedom to learn, 104–105, 173–174

Freedom to teach, 104–105
Frei, Eduardo, 200
Freud, Sigmund, 35–36, 273–274
Freund, Paul, 29
Future of America, 287–289

Geneen, Harold, 247–248
General Motors, 258
Generalizations
    description of, 206
    stereotypes versus, 206–207
Generation gap, 17–21, 52
Generations, 52–65
Genesis, Book of, 61, 277
Geneva Convention, 153
GI Bill, 171, 230, 281
Glass-Steagall Act, 282, 285
Global economy, 251–254, 256–257, 261
Globalism, 255
Globalization, 251–252
Glorious Entertainment, The, 31
Goethe, 135, 278
Golden Rule, 163, 164, 242, 249
Goldman Sachs, 282
Good life, 65, 69, 70–71
Good vs. personal preference, 162
Goodman, Kenneth S., 215
Gorki, Maxim, 63
Gray, Glenn, 32
Great books, 87, 178, 264
"Great Day, The," 26
Great Depression, 189, 265, 281
Greed, 250, 283–284, 287–288
Gresham's Law, 80
Gubernatorial campaign, xxiii–xxx, 116

Hamlet, 80, 231
Handwriting, 211
Harvard University, 208–209
Hawking, Stephen, 274
Hebert, F. Edward, 108
Hector, 181–182
Hedonism, 15, 62–63, 778, 124, 146
Hellenic traditions, 176, 179–180, 184, 237

Hillel, Rabbi, 164
Hindu scriptures, 60
Hiroshima, 150, 153–157
History of England, 99
Hitler, Adolf, 54, 106
Hobbes, Thomas, 143
Holmes, Jr., Oliver Wendell, 134, 145,
    284–285
Holocaust, 152, 156, 173
Homemaker, 64
Homer, 58, 183–184, 186
Hooking Up, 273
"Horses of Achilles, The," 184–185
House Judiciary Committee, 44–45
House of Intellect, The, 31
Housman, A. E., 64–65
Hughes Electronics, 260
Humanism, 28, 62, 237
Humanist secularism, 271, 273
Humanists, 28–29
Humanities, 28–31, 92, 177, 181, 236
Human worth, 174–175, 278–279
"Hyphenated Americans," 100

IDEA. See Individuals with Disabilities
    Education Act
Identity, loss of, 33
Ideological rigidity, 283
Ideologues, 173, 198, 202, 283
Ideology, 106–109, 173, 201–203, 281,
    283–284
Idyll, C. P., 276
Iliad, 181–183, 237
IMF, 251–252
"In Memory of Major Robert Gregory,"
    27
India, 253, 255, 259
Indians, American, 16, 215
Individuals with Disabilities Education
    Act, 220–221
Inductive education, 233–235
Instant culture, 5–21, 146
    eating habits affected by, 9
    marriage and, 10–11

pollution of time and, 9–12
science and, 7–9
Instantaneous gratification, 61, 160
Interdependence of old and young, 11,
16–18, 19–21, 63–64
Internet, 145, 253, 286
Iowa Test, 219
Irish, 93–101
Irving Independent School Dist. v. Tatro,
221
"Ithaca," 237–239
Iwo Jima, 154

Jackson, Jesse, xxiv
Jaeger, Werner, 177
James, William, 174
Japan, 150–157
Jaspers, Karl, 172–173
Jefferson, Thomas, 73, 75, 82
Jerusalem, 84, 87–88, 92
Jews, xxiv, 90–91
Journalists, 109, 111–112
Judaism, 88, 89–91, 152, 164, 273
Jury trials, 142–143
Juvenal, 282

Kairos, 236
Kant, Immanuel, xvii, xxxiii, 62, 103,
105, 164, 242–243, 252, 273, 277
Keeton, Dean Page, 192
Kennedy, John F., 22–23, 49, 100, 284
Kennedy, Robert, 22–23
Kimball, Roger, 188
King, Martin Luther Jr., 22–28
King Alfred, 96–97
King David, 25, 88
King Lear, 71
Kipling, Rudyard, 54
Kors, Alan, 197
Kozlowski, Dennis, 248

La Rochefoucauld, 11
Laing, R. D., 56–57
"Lake Wobegon Effect," 248

Law
domain of, 140–141
enforcement of, 142
erosion in standards of, 142–143
and nonviolent protest, 24
obedience to, 141–142
rule of, 40–51
Law of supply and demand, 33
Lay, Kenneth, 247–248
Lee, Peggy, 232
Left-wing objectives, 202
"Let It Rain," 180
"Letter from a Birmingham Jail," 23–24
Liberal education, 28, 76
Liberalism, 188–203
Liberation, 86
Limitations, knowledge of, 116–117
Lincoln, Abraham, 20, 264, 278, 288
Literacy testing of teachers, 212–213
Literalists, 278
Loral Space and Communications, 260
Loss of meaning, 166, 181, 232, 279
Love, 7, 11, 19, 27, 31, 55, 58, 60–61, 64,
67, 83, 90–91, 96, 98, 103, 186, 209,
232, 236, 270
Lucretius, 60
Luxury, 86, 160, 168, 232, 281–282, 283

Macaulay, Lord, 33, 99
Madison, James, 75
Maine, Henry Sumner, 237
Malcolm X, 22–23
Mann, Horace, 76
Manners, domain of, 141–142
Marcuse, Herbert, 203
Markham, Edwin, 148–149
Marriage, 10–11, 31, 52, 56, 61, 133, 161,
170, 184, 232
Marsh, Daniel L., 170
Marxism, xvii, 120, 197–198
Mass culture, 172
Massachusetts Comprehensive
Assessment System (MCAS), xli,
219

Massachusetts Educational Reform Act
of 1993, 218, 222
Materialism, 85, 144, 167, 174, 281
Mathematics, 29, 31, 37–38, 129, 138,
205, 211, 214, 218, 227, 233
Mayer, Jean, 79
McDonald's, 121–122, 253
McGuffey, William Holmes, 160,
180–181
McLuhan, Marshall, 12, 252
Meaning
goals for, 110, 174–175, 237–238, 264
literary, 122, 181
loss of, 181
quest for, 10
Means, Gardiner C., 245
Meditations, 54–56
Melian conference, 232
Melting pot, 77, 100
Memorization, 216–217, 237
Mercantilism, 254–257
Metcalf, Arthur, xxii, xxiii, 108,
197–198
Methodists, 169–170
Middle Ages, 57
Middle class, minorities in, 78
Mill, John Stuart, 188, 202
Milton, John, 178, 200, 239
Mitford, Jessica, 190
*Modern Corporation and Private
Property,* 245
Molotov–Ribbentrop pact, 106
Moore, Henry, 57
Moral education
description of, 160
liberal education, part of, 76
objective foundation of, 162–165
reintroducing of, 161–162
Moral equivalence, 106–107
Moral instruction, 162–163, 164–165
Moral principles, 165, 167
Moses, 17, 163
Moulton, Lord, 140–141, 143
Mozart, 128, 267, 278, 279

Mullen, Leo F., 248
Mullen, Peter, 123
Multiculturalism, 77, 135–139
Murlin, Lemuel, 170
Musicians, 190

Nagasaki, 150, 153–157
Nathan, prophet, 25, 88
Nation, The, 255
National Institute of Child Health and
Human Development, 215
Natural aristocracy, 73, 75
Natural Mind, The, 34
Nazi Germany, 106, 233, 273
New Deal, 189–191
New York Stock Exchange, 251
Nicomachean Ethics, 159–160
Nietzsche, Friedrich, 9, 121, 129–130,
272–273
Nihilism, 120, 123, 146
Nixon, Richard, 40–51
Nonviolent resistance, 24, 26–27
Norwich University, 114

Obedience, domain of, 141
O'Connor, Carroll, 79
O'Malley, Cardinal Sean, 269
O'Neill, Tip, 100
Odysseus, 183–184
Odyssey, 58, 181, 183, 184, 237
Oedipus, 184
Oedipus, 58
Okinawa, 154
Older generation, 16–17
Oligarchy, 284–285
Olivier, Laurence, 231
Ollam, 96
Omeros, 139
Ortega y Gasset, José, 172
Orwell, George, 120, 123, 217
Overqualification, 66–71, 74

Paideia, 177–178
Pardoning of Richard Nixon, 40–51

Parents, 7, 18, 20, 53–54, 57–58, 63–65,
  114, 117, 118, 123–124, 126–134, 144,
  145, 146, 159–162, 165, 209, 220,
  222, 225–226, 264
Pascal, 16–17
Patriotism, 80, 83
Patroklos, 181–182, 184–185
Pearl Harbor, 151, 153
Penelope, 183–184
Perfection, 43, 270–271
Personal Knowledge: Toward a Post-
  Critical Philosophy, 37
Personal nurture, 64
Petrarch, 28, 176
Pharmacology, 8
Philosophy, 15, 28, 30, 70, 92, 146,
  165–167, 236–237, 265–266
Phonemic awareness, 215–216
Phonics, 215–216
Picasso, Pablo, 57
Pietism, 62
Piracy, 253
Plato, xxxvi, 11, 60, 61, 68, 105, 137, 158,
  178, 180–181, 237
Platonic dialogue, 180
Pleasure, 62–63, 78–79, 80–81, 91, 124,
  144, 146, 161, 267, 278, 281
Pleasures of Reading in an Ideological
  Age, The, 121
Plotinus, 8
Plutarch, 75
Polanyi, Michael, 29, 30, 37
Politics of Authenticity, 196
Political correctness, 194, 201, 277
Pollution of time
  childhood myths and, 10
  in education, 12–14
  instant culture and, 9–12
  universities and, 14–16
Port Huron Statement, 5, 195
Positivism, 105
Poverty, 33–34, 160, 194, 255, 264, 285,
  288
Powell, Colin, 107

Power, 15, 26, 27, 35, 44, 48–50, 69, 77,
  88–89, 102, 111, 112, 116, 120, 143,
  148, 166–167, 174, 183, 195, 197, 232,
  236, 241, 245, 246, 251, 259, 261
Present lives, 53
Presidency of Boston University,
  170–175
Privatization, 256
Professional ethics, 242
Protagoras, 104, 165
Proverbs, 60–61
Public schools, xxiv, 192, 194, 226–227,
  271
Pursuit of happiness, 78–79
Pursuit of truth, 110, 172–173, 201–203,
  282

Quo Vadis Latin America, 200

Race, 82, 137–138, 170, 172, 234, 281
Ragnarok, 54
Random mutations, 275–277
Reading instruction, 215
Realism, 32–39, 124, 287, 289
Reality avoidance, 36
Recapitulative principles, 15
"Red Mass," 269
Reductionists, 277–279
Relativism, 104–105, 106, 138, 141, 281,
  283
"Repressive Tolerance," 203
Republic, 237
Responsibility
  corporate, 240–262
  definition of, 241
Restrepo, Lleras, 200
Revolt of the Masses, 172
Richardson, Elliot, 44–45, 48
Right and power, 77, 88–89, 166, 183
Right of self-determination, 20
Right Stuff, The, 114
Rigoletto, 13
Ripeness, 29, 71
Robin Hood, 6

Rockefeller, Nelson, 50
Romeo and Juliet, 18–19
Roosevelt, Franklin D., 189–190
Roosevelt, Theodore, 100
Rosenstein-Rodan, Paul, 29, 36
Rossinow, Doug, 196
ROTC, xvi–xvii, 107–108, 198–200
Rote memory, 216–217
Rouman, John C., 176–177
Roy, Arundhati, 255
Russell, Bertrand, 81

Sagan, Carl, 274
Samuelson, Paul, 29
Schenck v. The United States, 285
Schwartzmeister, 94–95
Science
    humanities use of, 28–31
    instant culture and, 7–9
    moral integrity of, 144
    reductionistic use of, 30
Scientific method, 200
Scientism, 29, 174, 269–279
Secularism, 110, 125, 235, 271, 273, 274
Self-consciousness, 163, 237
Self-determination, right of, 20
Self-discovery, 128, 263–267
Self-esteem, 194, 211, 216
Selfish Gene, The, 274
Self-knowledge, 114–118
Service economy, 259
Sex, 10, 61–62, 122, 127, 144–146, 146, 267
Sexual potentiality, 35
Shadow University, The, 197
Shakespeare, William, 18, 28, 29, 63, 80, 87, 139, 145, 175, 206, 217, 231, 264, 278, 282
Shannon, Bill, 100
Shaw, Peter, 122
Shaw, Robert, 278
Siebert, Muriel, 249
Silber, Jewell Joslin, xiii, 3, 67, 94, 189, 228, 265

Silber, John Robert
    and Barbara Smith Conrad, xiii–xiv, xvii, 192, 199
    Board of Trustees, confrontation with, xx–xxii
    census taker, 191
    childhood, xxxiv, xii–xiii, 188–190
    Chairmanship of Massachusetts State Board of Education, xli–xlii, 204, 209–220
    character, xi–xii, xvii–xviii, xxxi, xlii–xliii
    Chelsea Public Schools Project, xxxviii–xl, 223–225
    children, xiii, xviii, xxvi–xxviii, xxxiii, 128, 280
    Dean, University of Texas, xiii–xv, 195–197
    disc jockey, 230–231
    death of, xlii–xliii
    education, xiii, 190–192, 265–267
    and faculty, Boston University, xvi, xviii, xxii, xxiii, xxxvii, xl, 108, 127–130, 171, 199, 200, 218, xxxviii–xxix, xl–xli
    funeral home interviews, 190
    gubernatorial campaign (Massachusetts), xxiii–xxx, 116
    Kantian, xvii, xxiii, xxxiii, xlii
    humor, sense of, xix xx–xxii, xxxiii
    Jacobson, Natalie, interview, xxv–xxx
    liberal as a child, 188–190
    Northwestern Music School, 116, 265
    "One-arm Pete," xii
    optimism, 3, 65, 127, 208, 287–289
    presidency of Boston University, xvi–xxiii, xxxvii–xxxviii
    private life, xviii
    professor, xiii, xxxi–xxxiv, xxxv–xxxvi, 165–167, 192
    references to classical and other writers, xxxi–xxxii, 2–3

religion, 269–271, 277
School of Education, Boston
    University, xl–xli
"Slum Project," xxxvi
Society to Abolish Capital
    Punishment, xiii, 193–194
"shockers," xxii–xxv, 116
unions, importance of, 190, 222–223
Wolfe, Tom, honorary degree,
    xix–xx
Yale Divinity School, 190–191,
    269–270
Silber, Paul George, xii, xiii, xxiii, 3, 189,
    265, 266, 287
Silverglate, Harvey, 197
Simpson. O. J., 143
Singletary, Otis, 194
Skinner, B. F., 30, 274
Slavery, 82, 138
Smith, Adam, 33, 254
Smith, Al, 100
Smith, Barbara, xiv, 192–193, 199
Snow, C. P., 30–31
Social promotion, 216
Sociobiology, 274
Socrates, 23–24, 32, 70, 104, 125, 164,
    180–181, 200, 202, 236, 273
Solipsism, 62
"Solomon-Song," 89–90
Solzhenitsyn, Aleksandr, 80–82, 148,
    234
Sophocles, 58, 194
South Korea, 102–103
Speed reading, xxxii
Spinoza, 70
Spiritual formation, 229–239
St. Augustine, 70, 269
St. Patrick, 94, 96
St. Patrick's Day, 100–101
St. Paul, 186
St. Paul's, 229–230, 235–237, 239
St.-Exupéry, 179
Stalin, Josef, 106, 152, 199
Steffens, Lincoln, 250

Stereotypes, 206–207
Stevens, Wallace, 70, 101
Stevenson, Coke, 192
Stoicism, xi, xv, xxx, 65
"Stoned" thinking, 34
"Straight" thinking, 34
"Stretching the envelope," 114–118
Students. *See also* Colleges; Education;
    Universities
    parents of, 126–134
    phonemic awareness by, 215–216
    self-knowledge of abilities, 116
    social promotion of, 216
    "stretching the envelope" by, 114–118
Suffering, 17, 31, 85, 89–91, 106, 145,
    152–153, 230, 270, 281
Super PACs, 285–286
Supreme Court (U.S.), 46–47, 49, 75,
    192, 221, 284–285

Tacitus, 161
Teach For America, 289
Teachers. *See also* Education
    certification of, 211–212
    decline in intellectual ability of,
        207–208
    foreign language instruction,
        216– 217
    lack of preparation for, 214
    literacy testing of, 212–213, 218
    reading instruction by, 215
    salaries of, 205, 226–227
    testing of, 211–212, 218
Teachers' unions, 221–223
Telemachos, 183
Television
    advertising on, 79, 145–146
    as educational institution, 144–145
    historical description of, 231
    mass culture created by, 172
    moral instruction affected by, 165
    need for self-control, 147
    political candidate campaigns on,
        286

sexuality on, 145–146
societal effects of, 147
violence portrayed on, 144–145
world issues influenced by, 110
Temporal structures, 13
Tennyson, Alfred Lord, 273
Terrorism, 143, 145, 232–233
Texas Observer, 192
Third Reich, 54, 173
Third world, 251, 255, 261
Thought Police, 122, 194, 200, 201
Threepenny Opera, 89
Tillich, Paul, 62, 229–230, 231, 233, 234, 235–237
Time
    as independent variable, 14
    structuring of, 3, 9–11
    nonexistent present, 52–53
    continuity, 52–54, 61
Tocqueville, Alexis de, 109–110
Total immersion therapy, 35
Tower, John, 192–193
Tremble factor, 32–39
Trilling, Lionel, 29
Truman, Harry S., 80, 154, 191
Truth, 30, 73, 76, 102, 104–106, 110, 112, 113, 121, 137, 195–196, 200–201, 202, 275, 279, 281–282
    as matter of perspective, 121
    free pursuit of, 110, 173
    seeking of, 201, 282–283
Two-generation families, 11
Tyco, 248, 251

Unenforceable, obedience to, 3, 141–144, 251, 282, 286, 288
Unions, 190, 222
Universities. *See also* Colleges; Education
    academic freedom in, 104, 120
    church-related, 123–125
    commencement speeches, 5–21, 66–71, 114–118, 135–139, 140–149, 169–175, 263–268

crises in, 85, 123
curriculum proposals in, 87
ethical standards in, 124
failures of, 272
free, 109–110
free inquiry in, 107, 172–173
mission of, 84–92
moral equivalence doctrine in, 107
multiculturalism in, 138
parents and, 126–134
pollution of time and, 14–16
and the "real world," 69
"stretching the envelope" by students, 114–118
value-neutrality and, 105
USSR, 106, 233
Utilitarianism, 61

Value-neutrality, 76, 104–105
Vietnam War, 2, 5, 8, 20–21, 32, 193
von Moltke, Helmuth, and von Stauffenberg, Klaus, 234
Vyshinsky, Andrei, 199

Walcott, Derek, 139
Wallace, Henry, 191, 197
War Against the Intellect, 122
Warren, William Fairfield, 169–170
Watergate, 36, 40–51
Weill, Andrew, 34
Weimar Republic, 22, 287
Weinberg, Steven, 274
Weisskopf, Victor, 29
Weld, William, xxiv–xxvi, 204
West Indies, 135–139
White, E. B., 201
White, Kevin, 72
Whitehead, Alfred North, 178
Whole-language approach, 215
Will to Believe, The, 174
Williams, Eric, 136
Williams, Jerre, 191
Wilson, Edmund, 29, 178
Wilson, Edward O., 274, 279

Wilson, Logan, 192, 199
Wilson, Woodrow, 37
Wise, John, 75
Wolfe, Tom, xix–xx, 112, 114, 273
Women's' movement, xxvii, 74, 127,
    208–209, 231–2, 281
World Trade Organization, 251,
    255–256
World War II, 8, 26, 68, 80, 85–86, 171,
    230, 283
Wright, Charles Adam, 1

Yale Divinity School, 190, 266, 269

Yarborough, Ralph, 194
Yeats, William Butler, 6, 16, 26–27, 98,
    239
Young, Whitney, 22–23
Youth
    idealism of, 289
    older generation's responsibility,
        16–17

Zeffirelli, 18–19
Zinn, Howard, 200
Zion, 87–88, 91–92
Zoeller, Jerome, 192, 222

Seeking the North Star has been set in Minion, a typeface designed for Adobe Systems in 1990 by Robert Slimbach. It is among the more elegant and readable of the many "old style" faces that have their roots in the designs Aldus Manutius commissioned from Griffo and Garamond prepared for Estienne in the early sixteenth century. In basic appearance, it is very close to Bembo, with slightly heavier hairlines and serifs to accommodate the needs of offset printing. As Slimbach observed, "I like to think of Minion as a synthesis of historical and contemporary elements. My intention with the design was to make a progressive Aldine style text family that is both stylistically distinctive and utilitarian. The design grew out of my formal calligraphy, written in the Aldine style."

The sans serif types are from the Whitney family designed by Hoefler & Frere-Jones. Its compact forms and generous x-height use space efficiently, and its ample contours and open shapes make it clearly legible under any circumstances. Originally developed for New York's Whitney Museum, Whitney is the preferred typeface of Boston University for print and web communications as it comfortably contends with two different sets of demands: those of editorial typography, and those of public signage.

Both the book and jacket were designed by Michael Russem at Kat Ran Press in Cambridge, Massachusetts.